received from
Jack mills, L.A.T. Book Editor
11/13/1987

The Life and Times of James Willard Schultz
(Apikuni)

James Willard Schultz (Apikuni) as a young man in Montana. Courtesy Roland R. Renne Library Collection, Montana State University, Bozeman.

The Life and Times
of James Willard Schultz
(Apikuni)

by WARREN L. HANNA

Based in part on a manuscript by
Harry C. James

University of Oklahoma Press : Norman and London

Library of Congress Cataloging-in-Publication Data

Hanna, Warren Leonard, 1898–
  The life and times of James Willard Schultz.

    "Based in part on a manuscript by Harry C. James."
    Bibliography: p. 369
    Includes index.
    1. Schultz, James Willard, 1859–1947. 2. Indianists—
United States—Biography. 3. Indians of North
America—Montana. 4. Montana—History. I. James,
Harry Clebourne, 1896–   . II. Title.
E76.45.S38H36 1986   970.004'97'0072024 [B]   85–40944
ISBN 0–8061–1985–3

DEDICATED
TO
THE JAMES WILLARD SCHULTZ SOCIETY
AND ITS LOYAL MEMBERS
WHO HAVE LONG AWAITED
THIS STORY OF
THEIR HERO

Contents

Illustrations and Maps

Preface

To many he was known as Apikuni. But why Apikuni, one may ask, and why should he be of interest to the prospective reader of this book? He was born in the state of New York as James Willard Schultz, a name that was to become familiar in the literary circles of his day. But in the world of the red man, he was known as Apikuni, a name given to him by the Indians with whom he lived on the frontier of northwestern Montana; it was the name by which he liked to be called by his friends, red or white.

The story of Apikuni is a true story of adventure about an unusual man and his life in early Montana and elsewhere. When, as a lad not yet eighteen, he traveled up the Missouri by riverboat in the 1870s, he had hoped to see something of the hordes of buffalo and of the Indians of the region during a summer vacation. As it turned out, he stayed to see more of both than most men of his time. Not only did he live among the Piegan (or Pikuni)[1] people of the Blackfoot Nation, he learned to speak their language fluently and even married a Blackfoot girl.

On more than one occasion he was invited to, and did, join war parties of Blackfoot warriors in their forays against enemy tribes for the purpose of stealing horses and counting coup. In one of these raids, several of the party were killed and he himself suffered a serious wound. No wonder a later white wife called him "adventuresome, amazing Apikuni." More than that, as a young man he was so fortu-

---

[1] Because Schultz always used the term "Pikuni," it has been used herein.

nate as to gain the friendship of a well-known Indian trader and to work closely with him at his various Montana trading posts until the buffalo and other large game had disappeared from the plains.

Much of the foregoing has been recounted by Schultz in the pages of his best-selling book *My Life as an Indian.* However, his early years on the plains represented only the beginning of a career that was both colorful and checkered. On the one hand, he was a big-game hunter, rancher, explorer, writer of popular books, dabbler in anthropology, and ardent supporter of Indian rights and causes. On the other hand, he found himself charged at times with such offenses as game poaching and jumping a hotel bill, while at still other times he was in the position of a fugitive from justice, an involuntary drug addict, and for much of his life a borderline alcoholic.

Schultz was an early visitor to the St. Mary Lakes region, which now is part of Glacier National Park, first as a vacationing hunter and fisherman and later as an explorer and master guide. Barely had the buffalo vanished when he began to compile his impressive list of "firsts" in relation to this fascinating area. Not only was he the discoverer of Montana's two largest glaciers, Blackfoot and Grinnell, but it was he, in the company of George Bird Grinnell, who first visited and explored each of them. The first story of the Chief Mountain country to appear in a national publication was Schultz's *Forest and Stream* magazine article about his 1884 visit to the valley of Upper St. Mary Lake. He it was who brought the first boat to the St. Mary Lakes in 1884 and who built the first cabin there.

Not surprisingly, the nomenclature of Glacier National Park reflects the activities and the Indian name of James Willard Schultz. He had a special feeling for the mountains, lakes, and streams he explored, a feeling that inspired him to give them appropriate names. As a result, more than a dozen of the park's important natural features bear names that he gave them a century ago. His own name is reflected on park maps by Apikuni Mountain, Apikuni Falls, Apikuni Basin, and Apikuni Flat—more of the natural features within the park than have been named for any other individual. Far more impressive, however, is one of the park's major geological features, known as the Appekunny Formation. Composed of gray-green shale in massive layers of two thousand five hundred to three thousand five hundred feet thick, it is a part of mountains throughout the park. Its aggregate bulk, could it be computed, would exceed that of a dozen of the park's ordinary peaks combined.

Nor did his distinctions and activities stop at that point. Writing as James Willard Schultz, Apikuni became the author of many published articles and stories in addition to more than forty books having to do with the Blackfeet and other Indian tribes, and in some instances with Glacier National Park. As a matter of fact, apart from James Fenimore Cooper, Schultz is considered the leading writer of books of adventure dealing with the American Indian.

Schultz became an early and important contributor to anthropological knowledge about the Blackfoot people. At the age of twenty-four, he wrote for publication in *Forest and Stream* a series of sketches entitled "Life Among the Blackfeet," describing their traditions, history, and customs. For this accomplishment he received high praise from George Bird Grinnell, himself an able ethnologist, who also referred to Schultz as the "discoverer of the oral literature of the Blackfoot people."

Despite the foregoing, it is probable that Schultz himself would have felt that his greatest accomplishments were the result or results of his endeavors on behalf of Indian causes. For example, after taking the initiative in organizing a small group of people having a common interest in Indian welfare, he also headed their successful campaign to persuade Congress to grant the right to vote to the American Indian. At other times, whenever the Blackfeet or Hopis were in dire need or faced a crisis of some kind, it was Schultz who rushed to the rescue with aid and unrelenting zeal.

In his marital relationships, Apikuni was as adventuresome and amazing as he was otherwise. Of the eighty-eight years of his long and eventful life, sixty-three were spent in a state of matrimony or alternative togetherness. One of his

three wives came from Michigan in response to his advertisement for a wife, and two of them were really strangers to
him when he married them. The third lived with him in sin
for most of two years while he was still married to Wife
No. 2, as well as for several more months between the dates
of his Montana divorce and their marriage by a judge in Nevada. The three women who figured in those sixty-three
years ranged from an unschooled Blackfoot girl, who never
learned to speak English, to a cultured and literate college
professor, who not only earned a master's degree in anthropology and another in social studies but was awarded an
honorary doctor's degree for her outstanding work with the
American Indian.

Let us return to the questions of how Apikuni got his
name—of which, incidentally, he was quite proud—and its
significance. It was bestowed upon him, according to what
he has written, during his early years with the tribe by Chief
Running Crane, a noted Pikuni warrior, in recognition of
Schultz's bravery on the war trail and in token of the chief's
friendship for the young white man. At that time Schultz
chose to spell the name "Appekunny" and to translate it
"White Spotted Robe."[2] This, accordingly, was the spelling
used by the United States Geological Survey in making its
first map of Glacier National Park in 1912. However, Schultz
disavowed that spelling much later, insisting that it should
be "Apikuni" and translated as "Far-Off White Robe."[3]

Despite the biblical injunction that a prophet is without
honor in his own country,[4] Schultz has not been forgotten in

[2] As shown in the second installment of "Life Among the Blackfeet,"
published in *Forest and Stream* on December 6, 1883.
[3] James Willard Schultz, *Blackfeet and Buffalo*, 95. Yet Schultz's own published writings show that for more than forty years he himself spelled his
Indian name "Appekunny" (see, for example, the spelling he used in his
1926 book *Signposts of Adventure*). Although he translated it in his later
years as "Far-Off White Robe," some of the Blackfeet translated it "Scabby
Robe" and it appeared thus on the Blackfoot tribal rolls of 1907–1908. In
1976, because of the spelling used by Schultz in his later years, the U.S.
Board of Geographic Names changed the official spelling to "Apikuni"
for the park's natural features, with the exception of the Appekunny
Formation.
[4] Matt. 13:57.

the place of his birth. The year 1976 was a special one for the little town of Boonville in upstate New York, not only because it was the nation's bicentennial year but also because it was the year Boonville authorities paid homage to one of their native sons, "Willie" Schultz (1976, incidentally, was only a few months short of marking the one-hundredth anniversary of Schultz's departure from Boonville, as a teenager, to embark on his western adventure).

On October 1, 1976, the house where Schultz was born was dedicated as a New York State Historical Landmark by the placement of an appropriate plaque. The historical marker and accompanying ceremony were made possible by the efforts of Matthew J. Conway, father of the project, with the cooperation of the Boonville Bicentennial Committee and Mayor David J. Ernst, using funds contributed by Boonville residents and others, including the James Willard Schultz Society and Harry C. James, a longtime Schultz friend from California. Among the non-Boonville people at the ceremony were David C. Andrews, publisher of *The Piegan Storyteller*, from Andes, New York, and Mr. and Mrs. Donald Martin from Illinois, he being the nephew of Schultz's widow, Jessie Donaldson Schultz Graham.[5]

Much of what is told about Schultz in this volume has become available to the researching biographer only because two people (both deceased) who knew him intimately during the latter part of his life have independently left records of their association with him. His best friend, Harry C. James,[6] left an unfinished manuscript dealing with Schultz's life, and his widow, Jessie, left an unpublished autobiographical

---

[5] This report is based on an article entitled "Native Son Schultz Remembered" in the *Boonville Herald* of October 6, 1976; reprinted in *The Piegan Storyteller*, Vol. I, No. 1, 3.

[6] James (1896–1978) was a Californian who spent most of his life working with boys' clubs and schools. Among the books written by him were several dealing with Indians and the red man–white man relationship. Much of his final decade was devoted to preparation of a story of Schultz's life, in the course of which he carried on a considerable correspondence with Jessie in an effort to clear up various points. It is apparent, however, that neither of them had to clear up various points. It is apparent, however, that neither of them had anything more than hearsay knowledge of Schultz's first sixty years.

memoir which included much information about her husband. Although both manuscript and memoir were without
documentation, making their contents impossible to verify
independently, without these accounts the compilation of an
adequate biography would have been virtually impossible.

The other major source of information about Apikuni is
Schultz himself. He was a writer whose most frequent subject was the Montana scene; and a part of the charm of his
stories was the way he himself moved in and out of many
of them. His fascinated readers were entirely unconcerned
with whether he participated in the thrilling events he described or merely had discovered that the telling of a story
in the first person can be a useful device in heightening interest. In the early years on the frontier, the people with
whom he lived and worked were Indians and rough white
men, the exceptions being the eastern visitors for whom he
served as a guide in the St. Mary country. Consequently,
apart from what we are able to glean from reports by these
visitors, Schultz's tales of his early life in Montana, written
primarily for entertainment purposes rather than as autobiography, represent very nearly all that we have concerning
those years.

Scholars and historians having some familiarity with Schultz
suggest that it be remembered, in reference to his colorful
stories of his early adventures, that he was primarily a story-
writer who seldom let facts get in the way of a good story. As
to his reminiscences written fifty years or more after occur-
rence of most of the incidents they describe, these same
people suggest further that his memory for dates and similar details was remarkably unreliable and that what he has
written cannot be relied upon as history.

Mindful of the foregoing, I have tried to separate fact
from fiction, so far as possible, and have devoted an entire
chapter to setting forth some of the Schultz errors and inconsistencies in his published works. On the other hand, the
reader should appreciate the fact that there is really no
means of independent verification of most of the interesting
adventures of Schultz's early Montana years, as related by
himself, or of many personal incidents, such as Schultz's

marriage to his Indian wife by a clergyman. Despite Grinnell's comment in a prefatory editorial note in reference to *My Life as an Indian* that "in its absolute truthfulness lies its value," no one can really say with assurance that Schultz's fascinating reports of his early career are not, to some extent at least, the products of his genius as a writer of realistic fiction.

Apart from these three major sources, assistance and cooperation have been received from a variety of individuals and institutions and are hereby gratefully acknowledged. Outstanding in this regard is the Roland R. Renne Library at Montana State University at Bozeman, which is the repository for Schultz memorabilia and which, through its capable librarian, Minnie Paugh, has been very helpful.

Other great universities of the country have also provided assistance, including both Harvard and Yale. The Houghton Library on the Harvard campus has made available copies of the Schultz–Houghton Mifflin correspondence in its possession. The Beinecke Rare Book and Manuscript Library of Yale has furnished photostatic copies of the text of *Sport Among the Rockies*, a rare book which is the subject of Chapter 15 herein. From the University of Montana came the microfilm of the issues of *Forest and Stream* for the years 1879–94, all of which have been reviewed in search of Schultz material. Personnel of the Bancroft Library at the University of California at Berkeley have cooperated in arrangements for review of this microfilm, and credit is due Vivian Fisher and Jose Cuello, graduate student in history, for their cooperation.

I am particularly indebted to the Museum of the Rockies at Montana State University and to Anne Banks of its staff for her invaluable assistance with many puzzling aspects of the project. Also appreciated have been the advice and assistance of S. G. Ruth, curator of the Grinnell Papers at Southwest Museum in Los Angeles.

Other libraries have provided helpful information, including the Library of Congress, with the assistance of Mrs. Barbara Walsh, and the tiny library at Glacier National Park headquarters at West Glacier, Montana, with the help of

Miss Ellen Seeley. Special thanks are due the *Great Falls Tribune* for its prompt and willing assistance in tracing some of the Schultz articles that appeared in its columns during the 1930's and furnishing copies to me.

Both the Montana Historical Society and the Minnesota Historical Society have cooperated in the search for Schultz material. Thanks are due *Montana: The Magazine of Western History* for permission to quote and otherwise make use of material concerning Schultz from various of its issues.

A special acknowledgment is owing to *The Piegan Storyteller*, published quarterly at New Bern, North Carolina, on behalf of the James Willard Schultz Society, which publication has served to gather and present much useful information about Schultz the man and his literary career. David C. Andrews, editor of *The Piegan Storyteller*, has led the crusade to reestablish interest in Schultz and his life, and it was through him that a considerable volume of correspondence dealing with the publication of Schultz materials has been made available, it having been furnished to Andrews by Robert Martin of Glenview, Illinois, a nephew of Mrs. Jessie Schultz.

My interest in Schultz began with the acquisition of a copy of *My Life as an Indian* (Schultz's first book) nearly seventy years ago; it is still in my possession. My interest was enhanced through casual acquaintance with Schultz just after World War I when he made his annual summer visits to Glacier National Park, where I was working. I am satisfied that no one has done more to make the park beloved, as well as famous, than James Willard Schultz. By virtue of his pioneer activities as explorer, early guide, namer of many of its natural features, and author of books dealing with the region and its environs, he deserves to have the record of his accomplishments preserved for the benefit of his present admirers as well as for future generations of readers of his memorable stories.

Kensington, California   WARREN L. HANNA

The Life and Times of James Willard Schultz
(Apikuni)

CHAPTER 1

Growing Up in Boonville

Our western frontier sounded a clarion call for volunteers throughout much of the nineteenth century, a call that was heard by untold numbers of American youth. Many answered, of course, in response to the lure of gold and other precious metals, and for these it represented opportunity and the promise of a quick fortune. For others, however, it had the irresistible appeal of adventure and freedom, of mountain and prairie, of Indians and buffalo, an appeal that was not limited to the have-nots or the underprivileged.

Among those in whose ears the call of the West sounded loud and clear was a young man from a small town in upstate New York. The young man's name was James Willard Shults. The town was Boonville, and it was there, at 153 Schuyler Street, that James was born on August 26, 1859, the oldest son of Philander Bushrod and Frances Shults (as the name was then spelled). To this day there remains on the wall of the staircase leading to the attic a crude crayon sketch of an Indian in full regalia by Freddie Shults, James's younger brother, whose name also remains scratched on one of the window panes.

Boonville is rich in story and legend. It was founded in 1795 by Gerrit Boon, who was born in Holland and was an agent for the Holland Land Company. In time, Boonville became a shipping point on the Black River Canal, an important part of the intricate Erie Canal system. Barges laden with the varied products of the Great Lakes and the vast north country were stirring to a boy's imagination as they were drawn slowly past on their way to the markets and manufacturing establishments in and around the great cities of the East.

Then, as now, Boonville, with its many gracious homes on tree-lined streets and its historic and attractive old buildings, was a delightful place to live. It was an ideal birthplace for a boy, especially for a boy like Willie (as he was usually called) Shults. From the eastern edge of the village, the southwestern Adirondacks gave promise of high adventure, the mystery of deep hardwood forests, and the glory of autumnal coloring. There were lakes and streams, not only in the mountains, but throughout the surrounding countryside, for boating, swimming, hunting, and fishing.

Little is known of Willie's mother except that she was born Frances Joslin in Jefferson County, New York, and that she was a devout Presbyterian. Of his father's background, considerably more is known as a result of the diligent research of a third cousin, Mary E. Schultz. The name was of German origin, meaning "mayor"; indeed, in German, both *Schulze* and *Schultheis* refer to the mayor of a city.

Willie's great-great-grandfather was Jacob Schultheis, a member of a party of Palatinate Germans who took advantage of an alluring offer to Protestant Germans by Queen Anne of England: free passage and good farmland in her "province of New York." Jacob's son, and Willie's great-grandfather, John Johannes Shults, became a pioneer farmer at Stone Arabia, Montgomery County, New York, and was one of the patentees of the Stone Arabia Patent.

James Willard (as we shall call him) had chosen his parents well. They were educated, cultured, and prosperous people. Their home on Schuyler Street was a social center of the town, and they were popular with the habitués of Saratoga Springs, to which they made frequent and sometimes extended visits. Theirs was a home where stimulating conversation and good music were an important part of life. His father's produce business was a thriving one, and its warehouse on the Black River Canal was one of the busiest places in the district. From it produce was distributed over the far-flung network of the Erie Canal.

Philander Shults was a competent violinist, and his wife shared his devotion to music. Until his death, when James Willard was about ten, the father supervised his study of the violin. Often his parents took him with them when they visited New York City to attend the concerts of the New York and Brooklyn Philharmonic societies; all three were dedicated opera lovers.

James Willard Schults's earliest memory was of standing with his parents at a window of their home in Boonville watching troops march by on their way to the Civil War. When it came time for him to attend the public schools, he did so, but like many highly intelligent children he found the routine of much of the regular school day boring. He also showed a tendency toward being a nonconformist, as well as a prankster.

It is said that as one of his childhood pranks James Willard dressed up as an Indian to scare two little girls. When he found them walking along Charles Street one day, he began whooping and yelling. The girls started to run, and, yelling louder than ever, he gave chase. The chase did not last long. The girls stopped, faced the oncoming savage, and one of them declared: "We're not scared of you. You're not an Indian. You're only little Willie Shults."

Shults Senior had always understood and appreciated his son's love of the outdoors, and while James Willard was still a small boy he arranged with two competent men to take him into the nearby Adirondacks on camping and hunting trips. Thanks to these outings, James Willard not only became a skilled camper and an excellent shot but developed a deep appreciation of nature. His interest in the outdoors was encouraged by C. Hart Merriam, who lived at Locust Grove, only four or five miles from Boonville. Despite an age differential of four years, they became good friends.

To James Willard, the death of his father represented a deep tragedy, although his reaction to it was unusual. In fact, he shocked his relatives and family friends when he took his fishing pole and spent the day at the river, saying later: "I felt so damn bad that I had to be doing something. I wanted to be alone."

Upon the father's death, the mother was one of two guardians appointed for the two children, James, ten, and Frederick, five.[1] Bereft of the guidance of a father, James became something of a rebel against the religious teachings, educational practices, and social standards of the community. Taken in conjunction with a sensitive nature, some of his actions were of an unconventional or defiant character.

His mother, staunch Presbyterian that she was, insisted that James go to Sunday school. There he managed to make life miserable for the teachers by asking questions to which they were unable to supply satisfactory answers and by refusing to accept some parts of biblical lore as literal truth. When, for example, the teacher insisted that Jonah had emerged safely from the belly of a whale after three days of internment, young Shults questioned whether Jonah had ever been swallowed in the first place, producing data showing that the mouth of a whale would not have been large enough for Jonah to pass through. Before long he gave up Sunday school permanently.

James Willard had even more trouble with the authorities at the regular public school he attended. When he and some of the other boys violated a school rule by throwing snowballs during the noon hour at passers-by, the youngsters were lined up to be punished by having their knuckles rapped with a ruler. When his turn came, however, the lad rushed home and barricaded himself behind the front door, butcher knife in hand, ready to protect himself should the teacher come after him. This incident of total revolt ended his days in public school, and his education, so far as Boonville was concerned, was continued under private tutors.

While in his early teens, young Shults shocked some of the people who knew him by going into a saloon to drink a glass of beer with a few of the men of the town. He did not like the taste of it, but the talk of the men at the bar was more to

[1] The co-guardian with Mrs. Shults was Henry W. Bentley, a neighbor of the Shults family and highly respected member of the community. In fact, according to information secured by Matthew J. Conway, Bentley was the principal owner, or in charge at least, of the First National Bank of Boonville.

his liking than the prattle of youngsters his own age. More-over, it was a way of asserting his independence.

As he grew a little older, his endocrine system prompted him to engage in exciting adventures which gave his mother concern and caused talk among the good folk of Boonville. One day he persuaded a friend of his, Adam Finlayson, to go with him on one of the canal barges all the way to Rome, some twenty-two miles away. However, young Finlayson got worried and jumped ship at Lock 70, only two miles from Boonville. He ran home to be greeted with the punishment that in those days was usually meted out to small boys guilty of misconduct. Unfortunately, no one in Boonville seems to have any idea how James Willard came out: whether he got to Rome or what happened to him on his return.

After the death of the lad's father, his guardians decided that since James was so interested in wildlife and firearms he should be permitted to spend as much time as possible in the mountains with trusted guides, so long as he kept up his studies. In his fifteenth year they decided that because of his skill in shooting game and handling firearms he might well be prepared for a career in the army. Accordingly, he was sent to Peekskill Military Academy on the Hudson to pre-pare for West Point.

While he was at the academy, he enjoyed his courses in English and history and became editor of the school paper. He also developed considerable skill in drawing, as is shown by a picture of a deer he drew while at the academy. It was signed "J. W. Shults," and apparently it was not until some-time after he left the academy that he replaced the final *s* with a *z* and inserted a *c*. However, to this bright and indi-vidualistic young man there was little in the military life that appealed to him. During his stay at Peekskill, all he looked forward to were the vacation periods, when he could return to Boonville and again enjoy his hunting and fishing trips in the Adirondacks and his visits with Hart Merriam.

On many weekends, while at the academy, he went to New York City and stayed at the Fifth Avenue Hotel, where he had often been with his father and mother. There he would attend all the concerts and opera that he possibly could.

Schultz's birthplace in Boonville, New York. Courtesy Renne Library Collection.

There also he had a chance to enjoy a few beers at the hotel bar and to talk to men of experience. However, these week-end trips became so frequent and expensive that his guardians felt compelled to reduce his allowance. At the same time, the headmaster at Peekskill put a limitation on his off-campus leaves.

One weekend there was to be a particularly brilliant performance of *Aïda*,[2] and in spite of the newly imposed restric-

[2]This may well have been an early performance of *Aïda*, the premiere of which in the United States took place at the Academy of Music in New York City on November 28, 1873.

1859 - 1947

BIRTHPLACE OF APIKUNI
JAMES WILLARD SCHULTZ
BROTHER TO THE BLACKFEET
AUTHOR - EXPLORER - HISTORIAN
FRIENDS OF J.W.S.

Plaque at Schultz's birthplace. Courtesy Renne Library Collection.

tions, James Willard felt that he had to be there. He left school, planning to walk all the way to New York City, but when he encountered a band of hoboes eating beside a small fire, he accepted their invitation to join them, whereupon he ate with them, slept with them, and hopped a freight train with them, eventually arriving (without them) at the Fifth Avenue Hotel. As a token of appreciation of their hospitality, he gave them his gold watch. Somehow he managed to attend the performance of *Aïda*; and whatever the price he had to pay when he returned to Peekskill, he remembered that performance as being well worth it.

Young Shults's final day of his junior year at Peekskill in the spring of 1877 made academy history. To celebrate the occasion with a parting prank, he fired the campus cannon, thereby shattering innumerable windows and causing considerable commotion. It was now clear to his guardians that West Point was not for him.

Frances Shults, Schultz's mother. Courtesy Renne Library Collection.

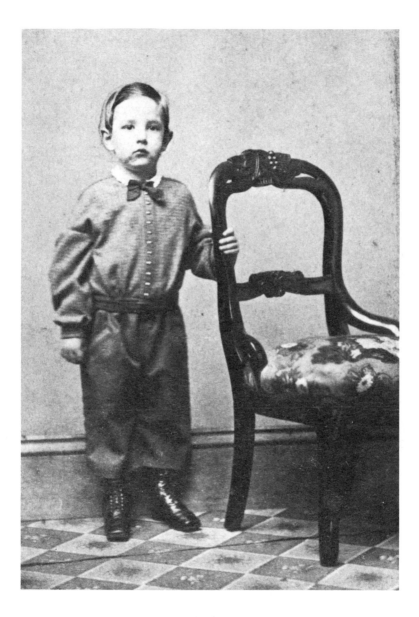

Schultz at age four. Courtesy Renne Library Collection.

Schultz at Peekskill Military Academy. Schultz is standing at the viewer's left of the tree. Courtesy Renne Library Collection.

Fortunately, the immediate problem of what to do with the young man was solved when he was invited to spend summer vacation with his uncle, Benjamin Stickney, who was the lessee and manager of the Planters Hotel in St. Louis, Missouri, home of Planters Punch and known for its catfish and crystal. Little did his guardians realize, when they agreed to his acceptance of this invitation, that they were helping him to take the decisive step toward a career they could never have imagined for him.

CHAPTER 2

St. Louis and the Broad Missouri

Y OUNG Shults,[1] although a small-town boy, had spent a good deal of time in New York City and enjoyed his visits there. But St. Louis entranced and excited him with its different atmosphere and its western flavor. The streets were crowded with trappers, traders, officers, and crewmen of the Mississippi and Missouri steamboats. He saw richly dressed plantation owners and their families, even Indians from various tribes in native dress.

In the lobby and at the bar of the Planters Hotel, Uncle Ben Stickney introduced him to some of the well-known men of the early western trade, such as Conrad and Baker. He listened to exciting stories, and there were plenty to hear: wrecks and near-wrecks on the tricky Missouri, narrow escapes from Indians and grizzly bears. One trapper told of being scalped, not by Indians but by a grizzly, and took off his cap to prove it. There were stories of buffalo hunts and escapes from stampedes. Tall tales without number brought guffaws as one yarn led to another, each tale taller than the one before.

Schultz spent much time along the levees; there the loading of the great steamboats of the Mississippi and its tributary rivers was of lasting interest to him. Every day he made a point of going to the levee where the riverboats plying the Upper Missouri docked. Sometimes he got a chance to talk

---

[1] Just when young Shults changed the spelling to *Schultz* is not known, although it was sometime after he left Peekskill Military Academy. However, from this point forward in this book the name is spelled *Schultz*.

with the captain or the pilot about the buffalo country and life and adventure in the Northwest.

Little wonder, then, that it was not long before the young man's mother back in Boonville received a letter asking that five hundred dollars be sent to him so that he could travel by steamboat up the Missouri to Fort Benton, head of navigation in the territory, his purpose being to go buffalo hunting. It seems likely that his mother's misgivings about such an adventure were somewhat allayed by assurances from Uncle Ben that he would supply the lad with letters of introduction to responsible friends in Fort Benton. Moreover, teenagers were not considered "kids" in those days, so, on condition that he would return home and to school after his Fort Benton visit, his mother sent him the requested funds.

At last came the day when he purchased passage on the next boat headed for Montana and left St. Louis, never to return to school. Long had he dreamed of the Far West! He had read and reread the Lewis and Clark *Journal*, Catlin's *Eight Years*, *The Oregon Trail*, and other thrilling stories. Now he was to see something of the country and the life about which they told. Perhaps he might even see some wild Indians and perhaps have a chance to shoot a buffalo; but at this point it was all a dream.

Once the boat got under way, every day was a new experience. The pilot of the boat became his hero, for it was only by his alertness, his unfailing skill, and his constant watchfulness that innumerable snags and river obstacles were avoided; half-sunken logs had wrecked many a valuable steamboat and its cargo. Time after time the pilot would order the engine stopped to avoid the hazards of floating logs and even thick blocks of ice being swept toward the boat by the raging waters.

Schultz remembered a crossing where the boat had to cut directly across the full current and consequently, in spite of the pilot's skill, was swept back downstream. Only on the third try was she able to force her way upstream once more. On the Missouri, as Schultz would explain, a crossing was a place where the current swept from one side of the channel to the other. These crossings and the river bends were graveyards for many a steamboat. Others were wrecked by the explosion of their mud-clogged boilers. The Missouri was well-named: Big Muddy.

Sometimes the boat on which Schultz was a passenger got stuck on submerged sandbars but usually was able to back off in short order. One time, however, she got stuck badly, and no amount of maneuvering would set her free. Finally the pilot ordered that strong, tall spars be lowered to the bottom of the river on each side of the boat, their tops angled toward the bow. A block and tackle with heavy manila ropes was attached to each spar; one end was then fastened to a sturdy portion of the gunwale, and the other was wound around the capstan. When everything was ready and at the pilot's order, the big stern wheel began thrashing the muddy water as the crew manned the capstan. Slowly the boat rose above the mud that had held her fast and jerked forward a short distance, only to become stuck again. The spars and their rigging were replaced some distance forward and the process was repeated until at last she floated free. The passengers cheered, but this grasshoppering, as it was called, was slow business and hard work for the crew.

The going was difficult in the daytime, even with full visibility, and it was necessary when darkness came to tie up for the night. Navigation on the Missouri was too tricky for night travel, and the boat's ravenous boilers consumed fifteen to twenty cords of wood a day, so the crew had to spend much time loading wood. If it seemed a likely place for fish, night lines would be set out in the hope of catching enough to afford a change in the otherwise monotonous diet. The overnight stops occasionally gave the passengers a chance to do a little hunting. If luck was with them, they might get ducks, geese, venison, or bighorn sheep to feast on.

Some parts of the river were picturesque, and for Schultz there was always something different and interesting to see. Particularly scenic were some of the rock formations for hundreds of miles along the river beyond Fort Peck, likenesses of which have been preserved on canvas by Catlin, Bodmer, and other artists of that period.

One of Schultz's most vivid memories was of a day when

the boat tied up to the bank directly below a massive yellow
sandstone hill which they had been able to see shortly after
passing Council Bluffs. The captain offered to lead a group
of the passengers to the summit to examine the curious
mound which capped it. The mound proved to be about
twelve feet in diameter and six feet in height. The captain
explained that an Omaha Indian named Blackbird was buried there.

As the story went, Blackbird as a youth had been an admired and famous warrior, but in later years he became the
tool of certain unscrupulous white traders. These traders
told the Omaha people that they had made Blackbird a very
great chief and had invested him with mystical and dreadful
powers. In a short time Blackbird became so arrogant and
brutal in the methods he used to force the Omahas to trade
only with his friends that several of the chiefs protested and
encouraged their people to trade wherever they wished.
This made Blackbird very angry and he reminded the chiefs
of the great powers he possessed. As a result of his powerful
medicine, every person who spoke against him died myste-
riously. Actually, they were poisoned with arsenic, applied
by his white trader friends.

Years later as Blackbird was dying of smallpox, he ordered
the Omaha people to bury him in accordance with his instructions; fearful of his mysterious powers, they complied.
He demanded that they dig a large, sloping pit on the summit of the yellow hill. Then he had himself dressed in full
regalia, wearing a sweeping warbonnet, tied upright to the
back of his favorite horse, and placed in the deep pit, after
which the people obeyed his final order: to pile rock and
earth upon him and his horse until they had made a great
mound. The mound was visible for several miles, and Blackbird was long remembered as a villainous, double-dealing
rascal.

The steamboat, as Schultz has described it, was a sturdy,
flat-bottom, shallow-draft stern-wheeler from the deck of
which he said he saw every foot of the Missouri's hundreds
of miles of shore between the Mississippi and Fort Benton.
He saw the beautiful groves and rolling green slopes of the

lower river, as well as the picturesque cliffs and walls of sandstone along portions of the upper. Sometimes he saw tribes of Indians camped on the banks, and he saw more game than he ever thought existed. Great herds of buffalo swimming the river impeded the boat's progress, and many bears, wolves, and coyotes, as well as antelope and bighorns, were seen. Most impressive, of course, were the vast herds of buffalo. From South Dakota on, they were constantly in evidence. Hundreds and hundreds of them—drowned, swollen, in all stages of decomposition—lay on the shallow bars where the current had cast them. The treacherous river, with its quicksands and its unevenly frozen surface in winter, apparently played as much havoc with the herds as did the Indians living along its course.

One would naturally think that animals crossing a stream and finding themselves under a high cut bank would turn out into the stream and swim down until a suitable landing place appeared, but many of the animals did not seem willing to do this. Having made up their minds to land at a certain place, those that were seen dead and dying under the cut banks seemingly chose to die there rather than make a short detour to reach their destination.

After the boat entered the buffalo country, there were many places which Schultz passed with regret, since he would have liked to go ashore and explore them. The captain, however, warned him not to become impatient, since if he went ashore he might not keep his scalp for two days because the groves along the river sheltered many a war party. Schultz found this good advice hard to accept until one day, somewhere between Round Butte and the mouth of the Musselshell River, they came upon a ghastly sight. On a shelving, sandy slope of shore, near a still-smoldering fire of which their half-burned skiff formed a part, lay the remains of three white men. The term *remains* was appropriate, for they had been scalped and literally cut to pieces, their heads crushed and frightfully battered, hands and feet severed and thrown promiscuously about. The steamboat party stopped and buried them, and Schultz did not again ask to be set ashore.

The trip from St. Louis to Fort Benton was reckoned by
old rivermen to be three thousand miles, but later surveys
showed the distance to be slightly under two thousand three
hundred miles.[2] Because travel was restricted to daylight
hours, the length of the average trip was forty to forty-five
days.[3] The head of navigation for the Upper Missouri was
Fort Benton except in times of low water late in the season,
when the boats could not get beyond Cow Island.

To many Schultz aficionados, no phase of his early career
has been of greater interest than his arrival at Fort Benton,
sometimes referred to as the "world's innermost port." Yet
few of them have become aware that a curious though in-
consequential dilemma in reference to this very subject has
arisen by reason of the differing versions of that event given
us by Schultz himself. As a matter of fact, few of Schultz's
readers have become aware of more than one version of his
arrival: that set forth in *My Life as an Indian*.[4] What it tells us
is that "one warm April morning" Schultz "left St. Louis on
a Missouri River steamboat, bound for the Far West," and
that "ours was the first boat to arrive at Fort Benton that
spring." What it does not tell us, whether by oversight or in-
tent, are the date of his arrival and the name of the first boat
to arrive at Fort Benton.

Few readers of *My Life as an Indian* have been aware that
Fort Benton records are available to show the name of each
riverboat arrival in the 1870's, as well as the arrival date and
point of origin for each. For the year 1877, these records
show the first arrival to have been the *Benton*, the date of its
arrival May 7, 1877, and its port of origin Yankton, South
Dakota. This means that since Schultz came from St. Louis,
it was unlikely that he would have reached Fort Benton on a
boat originating at Yankton and even more unlikely that he
would have reached Fort Benton on May 7, 1877.

An earlier Schultz version of his arrival really adds confusion to the picture. It appeared in an article entitled "On the

[2] Information supplied by Joel F. Overholser, retired editor of the *Fort
Benton River Press*, from records in his possession.
[3] *Idem.*
[4] *My Life as an Indian*, 4–6.

War-Path with Redskins" in the September, 1899, issue of *World Wide Magazine* of London, England.[5] So far as is pertinent, it reads as follows:

> There were but one or two passengers on the boat, and they, like myself, were bound for Fort Benton, a trading post of the American Fur Company. The boat, however, was not to reach there that year, for the water was falling rapidly; and at Cow Island, several hundred miles below our destination, it could go no further. At that point we found some bull trains awaiting us; the freight on the steamer was loaded onto the heavy wagons, and we proceeded overland. This part of the trip occupied two weeks, but every day of it was a delightful experience for me. One of the bullwhackers lent me his pony, and I used to ride ahead of the long train and shoot buffalo and antelope for the ever-hungry men. We arrived at the Fort at last, and this itself was worth traveling a long way to see.

Thus Schultz creates conflict by telling us in 1899 that his 1877 arrival at Fort Benton was by land and telling us a few years later that it was by water. Naturally, only one of these versions can be correct. Yet even if we accept the latter as the more likely happening, there is still no way, seemingly, to reconcile the assertion that "ours was the first boat to arrive at Fort Benton that season"[6] with historical records showing that the first boat did not come from the place Schultz came from, to wit, St. Louis.

Schultz's third version of his coming to Montana did not come to light until the publication in December, 1983, of *Bear Chief's War Shirt*, a book left unfinished at the time of his death and later completed by a friend. On page 2 of that interesting story, Schultz wrote: "On June 10th, 1877, in St. Louis, I boarded the Missouri River steamboat *Far West*, and in due time arrived in Fort Benton, Montana."

Records of steamboat arrivals at Fort Benton for 1877 do not list the *Far West*. As a matter of fact, that historic vessel was to spend her time that summer largely on the Yellow-

---

[5] The story was reprinted in *The Piegan Storyteller*, January, 1979, p. 1.
[6] *My Life as an Indian*, 6.

stone and Bighorn rivers.[7] Consequently, it was necessary
for passenger Schultz to disembark at Bismarck and transfer to the next boat headed for Fort Benton. Records from
the latter port show that the next boat would have been the
Benton, which had spent the summer plying between the
railhead at Bismarck and the head of navigation at Fort Benton,[8] its fourth departure from Bismarck having been about
July 9 or 10, with arrival at Fort Benton on July 20.

The possibility or probability that Schultz was on the *Benton* when it left Bismarck has been confirmed by Joel F.
Overholser, editor emeritus of the *Fort Benton River Press*,
who has stated that a steamboat leaving St. Louis on June
10, 1877, could be expected to reach Bismarck about July 9
or 10 and that the usual running time of the *Benton* from
Bismarck to Fort Benton was eleven days or less.[9] Assuming,
accordingly, that Schultz had arrived at Bismarck on the *Far
West* on July 9, 1877, and had made an expeditious transfer
to the *Benton*, he would have "in due time arrived at Fort
Benton" on July 20, 1877.

Apart from the close correlation of the time factor, other
circumstances point to the probability that this was what happened. In the excerpt from *Bear Chief's War Shirt*, Schultz's
wording leaves an implication that the *Far West* did not go all
the way to Fort Benton without explaining why. In conversations with his wife and friends in the 1920's, Schultz always
referred to his Fort Benton arrival as having been on board
the steamboat *Benton* in spite of the fact that he made no
mention of the name in earlier accounts.

Chronologically, a June 10 departure from St. Louis would
have been much more likely than the "warm April morning"
mentioned in *My Life as an Indian*, since it is improbable that
his school term at Peekskill had been concluded before mid-
May, after which he still had to travel to St. Louis, become
familiar with the riverboats, and ask for and receive from
home the funds needed for his Montana excursion.

[7] Joseph Mills Hanson, *The Conquest of the Missouri*, 353 N36.
[8] From record of boat arrivals in *Fort Benton River Press*, furnished by
Joel F. Overholser.
[9] Letters from Overholser dated January 5 and 16, 1984.

Curiously, when one reviews Schultz's language in *My Life as an Indian*, he writes of leaving St. Louis "bound for the Far West" (possibly a Freudian slip in view of the fact that the name of the boat was the *Far West* and that Montana was the Northwest, not the Far West). His statement that "ours was the first boat to arrive at Fort Benton that spring" was true in reference to the *Benton*, although he himself did not reach his destination until that vessel had made its fourth visit of the season to Fort Benton.[10] All in all, the evidence seems to show rather conclusively the means as well as the date of Schultz's arrival at Fort Benton in 1877.

[10] Fort Benton records for the *Benton* in 1877 show the following:

ARRIVALS AT FORT BENTON	DEPARTURE DATES
May 7 (from Yankton)	May 11
May 31 (from Bismarck)	June 3
June 27 (from Bismarck	June 30
July 20 (from Bismarck)	July 22
August 15 (from Bismarck)	August 17

CHAPTER 3

Fort Benton

OR ME life really began that day in 1877 when I jumped from the deck of the steamer *Benton* to the levee at Fort Benton." Thus did James Willard Schultz refer to his arrival at Fort Benton in conversations with his good friend Harry C. James in the 1920's. Occasionally he would add: "I just couldn't wait for the gangplank to be lowered. People crowded around me and some one hoisted me to the top of a pile of baled buffalo robes. Buffalo! that was what I had come for! One of my fellow passengers called out to me, 'Good luck, Willie, don't let any Indians get your hair!'"

Fort Benton was an important trading post built by the American Fur Company in 1846 in what was then the far distant territory of Montana. Adjacent to it a town was laid out in 1865, although it was not incorporated until 1883. As head of navigation on the Missouri, the town of Fort Benton had become the entry port for all kinds of adventurers, hunters, trappers, traders, cattlemen, and gold seekers.

The arrival of the first steamboat in the spring of each year was an event of great importance in Fort Benton. For days people from the surrounding countryside would crowd into the small town to celebrate her arrival. Her smoke was seen as she steamed into a large bend in the Missouri some distance downriver. Shouts went up from the crowd assembled on the levee to give her a rousing greeting. Flags were flying and cannon were booming as she moved toward the levee.

In the forefront of the crowd on one such occasion were two important-looking men, traders who were now building their own empires on the ruins of the once-prestigious

American Fur Company. They were dressed alike in suits of blue broadcloth with high-collared, long-tailed coats fastened with large brass buttons. Their neatly combed hair hung down to their shoulders. With them were their chief employees, who also wore their hair long and whose rawhide moccasins were bright with brilliantly colored Indian beadwork. They waited anxiously for the cargo to be unloaded so that they could check their shipments of trade goods and supplies from St. Louis or other points of departure.

Scattered among the townspeople were French boatmen from St. Louis and the Lower Mississippi who had spent their lives cordelling many a boat up the Missouri. They stood out among the crowd because of their capotes, and their buckskin or fustian trousers held up by bright red sashes. Nearly all the men had knives and Colt six-shooters stuck in their belts, and many of them, especially the hunters and the trappers, wore headgear made of fox skins, the tails hanging down their backs.

When the hawsers had been made fast and the gangplank lowered, the *Benton's* passengers began to come ashore. Two of the local madams and their girls added more color to the scene as they pushed forward toward the gangplank to welcome returning customers. As one of their well-known patrons started down the gangplank, they gave him a loud and bawdy greeting. He ducked and tried to lose himself in the crowd.

Interesting as all this was to young Schultz, he was far more interested in the crowd of Indians in the background. They were in their everyday attire. The men wore cow-buffalo leggings, calico shirts, and blankets or buffalo leather robes. Their faces were painted with reddish-brown ocher or vermilion, and their hair was neatly separated in two braids. Some of them carried flintlock rifles; others, bows and quivers of arrows. Riflewise James Willard noted that a few of the men had the more modern caplock rifles. He saw, too, that although most of the Indian women wore calico dresses, some of them were conspicuous in silk dresses and vividly colored shawls. These, he found out later, were the wives of traders, clerks, and skilled workers of the trading companies.

As soon as cargo unloading began, long teams of mules and oxen moved along the levee toward the steamboat, where their great wagons were loaded with general merchandise, which included just about everything from traps and rifles to sewing machines; trade goods for the Indians; mining equipment, from picks and shovels to massive machinery; and cask after cask of whiskey. As each cask was hoisted from the hold, it was greeted with cheers from the bystanders.

Some of the cargo was destined for the warehouses of the Fort Benton merchants and traders, but much of it would be hauled all the way to Helena and even on the wagon trail through the "Whoop-Up Country" as far as Fort Macleod in Canada, two hundred forty miles northwest of Fort Benton. Indeed, trails soon were to radiate from Fort Benton in many directions, for it quickly became the business center of a large area. By some it was being called, "the Chicago of the West."

As the crowd was beginning to move away from the levee in the direction of the town, Schultz jumped down from the buffalo hides and followed along, his eyes ranging far and wide.

Beyond the town the river valley ended in a series of breaks and coulees leading up to the vast short-grass plains—buffalo country. The adobe walls and the two high blockhouses of Fort Benton dominated the town. Front Street was a heterogeneous collection of false-front stores, saloons, hurdy-gurdy houses, warehouses, a blacksmith shop or two, and a scattering of houses between Front Street and the fort.

Fort Benton had the reputation of being a wild and lawless town, but by 1877 much of the crudity and lawlessness of frontier life were on their way out. However, with the arrival of the *Benton*, Front Street was as wild and woolly as Schultz could have wished it. On the long trip from St. Louis, he had heard many a wild tale of Fort Benton; now he was in the middle of it, and it was living up to his expectations. Half a dozen curs got into a fight in the middle of the street. A cloud of dust went up and a crowd gathered, Schultz among them. A couple of fist fights added to the commotion. Someone set fire to a pile of rubbish, which increased the confusion.

Schultz walked on to the Chouteau House,[1] the hotel his Uncle Ben had suggested to him, but every room had been taken by a group of United States Army officers. The clerk suggested that he try the Overland Hotel, so he walked back down Front Street to the Overland and was able to get a room in one of the log cabins connected with the main building. Dinner was announced as he was registering. Fittingly, the young would-be buffalo hunter was served boiled buffalo boss ribs at his first meal in the land he had traveled so far to reach.

After dinner he sauntered back to the *Benton* to get his baggage and his Henry rifle, in which he took such pride. These stowed away in his room, he joined some of the other Overland guests on the porch. Front Street was still filled with the crowd celebrating the arrival of the first boat of the season. His eye caught three Indians walking toward the Overland: a man, a woman, and a little girl of about ten, all neatly dressed with their hair in long braids. They paid no attention to the noisy crowd milling about them. Schultz had by now become accustomed to seeing Indians, but there was such an impressive dignity and an aloofness about this decidedly handsome little family that he asked the man next to him what Indians they were. "Blackfeet, Pikuni Blackfeet, the meanest, most bloodthirsty bastards in all Montana!" was the reply. It came as a shock to Schultz, since the Indians did not look the part to him.

It is not likely that Schultz slept much during his first night in Fort Benton. With whiskey at its normal price of two bits a glass, the celebration went on all night, and his room at the Overland was far from soundproof. But there he was, at long last, in buffalo country.

With breakfast under his belt, he pocketed his letters of introduction and started off to present them and get ac-

---

[1] But the town of Choteau, Montana, is spelled without the extra *u*.

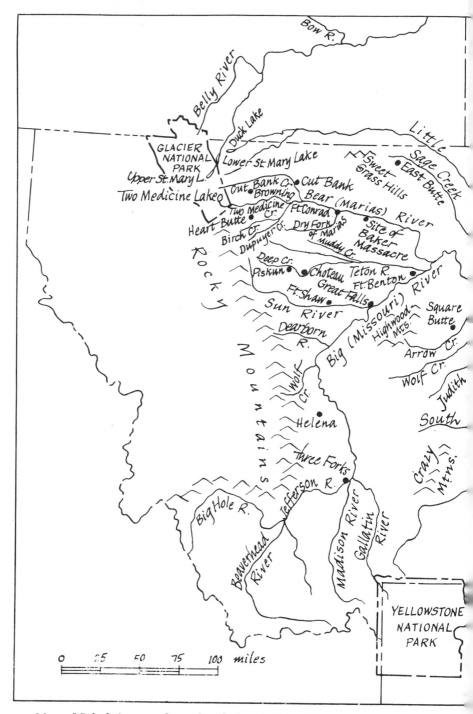

Map of Schultz's area of travel with the Blackfeet (Montana and surrounding areas). From James Willard Schultz (Apikuni), Blackfeet and Buffalo: Memories of Life Among the Indians, *ed. and*

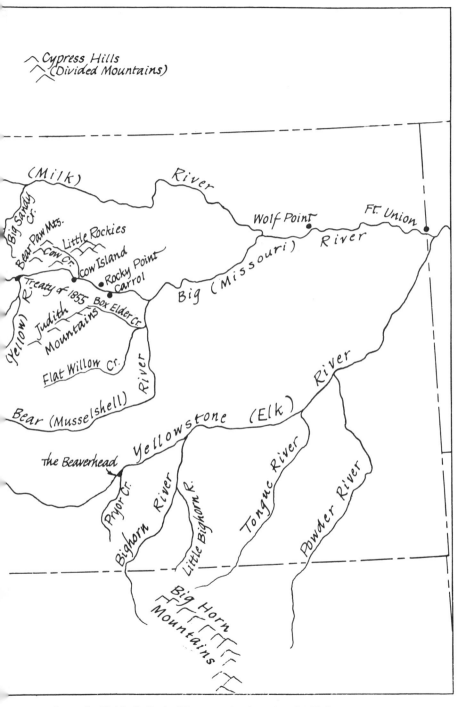

intro. by Keith C. Seele (Norman: University of Oklahoma Press, 1962).
Reprinted by permission.

quainted. One was addressed to the management of the
I. G. Baker Company; his Uncle Ben had suggested that he
call there first. The Baker establishment was a small store
with a porch across the front and a commodious adobe
warehouse at the back. A sign in front read:

I. G. Baker and Co.
Wholesale and retail
Dealer in
DRY GOODS GROCERIES
Hats Caps Boots and Shoes
Gents Furnishing Goods
Carpets Tents etc.

In *My Life as an Indian*, Schultz told of his hospitable re-
ception.[2] After he met the employees, one of the members
of the firm took him up to old Fort Benton to meet some of
the officers there, then back to town, where he was introduced to many of the leading citizens as well as a number of
trappers and traders who had come to town for the arrival
of the steamboat.

With the dissolution of the historic American Fur Company, the T. C. Power and the I. G. Baker companies of Fort
Benton proceeded to build their own vast commercial empires with and on its ashes. Two years before Schultz arrived
at Fort Benton, George Baker, the junior member of the
firm, had sold his interest to the three Conrad brothers
from Virginia: William, Charles, and John. About that same
time, the senior partner, Isaac Gilbert Baker, established in
St. Louis an office from which to supervise the purchasing
and financing activities of the company. Under his knowledgeable direction, assignments of goods intended for the
firm's western headquarters at Fort Benton were assembled
and shipped. With I. G. Baker in St. Louis and the Conrad
brothers at Fort Benton, it is small wonder that theirs was
one of the most successful business enterprises of the period. Schultz was in good hands, and he and Charles Conrad became and remained close friends.

For Schultz, however, the most important meeting of the

[2] Pps. 9-10.

day, and one which was to influence his whole life, was with
trader Joseph Kipp, named Raven Quiver by the Blackfeet.
Kipp was ten years older than Schultz, but they took to each
other at once. Kipp, referred to in *My Life as an Indian* as
Berry, was a remarkable man. In fact, he was the remarkable son of a remarkable father, James Kipp, who was born
in Canada about 1798. As an employee of the Columbia Fur
Company, he came to the Upper Missouri country in the
early 1820's and built the first trading post for the Blackfoot
Indians in 1831. He remained in that part of the country
until he retired in 1859 or 1860. He had several Indian
families, as well as a white wife and children who lived on his
farm near Independence, Missouri. Joe Kipp's mother was
Earth Woman, daughter of Mandan Chief *Mahtotopa*, of
whom George Catlin wrote such extravagant praise.

Schultz spent the rest of the day with Kipp, who seemed
to know almost everyone in Fort Benton. Late in the afternoon they entered one of the town's many saloons just as a
violent argument was commencing between two men at one
of the gambling tables. As the gamblers reached for their
guns, Kipp yelled, "Down!" and at the same instant pulled
Schultz with him to the floor. Guns blazed and when the
shooting was over, one of the men lay back in his chair dead.
Realizing that his young friend was somewhat shaken by the
incident, Kipp led him out and up the street toward the
outskirts of the town and an adobe cabin where, Kipp explained, a group of trappers and traders were holding a
dance. A violin and a concertina supplied the music, and
Kipp and Schultz, much to be the latter's surprise, were soon
taking part in a lively square dance with handsome Indian
women partners.

When the dance ended, Schultz's partner, who did not
speak English, led him over to Kipp, who was talking in
Blackfoot with another man. Kipp greeted her in Blackfoot
and she immediately responded, talking first to Kipp and
then to the other man. Kipp turned to Schultz and introduced the man he had been talking to as his friend Sorrel
Horse and explained that it was his wife who had just been
Schultz's dancing partner. Kipp went on to say that Sorrel

Horse had invited them to come over to his lodge to have
something to eat.

The light inside the cabin where they had been dancing
was poor, so Schultz was surprised when they stepped outside into the sunlight to find that Kipp's friend Sorrel Horse,
with whom he had been conversing freely in Blackfoot, was
not an Indian but a tall, pleasant-faced white man. He had
blue eyes, a thick head of hair, and a full beard of reddish-
brown color. As they all walked toward the lodge of Sorrel
Horse, Kipp explained that the Pikunis had named him Sorrel Horse because of the color of his hair and that, like Kipp,
he was a trader with the Blackfoot tribes.

Sorrel Horse's lodge turned out to be large and beautifully
decorated. They entered, and Mrs. Sorrel Horse soon had a
small fire burning briskly in the fire pit directly under the
smoke hole at the top of the lodge. As it began to smoke, she
stepped outside and skillfully adjusted the two flaps, or ears,
to the wind and in a moment was back arranging her pots at
the fire. From a gaily painted parfleche, she took several
small bags and was soon busy cooking.

At each side and at the back of the lodge were couches
covered with buffalo robes and blankets, their backrests
made of supple, tough wooden rods covered with buffalo
robes. A decorated drop curtain was suspended behind and
above the couches. Schultz noted that it not only prevented
drafts across the couches and the floor but also supplied
ventilation. Both the tentlike lodge covering and the drop
curtain were made of buffalo hides skillfully prepared and
neatly sewn with split-buffalo-sinew thread. Even the slender
lodge poles had been smoothed and tapered with nicety.
While the meal was being prepared, the men lay back among
the buffalo robes on the couches, smoking and talking. Mrs.
Sorrel Horse, as Schultz found himself calling her, joined in
the conversation from time to time.

The neatness, the cleanliness, the good workmanship, the
general "rightness" of everything about the lodge, along
with its quiet comfort, gave him a deep sense of contentment and comradeship despite the handicap of an unfamiliar language. Schultz mentioned this to Kipp, who trans-

lated what he had said for the benefit of Mrs. Sorrel Horse.
She looked over at their young guest and, with Kipp still
translating, told how Sorrel Horse had shot eighteen
buffalo, the hides of which she had tanned and cut so that,
in addition to the lodge, she might have enough for the curtain around its interior and for the thick, warm robes that
covered the couches. With simple sign talk, she indicated
that her husband was a great hunter.

The men laughed and she, laughing too, began to serve
dinner. Schultz realized that it was a meal to suit the occasion: light biscuits baked in a Dutch oven, stewed buffalo
berries, and that great delicacy of the plains, boiled buffalo
tongue, all washed down with cups of pungent hot tea. Re-
clining against the backrests, they ate leisurely. And as it began to get dark, a few small sticks were tossed on the fire
and the flames gave them a flickering light.

As they chatted by the fire, Schultz learned that both Kipp
and his hosts were leaving in the morning, although separately. With his long bull train, its wagons laden with supplies, Kipp would be heading for the gold fields at Helena.
As for the Sorrel Horses, their wagons were loaded in readi-
ness for joining a band of Pikuni Blackfeet on their summer
buffalo hunt. To Schultz's amazed delight, Sorrel Horse invited him to join them and Kipp tried to persuade him to go
along to Helena and try his luck as a miner—he might strike
it rich and make a fortune.

It did not take Schultz long to reach a decision. In joining
Sorrel Horse and the Pikunis, he would be able to hunt
buffalo, and that had been his purpose in making the long
trip from St. Louis. On the other hand, he and Kipp had
become very good friends in the brief time they had spent
together, and before they went their separate ways the next
morning, they agreed to meet again in Fort Benton after
Kipp had returned from Helena and Schultz from his
buffalo hunt with Sorrel House.

CHAPTER 4

In the Lodges of the Blackfeet

A	T DAWN the Sorrel Horse camp was a scene of great activity. The lodge had to be taken down and packed in one of the wagons, and the long slender lodge poles had to be tied securely along the sides of the wagons. As this was in progress, a slim young Indian, about the same age as Schultz, rode up driving a small herd of horses ahead of him. As he swung out of the saddle, Sorrel Horse introduced him as his brother-in-law, *Iś-sis-tsi*, or Wolverine, who would help Schultz buy what he would need for the summer. In short order they had purchased a horse well trained for buffalo hunting, a bedding roll, a supply of tobacco, and cartridges for Schultz's treasured Henry rifle.

The two wagons, linked together and drawn by an eight-horse team, were laden with provisions and trade goods. Sorrel Horse and Wolverine took turns driving while Schultz herded the extra horses. Sorrel Horse's wife rode in the front wagon, but sometimes she would join in herding the horses. Sorrel Horse intended to find the Small Robes band of the Pikunis and to follow along with them, hunting and trading as they slowly moved along the foot of the Belt Mountains by Warm Spring Creek and through the valley of the *Otokwi Tuktai*, or Judith River.

Schultz and Wolverine soon became close friends and often participated in the buffalo hunts organized among the Small Robes. Mounted on the fine buffalo horse Wolverine had chosen for him and with his ability as a marksman, Schultz soon began to learn some of the finer points in this special type of hunting, and shot the buffalo he had come all the way from St. Louis to shoot. As a matter of fact, he was delighted to find that his skill with the rifle, his ability as a horseman, and his friendly interest in everyone he met soon won for him a welcome among the many members of the Small Robes band with whom he came in contact. Game was plentiful, and he and Wolverine went frequently on hunting trips for bighorn, bear, antelope, and elk. They not only kept the Sorrel Horse lodge well supplied with meat but frequently helped supply the needs of some of the old people among the tribe.

The hunting trips with Wolverine were of inestimable value to Schultz. Both spent much time sitting in the sun high on some mountainside, watching herds of game far below or silently gazing at the massive ranges of snowcapped mountains that fretted the not-too-distant skyline. For Schultz this was sheer delight, and Wolverine, too, could be heard to murmur, *"I-tam-ap-i,"* the Blackfoot exclamation of happiness.

It was at such a time that Schultz began to make a serious study of the Blackfoot language—he never failed to have a notebook with him. Although Wolverine had slight knowledge of English, he frequently resorted to the versatile sign language in common use among the Plains tribes. He would make a sign; if Schultz did not grasp its meaning, he would explain it by pantomime or sometimes by a word or two in English complemented by pantomime. At times it was an amusing performance and they welcomed every opportunity to engage in it. As Wolverine made a sign, he would simultaneously use the Blackfoot word the sign represented. Schultz found this helped him learn the Blackfoot spoken language while he was becoming familiar with sign language.

Wolverine seemed to be such a carefree chap that Schultz was surprised when one day he confided that he was in deep trouble. He explained that while visiting in the camp of the Gros Ventres, with whom the Pikunis were then at peace, he had met a girl with whom he fell deeply in love. Her mother was a Pikuni, but her father was a Gros Ventre whose brother and son had been killed by the Pikunis when the tribes were at war some years earlier and who had sworn that his daughter would never marry a Pikuni. Wolverine

knew that the girl, whose name was *Piks-ah-ki*, loved him
and that her mother would be in favor of his suit. Her father, whose name, appropriately enough, was Bull's Head,
was adamant in his determination that *Piks-ah-ki* would
never marry Wolverine or any other Pikuni. Knowing that
Piks-ah-ki loved him in return, Wolverine had decided that
he would find some way to abduct her, and he asked Schultz
to go with him. Schultz agreed gladly as it gave promise of
being a unique adventure.

They rode by night and hid and rested by day, Wolverine
leading a gentle pinto pony for the girl. At dawn one morning they came to a large grove of cottonwood trees along a
small stream, an excellent place to hide for the day. To their
concern they discovered fresh footprints in the wet sand.
Leaving Schultz with the horses, Wolverine stealthily reconnoitered the area and returned to report that from the
tracks of the moccasins they were wearing, it was evident
that a war party of Crees, or some tribe from the other side
of the mountains, recently had passed through the grove
and down the valley. He concluded that they were on their
way to steal horses from the Gros Ventres and that, being on
foot, it would take the party at least two days to reach the
Gros Ventre camp.

This discovery led Wolverine to formulate a plan which he
discussed with Schultz. As there was now peace between the
Pikunis and the Gros Ventres, the next morning they rode
boldly into the Gros Ventre camp and directly to the lodge
of Chief Three Bears. When invited to enter, Wolverine
presented the chief with tobacco and told him that Big Lake,
chief of the Pikunis, had sent them to warn him that there
was a large war party of twenty or thirty apparently on its
way to raid the Gros Ventre camp. Three Bears expressed
his gratitude for this warning and sent word throughout the
camp. He treated Wolverine and Schultz as honored guests
and gave them the freedom of the camp.

Wolverine managed to have a few words with *Piks-ah-ki*,
and she gladly agreed to be ready to leave with them. At
dusk Schultz and Wolverine saddled their horses, Wolverine
putting his saddle on the pinto pony he had brought for
Piks-ah-ki. Then they waited.

Schultz and Mrs. Bear Head about 1918. She is Piks-ah-ki, whom Apikuni helped Wolverine steal from her Gros Ventre family in 1877. Courtesy Renne Library Collection.

Sometime during the night the enemy war party attempted to enter the Gros Ventre camp, and the alarm quickly spread. Being well prepared, the Gros Ventres opened fire on the raiders. In the confusion, Bull's Head, worried about his horses being stolen, ran out to protect them. In the meantime, Wolverine found *Piks-ah-ki* and her mother and they quickly joined Schultz, who was waiting with the horses. *Piks-ah-ki* bade a sorrowful farewell to her mother, Wolverine promised that he would take good care of her, and away the three of them rode. Just as they thought they were free of the camp, a gun was fired from some bushes directly in front of Wolverine and down went his horse. The girl screamed, thinking he had been killed, but he quickly scrambled to his feet and fired several shots into the brush, killing the man who had shot at him. Seizing the old gun that had been fired at him, he jumped up behind *Piks-ah-ki.* Suddenly her father appeared, shrieking abuse at Wolverine. Wolverine jumped upon him and flung his gun far into the brush, then once more leaped up behind *Piks-ah-ki.* The three of them were soon well out of danger.

Realizing that they might be followed, they took a long, circuitous route back to the Pikuni camp. They were not too surprised to find Bull's Head already there. His attitude had changed entirely. He fairly fawned upon Wolverine, extolling his daughter's virtues and pleading his great poverty. To appease him, Wolverine gave Bull's Head ten horses and the old gun that had belonged to the man who tried to kill him. Bull's Head was quite satisfied and soon was on his way back to the Gros Ventre camp. When Sorrel Horse heard about Schultz's helping to steal an Indian girl, he laughed heartily. "Only three months in the country and going with an Indian to steal a girl!" he said.

Those wonderful few months with Wolverine and Sorrel Horse passed quickly. All too soon Schultz was back at Fort Benton, eagerly waiting for Kipp to return with his bull train from the long haul along the Whoop-Up Trail. There is no record of when Kipp got back to Fort Benton, but we do know that when he did he had plans to spend the autumn and winter trading with the Pikunis, wherever they planned to spend those seasons.

When Kipp had assembled the necessary supplies and equipment and pulled out of Fort Benton, Schultz was with him. Kipp's outfit was an impressive one. His bull train consisted of eleven wagons filled with trade goods supplied by I. G. Baker Company in Fort Benton, with which Kipp had become affiliated. Experienced bullwhackers drove ox teams, while Kipp and his other employees usually rode to keep the sizable herd of horses from straying. Besides overnight camps, longer stops were made from time to time when Pikuni scouts reported opportunities for good hunting. At all these stops a certain amount of trading was carried on by Kipp and his helpers. The slow pace of the bull train gave

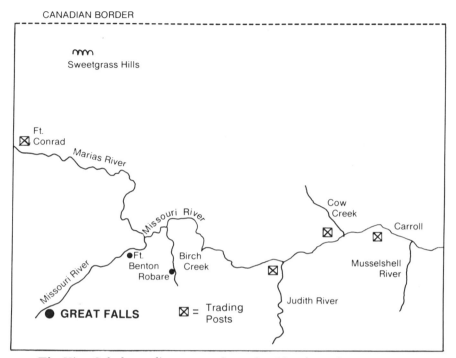

The Kipp-Schultz trading posts, 1877–82. Map by author.

Schultz opportunities to range far and wide to investigate everything that caught his eye. At Kipp's suggestion he took advantage of every occasion that came his way to gain fluency in the difficult Blackfoot language, as well as in the remarkable sign language that served the Plains tribes so well as a lingua franca.

In late autumn the Pikuni chiefs decided the tribe should winter in the open valley of Cow Creek, a small tributary of the Missouri between the Bear Paws and the Little Rockies. Scouts had reported that antelope and buffalo were thick upon the plains above the valley, as were deer and elk in the valley and in the surrounding mountains. It gave promise of being a good winter for the Pikunis and a rewarding one for James Willard Schultz, plus good trading for Kipp.

It was late November by the time the Pikunis reached the
valley of Cow Creek and began to erect their lodges in areas
which would provide some protection against the winter
blizzards and yet be open to the warm chinook winds when
they happened to smile upon the Pikunis in the depth
of winter. Close by, where the Kipp party had erected its
lodges and drawn up its wagons to establish a trading post,
were the lodges of some of Kipp's friends, among them old
Hugh Monroe (Rising Wolf to the Blackfeet) and William
Jackson, Monroe's grandson, often called *Siksikaikwan* (Blackfoot Man) because of his close association with them. Also
nearby was Kipp's friend old Charles Rivois,[1] known among
the Blackfeet as a storyteller; his tales would help pass many
a long winter evening. During his stay with Sorrel Horse
and his family Schultz had begun to appreciate the store of
thrilling tales known to the Pikunis, but it was during the
long winter at Cow Creek, when he listened night after
night, as the tiny lodge fires flickered down to glowing em-
bers, to epic tales of adventure told by the participants
themselves, that Schultz came to understand what a treasure
trove of material lay here for a writer.

Kipp and his wife, Double-Strike Woman, daughter of
Chief Heavy Runner of the Pikunis, were popular among
the Blackfoot tribes. As a protégé of Kipp, Schultz enjoyed
the freedom of the camp along Cow Creek and was greeted
in friendly fashion wherever he went. As his familiarity with
the Indians' language increased, he saw into their way of life
and began to understand the significance of their various
religious rites. The lad who as a youngster in Sunday school
had found the story of Jonah and the whale ridiculous now
found himself deeply impressed by, and in some strange
way emotionally involved with, the religious observances of
the Pikunis. He had not been with them very long at Cow
Creek before he realized that he felt himself a part of this
community in a way that he had never felt a part of Boon-

---

[1] See James Willard Schultz, *Friends of My Life as an Indian*, 135; *Blackfeet
and Buffalo*, 347.

ville. As yet, however, there was nothing to indicate that he had made a decision to renege on the promise he had made to his mother to return to Boonville, and there are no records or letters to indicate just when that decision was made. It is probable that his mother was kept informed by Ben Stickney and the latter's sources of communication that her son was under the wing and informal guardianship of a responsible individual in the person of Joe Kipp.

At the Pikuni camp Schultz formed strong ties with many of the young men of the tribe and frequently rode with them up onto the plains to hunt buffalo and antelope and thereby help keep the tribe in meat. They also made occasional trips into the mountains after bighorn sheep, and possibly to trap for beaver, mink, and otter. Among the life-long friendships made on trips of this kind were those of William Jackson, mentioned earlier, and a young Pikuni by the name of *Apsi*, or Arrow. In later years, after a successful raid on the Assiniboines during which he counted coup three times, *Apsi* took the name *Stumkis Otokamp*, or Bull-Turns-Around. One of the hunting trips was of significance to both *Apsi* and Schultz but particularly to Schultz.

For a long time the Pikuni camp was virtually immobilized by bone-chilling cold and deep snow. One evening the revered old medicine man Red Eagle brought out his sacred thunder medicine pipe and made sacrifice and prayers to the gods to take pity on their children. At midnight a warm chinook wind started to blow; next morning the sun shone and the snow began to melt. The people of the camp called out their thanks to Red Eagle, and the hunters were quick to take advantage of the soft, warm wind. After pledging Red Eagle the highly esteemed tongue of every buffalo they might kill that day, they mounted swift buffalo runner horses and started down the valley.

Before the bad weather had descended on the Pikuni camp, *Apsi*, with the help of Jackson and Schultz, had killed a buffalo and an antelope or two some distance from camp. These they poisoned with strychnine to serve as bait for the great gray wolves which followed the buffalo herds in large packs.[2] Traders paid five dollars for a prime gray-wolf pelt. As he had no chance to visit these poisoned baits after the blizzards had struck the camp, *Apsi* also decided to take advantage of the chinook. He invited Schultz and Jackson to join him, and the three of them followed the hunters as they rode down Cow Creek toward the Missouri. Several miles below camp the hunting party divided to take advantage of the many coulees. Thus *Apsi*, Jackson, and Schultz had the valley to themselves.

After riding a few miles they turned up a certain coulee and at its head found their first bait, a bull buffalo carcass laced with three-eighths of an ounce of strychnine. Small as the amount of poison was, it had done its work well. Surrounding the carcass were the bodies of eleven wolves and several coyotes, all frozen stiff. It would be impossible to skin them until a long thaw had set in.

Pleased at this success, they rode on to the next bait, an antelope carcass around which were scattered the frozen bodies of several coyotes and foxes. Near the body of a fox lay a large golden eagle, evidently killed when it ate the strychnine-contaminated liver of the fox. *Apsi* was thrilled at the sight of the big eagle; its tail feathers were worth at least three horses, but he would not consider such a trade for his war shield had only a dozen such feathers around its rim and these three would complete its decoration.

The third bait was about three miles south of the antelope carcass. As they came close to it, they were startled as, with a thunderous rush, a herd of buffalo poured in a sea of brown bodies down the steep slope of the valley. When the leaders of the herd sighted the precipitous cut bank of Cow Creek, they veered and the entire herd came dashing toward them. Suddenly the leaders saw the three horsemen, wheeled instantly, and shot off down the valley. *Apsi* and his companions were so close to them that they could see their gleaming black eyes. Momentarily the herd opened up before them

[2]The practice of poisoning wolves, sometimes referred to as wolfing, was not commonly carried on by Indians because of the danger to their dogs. In this case, it will be noted, the poisoned bait was several miles from camp.

and in the middle of it the men caught a sight so rare that they could hardly believe their eyes: a snow-white young buffalo. They all knew the reverence in which the Blackfeet held such a rare animal. With a cry from *Apsi* they dashed after the herd, but because they were not riding their swift buffalo runners, the chase proved hopeless. *Apsi's* disappointment was beyond measure.

As they slowed their fruitless chase, Jackson shot a fat cow, the meat of which was preferred by the Plains Indians. At least they would not return to camp emptyhanded, and the tongue, as they promised, would be given to old Red Eagle.

As they were packing the meat of the buffalo, *Apsi* planned with Schultz and Jackson that he would remain behind and track the herd until dark while they would return to camp with the meat, present the tongue to Red Eagle, and ask him to pray for *Apsi's* and their success in the hunt for the white buffalo. In the morning they were to rejoin him, riding their swift buffalo runners and bringing *Apsi's* with them.

When Schultz and Jackson arrived in camp, they made their way at once to Red Eagle's lodge. Sensing that they were bringing news of importance to him, a crowd of Indians assembled. When Schultz and Jackson told him about the white buffalo, Red Eagle cried out in amazement and tears filled his eyes. As the news spread through the camp, cries of joy echoed through the valley.

Schultz and Jackson presented the buffalo tongue to Red Eagle and told him of *Apsi's* hope that his prayers for success would go with them when they resumed the hunt. To this the old man readily assented, inviting them into his lodge to join him in his prayers. There, with the help of his wife, he began the unwrapping of his famous thunder medicine pipe and the long ceremonial prayers for success on tomorrow's hunt for the sacred white buffalo.

Shortly after sunrise, riding their buffalo runners and taking turns at leading *Apsi's*, Schultz and Jackson started down the valley. As they approached the spot where they had left *Apsi* the afternoon before, they began to follow the trail of the buffalo herd up onto the plain. The chinook had softened the ground so that here and there they could easily see the tracks of *Apsi*'s horse. For a distance the herd's trail was easy to follow, but later it joined the trail of another herd and still later the combined herd evidently divided. The two young men became confused as to which to follow, for there was still no sign of *Apsi* or any signal from him. They were just about to give up the search when they came upon a pile of small stones with a branch of greasewood, freshly broken off, stuck in the top. They did not doubt that *Apsi* had placed the sign to indicate the direction they should take. Reassured that they were on the right trail, they hurried on and by late afternoon came to a similar trail sign. However, soon afterward they came to a long ridge which led down through the breaks above the Missouri. Just a quarter of a mile beyond that point the ridge forked; there the herd seemed to have separated. They could not find the trail of *Apsi*'s horse down either fork.

As it would soon be getting dark, they made camp in a small grove of trees not far from the frozen Missouri in the hope that when dawn came they might be able to pick up *Apsi*'s trail. As they were making camp, they noted that elk attempting to cross the Missouri had slipped and fallen easy prey to a pack of wolves. Knowing the value of wolf pelts, Jackson and Schultz managed to shoot five of them. Their shots served to indicate to *Apsi* where they were, and by nightfall he had joined them. As they ate he told of his long and difficult attempt to keep in sight the herd with the white buffalo and how he was able, as the sun was setting, to find that it was still grazing with the herd in the bottomlands only a short distance above the place where they were camping.

At daylight the men began moving cautiously up the valley. Soon they were in sight of the open flat where *Apsi* had sighted the herd and the white buffalo the evening before. There they saw the herd and the white one still grazing peacefully. They also observed that the spot where the white buffalo was could be approached, without alarming it or the herd, by means of a long coulee which ran down to the end of the flat where the white one was grazing.

Schultz and Jackson had a hard time persuading *Apsi* that he and he alone must have the honor of shooting it. Finally, with reluctance, he began his stealthy approach. Schultz and

Jackson watched in suspense, fearful that at any moment a change in wind or some slight noise might warn the herd of *Apsi*'s approach. It seemed hours before they heard the shot and saw the white buffalo fall. Thereupon they jumped on their horses and dashed across the flat to join *Apsi* as the frightened herd scattered out before them. *Apsi* was standing by the dead buffalo, speechless with emotion. The hide was without blemish. There could not be a more perfect offering to Sun.

It was some time before *Apsi* could calm himself and ask his friends to help him remove the hide, which, he explained, must be done with its hoofs and small horns still attached. The tongue must be taken out carefully, for it would be used by Red Eagle in the ceremonies, which *Apsi* knew would be performed in offering Sun the hide of the white buffalo. The meat was to be left where it was because it, too, was considered sacred to Sun.

It was late afternoon when they reached the Pikuni camp and rode directly to Red Eagle's lodge. After dismounting, Schultz and Jackson made *Apsi* take the sacred hide and walk ahead of them to the door of the lodge, which was open, and about which people began to gather. Hearing the approach, Red Eagle stepped out. When *Apsi* handed the hide to him, hands trembling with emotion, Red Eagle took it and raised it high above his head. As he did so, the crowd became silent as Red Eagle began a fervent prayer to Sun, asking for mercy and beneficence. Deeply moved by his eloquence, the whole crowd, including Schultz and Jackson, joined in the old medicine man's plea.

That night the whole camp rejoiced. There were feasting, singing, and countless prayers to Sun. There were prayers of thanks to Red Eagle, whose thunder medicine had brought the chinook wind, without which the white buffalo would never have been discovered. The date was December 23, 1877. In his notebook for the winter of 1877–78, Schultz made this entry for December 24:

Trade fair today; 67 robes and some antelope, deer, wolf and elk hides. Cold as the weather is, Red Eagle's daughter has the white buffalo hide on a stretcher and is chipping it. I watched her for a time this morning. Before getting up on it with her little elk horn, steel-bladed hoe or chipper, she made a short prayer which I was close enough to hear: "Oh Sun, I am indeed pure; I am worthy to prepare this sacred robe for you; have pity on me. Continue to keep me in good health and strength that I may make the robe fit for your acceptance!"

The next day was Christmas, an eventful one for the youthful Schultz which contrasted with other experiences of that winter. He and Kipp had been invited for Christmas dinner to the enormous lodge of Hugh Monroe (Rising Wolf). Being in his way a good Christian, Rising Wolf insisted that the birthday of Christ be fittingly celebrated.

As the sun went down, Schultz and Kipp were called to the Monroe lodge. There they found other guests already assembled, most of them members of their host's family. These included his two sons, their wives and children, and his grandson, William Jackson. Also present were old man Rivois and his wife, medicine man Red Eagle, and the young couple who kept house for their host, who, old as he was, was too independent to live with any of his family.

The women of the three families, assisted by Rivois' wife, had worked hard to prepare a truly great feast: boiled fat-cow boss ribs; stewed dried camas roots (traded from the Flatheads); chokecherry pemmican; dried backfat; Labrador tea[3] from the muskeg country to the far north; and that fine, light, wholesome bread that the Red River half bloods called *gollette*, made by mixing flour, marrow fat, salt, and water into a thin dough, which is then beaten for several hours with a club and cooked in thin cakes before the fire. Schultz and Kipp added several cans of sweet jelly for the children.

Sated, the guests lolled on couches of buffalo robes and blankets and sipped Labrador tea. Red Eagle lit his large stone pipe; the time for stories had arrived. As the pipe was making the rounds, Red Eagle asked their host to tell them the story of the black antelope. There was a chorus of agree-

---

[3] Labrador tea is made from the leaves of the shrub *Ledum groenlandiicum*.

ment. After a few moments of thought, Monroe straightened up and began his tale of the hunt for the black antelope, that other rare animal which, like the albino buffalo, was considered sacred to Sun.

When Schultz and Kipp finally made their way back to their own lodge, Schultz could not help but compare this Christmas dinner with those he had enjoyed in Boonville: turkey and mince pie rather than buffalo boss ribs and *gollette* eaten while sitting in the circle of an Indian lodge as the guest of a man who had been a long-ago pathfinder in a still very wild West.

It should be noted, incidentally, that Schultz had determined that one of his new friends should have a special Christmas, this being *Apsi*, of white-buffalo distinction. On the day before Christmas, Schultz secretly rode out to the place where he and *Apsi* had left the frozen wolves and brought four of them back to camp. At dawn on Christmas morning while the camp was still asleep, he managed to carry them, one by one, to *Apsi's* lodge. There he planted them upright in the snow to greet *Apsi* when he emerged. Needless to say, when *Apsi* saw them he let out a shout and soon they were being viewed by dozens of people.

With him to the Hugh Monroe lodge Schultz brought his notebook in anticipation of recording items and stories of interest. That he had brought it with him to Cow Creek Valley suggests that he planned to make good use of it that winter, undoubtedly a fact of some significance to future generations of Schultz readers, and it may have proved to be an even more rewarding experience than he had dared to hope for. Much of his future work had its genesis in what he learned that winter at Cow Creek Valley.

Once Christmas had passed, Schultz began to dream of holiday vacations spent in the Adirondacks and decided to return to that area for the remainder of the winter, that is, for all or most of January, February, and March, 1878. He spent this time at the Jack Sheppard camp on the south shore of Fourth Lake, Fulton Chain of Lakes, Old Forge, New York, approximately seventy-five miles northeast of Boonville. During this time he hunted panthers and suc-

ceeded in killing three full-grown ones, the largest of which
was more than eight feet long.[4]

With the approach of spring, Schultz returned to Montana and the Pikuni camp at Cow Creek in time to find some
of his friends striking their winter lodges in preparation
for a return to the plains. As for himself, his outings with
Sorrel Horse and Kipp were drawing to a close, and he kept
busy by helping Kipp, for whom the trading season had
been only a fair one (two thousand robes and a profit of six
or seven thousand dollars), prepare for the return to Fort
Benton.

What did the future hold for Schultz so far as Montana
was concerned? Would he continue his relationship with
Kipp after returning to Fort Benton, or would their paths
diverge?[5] Neither of them then knew that Kipp soon would
acquire Fort Conrad to have and to hold for the next eight
years.

---

[4]It was in his first *Forest and Stream* article, appearing on October 14,
1880, that Schultz told how "I spent nearly the entire winter of '77 and '78
in the Adirondacks" with "Mr. Jack Sheppard and Ed. Arnold" and killed
the three "varmints" referred to. Schultz's Adirondack adventure was confirmed in the *Boonville Herald* issues of February 21 and March 7, 1878.
According to the item of February 21, 1878: "We found our young friend,
Will Schultz, robust and hearty from his forest-life exposure" (information from the files of the *Boonville Herald* furnished by Matthew J. Conway
to *The Piegan Storyteller*, Vol. VII, No. 3, 16).

[5]The answers, or some of them, to these questions will begin to emerge
in Chapter 5.

Fort Conrad Becomes Home Base

Wᴴᴇɴ Kipp and Schultz returned to Fort Benton upon completion of the winter trade at Cow Creek, they went directly to the I. G. Baker Company office, where Charles Conrad greeted them heartily and handed Schultz a sizable bundle of mail. While Kipp discussed his trading operations during the past season with Conrad, Schultz moved to a spot by himself and began reading his letters. As he had anticipated, there were several from his mother, all urging him to keep his promise to return home. One from his guardian reminded him that he was still a minor and obligated, as such, to follow the request of his guardians that he return to Boonville.

When Kipp finally finished his business with Charles Conrad and other key people, he sought out Schultz and, sitting down next to him, told him that he had just made an important decision: he had bought Fort Conrad, a trading post built by Conrad in 1875. Constructed primarily to serve the Blackfeet, it stood on a high south bank of the Marias River, close above the mouth of its Dry Fork, eighty miles northwest of Fort Benton. Neither the building nor its site exist because the changing currents of the river have long since cut away the bank and carried away the logs.[1]

Schultz had often heard Kipp talk about Fort Conrad and say that it was well patronized by the various Blackfoot tribes. Kipp now explained that it would also serve as a headquarters for trading parties moving with the tribes. He of-

---

[1] *Blackfeet and Buffalo*, 3; adapted from the *Great Falls Tribune* of October 8, 1939.

fered young Schultz a share of the venture, but Schultz
turned it down, giving as an excuse that he wanted to remain free and independent for a few more months. The
letters he had just received reminded him all too well that he
was still a minor and as such could not enter into such an
agreement. Kipp, however, urged him to remain as an employee, and Schultz agreed to do so.

Kipp, called Raven Quiver by the Blackfeet, was anxious
to take possession of Fort Conrad as soon as possible. Schultz
and the other employees were kept on the run day after day,
assembling the multitude of things Kipp deemed essential
to equip, stock, and provision the new operation adequately.
At last all was ready and they left Fort Benton in September,
1878, with a bull train of four eight-yoke teams of oxen
hauling twelve large, heavy wagons, or prairie schooners,
loaded to capacity with fifty thousand pounds of trade goods,
provisions, and a thousand and one other things. The bull
train, with Long John Forgy as wagon boss, had been taken
off its usual profitable run on the trail to Fort Whoop-Up,
which ran from Helena to Fort Benton and on to Fort Macleod in Canada. Three young Pikunis, steady employees
of Kipp, served as bullwhackers: Comes-with-Rattles, Red
Eyes, and Takes-a-Gun-at-Night. Accompanying the wagon
train were men for night herding and caring for the extra
oxen and horses.

Kipp and Schultz, with the many members of the former's
family, as well as his several employees, rode as a protective
escort for the wagon train. The slow pace of the oxen made
it easy for some of the riders to scout constantly ahead and
give warning of possible danger. A few brought up the rear
to urge on the slowpokes, while others, usually including
Schultz, ranged far and wide across the rolling plains on either side of the snail-paced bull train. Schultz's skill with the
rifle made it possible for him to add much good meat to the
train's larder.

To cover the distance from Fort Benton to Fort Conrad required three days of travel. At the end of their second day,
as was customary, they made a corral of the wagons to protect their horses and men. The big new lodge of the Kipp

family was erected, and Schultz was invited to spend the night with them; other employees slept under the wagons. In the middle of the night, and it was a particularly dark night, the camp was thrown into chaotic alarm. Something was bumping and banging against the wagons, terrifying the horses and oxen. The men under the wagons were calling out to find out what was happening. The darkness added to the confusion.

Kipp and Schultz reached for their rifles as something hit the side of the lodge. The women screamed as the lodge poles cracked and the buffalo-skin covering fell and blanketed them all for a brief moment. Suddenly it tore apart and the major portion of it went crashing back and forth around the corral. Men began shooting wildly at the weird white monster, and it finally fell to the ground. When a corner of the badly torn lodge covering was lifted, they found an enormous old dead buffalo! Much of what was left of the night was spent wondering how it managed to get into the corral, while Kipp's wife, Double-Strike Woman, his mother, Earth Woman, and her friend, Crow Woman, bemoaned the destruction of the new lodge they had worked so hard to make.

The next day, Schultz got his first view of impressive 150-foot Fort Conrad on a bluff above the river, which had been named Marias by Captain Meriwether Lewis for his cousin, Maria Wood, but was known to the Blackfeet as the Bear. Fort Conrad was indeed strategically located. A hundred yards below the fort was the crossing of the Whoop-Up wagon trail, where the fort maintained a ferry. The fort also was situated on the route favored by the Blackfoot tribes as they followed the buffalo herds over the vast prairies, which spread far and wide in every direction. Here, too, Blackfoot war parties passed back and forth on raids against their enemies or to capture horses, the popular currency exchange of the period.

Kipp knew Fort Conrad well and would soon have his wagonloads of trade goods and supplies stored away in the spacious warehouse, so that Long John Forgy and his bull teams could be on their way to carry on with Kipp's profitable freighting business along the Whoop-Up trail. Schultz was assigned living quarters in the office adjoining the trade room and warehouse in the south row of cabins. Kipp, his extensive family, and Hiram Upham, the clerk, as well as several other employees, were housed in the north row of cabins about fifty feet across the open courtyard.

Trading began immediately, but living a sedentary shop-keeper existence in a stout log cabin, rather than an Indian tipi, was not the type of life that Schultz had in mind; nor was it to be that which was in store for him or for most of the other people living at Fort Conrad.

It was at Fort Conrad that Schultz came to know inti-mately two Indian women who would play such an impor-tant part in his life. One of these was Joe Kipp's mother, *Sahkwi Ahki*, or Earth Woman, who was the daughter of Mandan Chief *Mahtotopa* (Four Bears), of whom Catlin painted a full-length portrait. The other was Earth Woman's friend and constant companion, an Arikara woman whom the Blackfeet called Crow Woman, who, when very young, had been taken captive by the Crows; later she was captured again, this time by the Bloods. She became the fourth wife of Spotted Elk and passed many unhappy years with little more than the status of the mistreated slave of his other three wives.

One day when Crow Woman was with some Bloods who were trading in Fort Benton, by chance she came face to face with Earth Woman. They had been very close friends when they were small girls, and their meeting was an emotional one. When Earth Woman learned of the treatment to which her friend was being subjected, she went at once to Spotted Elk and, offering him a much-desired Henry repeating rifle, demanded Crow Woman's release. When he refused, Earth Woman threatened to call the white soldiers at Fort Benton to arrest him for stealing Crow Woman. Spotted Elk capitu-lated. From then on, these two outstanding women remained inseparable. They both acted like mothers toward young Schultz, nursing him when he was sick, washing and mend-ing his clothes, advising him, and at times scolding him.

That first winter at Fort Conrad (1878–79) was another

rewarding and pleasant experience for Schultz. Sorrel Horse and his family also spent the winter there, and Schultz passed many evenings with them. He continued to be impressed by the warmth and joyousness of their relationship. Several times he accompanied Sorrel Horse when the latter made the rounds of poisoned baits he had set out for wolves. Frequently, Schultz went hunting with the Pikunis. His knowledge of them was broadened and enriched by the long winter nights around the lodge fires, listening to the stories of the older men, who were well versed in the traditions of their people. For the first time, Schultz had an opportunity to become well acquainted with the Bloods, the most northern of the tribes in the Blackfoot Confederacy. His notebooks bulged with his copious notes, and his astonishing memory captured and stored away details of their customs, religious beliefs and ceremonies, and the manner in which these differed from those of the Pikunis.

CHAPTER 6

On the Warpath

IN THE WINTER OF 1878–79, Schultz was associated with
Joe Kipp at Fort Conrad, Kipp's trading post on the Marias River. Kipp carried on a good trade with the Blackfoot tribes, the Pikunis, Blackfeet, and Bloods, getting from
them two thousand buffalo robes and several thousand hides
of other animals. When spring came, the tribes left, some to
return to Canada, the Pikunis to summer-hunt along the foot
of the Rockies seventy-five miles west of Fort Conrad.

A hundred yards below the fort was the Marias River
crossing of the Fort Benton–Fort Macleod wagon road,
along which flowed considerable traffic in supplies brought
up the Missouri to Fort Benton and transported from there
by bull train, mule train, and sometimes horse train. In June
of 1879 a train comprised of several spans of horses and
wagons with supplies for Fort Macleod was encamped twenty
miles south of Fort Conrad when it was attacked by a war
party of Indians who made off with all the horses. A few
nights later thirty miles to the north, a similar attack resulted in the death of two teamsters and the loss of most of
the horses in a large wagon train. In quick succession and
like manner, several smaller freighting outfits lost their
horses at various points along this route, with the result that
governmental action became necessary. Patrolling of the Canadian part of the road by the Northwest Mounted Police
was instituted, while a company of mounted soldiers from
the Third United States Infantry under command of Lieutenant J. H. Beacom was assigned to provide security on the
Montana side of the line.

Lieutenant Beacom's men made camp a few hundred yards from Fort Conrad, and he came over to confer with Joe Kipp, seeking information as to the identity of the raiders. Kipp strongly suspected that they were Assiniboines, with a possibility that they might in some cases be Crees or Crows or Sioux. He was positive that none of them were Blackfeet, since they would not undertake to raid the whites in the middle of Blackfoot country. Kipp was unable to offer any bright ideas for Beacom's use in catching or punishing the raiders.

After the soldiers moved in, the offenders became even bolder and began to direct their efforts at the horses and mules of the army detachment. The animals were turned out to graze each night with chain-and-leather hobbles and were herded by two shifts of men. Nevertheless, the Indians got away with five horses one night and came back the next for five mules. In desperation, Lieutenant Beacom again came to Kipp for help, whereupon Kipp and Schultz circled and recircled the area without finding a trace of the missing animals. Continued search, however, uncovered evidence to indicate that the guilty parties were Assiniboines.

Finally, adding insult to injury, a notorious Assiniboine named White Dog came almost into the camp of the soldiers guarding the animals, taunting them in the Blackfoot language with the fact that he, White Dog, had stolen their horses and mules and challenging them to come and get him. As the soldiers rushed out of their tents in pursuit of White Dog, it was too dark to see anything, but they could hear the hoofbeats of the stolen mules becoming fainter and fainter as the thieves rode them off.

On the following morning, purely by coincidence, a small Pikuni war party arrived at Fort Conrad. They were on foot, traveling only at night and resting in some secluded spot during the day. Kipp suggested that they spend the day resting at the fort's big warehouse, which they were glad to do. During the day Schultz visited them and talked with their leader, Many-Tail-Feathers, whom he knew to be both a respected medicine man and a leader of many successful war parties. With him were Weasel Tail, Red Plume, Little Otter,

White Antelope, Running Wolf, and Bear Head—all experienced warriors with whom Schultz was acquainted. Many-Tail-Feathers said that he and his party were out to raid the Crows for horses but had made this side trip to trade for tobacco and ammunition. Schultz told them of White Dog's recent raid on the horses and mules of the nearby army camp.

At the mention of White Dog, the face of Many-Tail-Feathers clouded and he explained to Schultz that White Dog seemed to lead a charmed life. He had killed Many-Tail-Feathers' father and grandfather and Many-Tail-Feathers' grandmother had died of grief as a result. White Dog had stolen their horses and the Pikunis had been unable to track him. Five times, he told Schultz, he had led war parties to kill White Dog, but without success. They would aim very carefully, but their bullets never touched him. As the two men talked, members of the war party voiced their own hatred of the wily Assiniboine, whereupon Many-Tail-Feathers suggested that they change their plan to raid the Crows and go after White Dog instead. At this, Schultz urged Many-Tail-Feathers to allow him to go with them; Many-Tail-Feathers agreed.

Kipp, his mother, and Crow Woman protested vehemently, but they soon realized that it was no use, for Schultz was determined to go. When they realized this, Earth Woman and Crow Woman called him into their room and talked to him very seriously. They explained to him that Many-Tail-Feathers was one of the wisest and most successful of all Pikuni leaders, one whose orders must never be questioned. He must be obeyed instantly. Crow Woman gave Schultz her most treasured sacred object, a buffalo stone, which many times had protected her from disaster, and she urged him in time of danger to pray to it for protection. Knowing how she treasured it, Schultz was sincerely grateful and promised to do as she suggested. Later he learned that the buffalo-stone fetish, shaped naturally like a buffalo, was probably part of a fossil ammonite.

Schultz went to his quarters at Fort Conrad to make ready for his adventure. To dress much like the other members of the war party, he wore a breechclout, a woolen shirt, fringed buckskin leggings, beaded moccasins, and a blanket capote for his '73 Winchester repeating rifle. He strapped two belts of cartridges around his waist, and over his shoulder he slung a braided rawhide lariat. Into a pouch by his side went extra moccasins, tobacco, matches, needles and thread, and some salt tied up in a bit of buckskin. Thus accoutered, he joined his first war party.

In the afternoon the entire party went down to the river and bathed. When they returned, the women had a substantial meal ready for them. As they were finishing it, Lieutenant Beacom came over to them and, with Schultz as interpreter, asked Many-Tail-Feathers and his war party if they would try to recapture the army's horses and mules while they were in Assiniboine country. He assured Many-Tail-Feathers that the Indians would be suitably rewarded if they succeeded.

It was late afternoon when Kipp ferried the war party across the Marias. Once more he tried hard to persuade Schultz not to go, but to no avail.

It was a clear, moonlit night. They had gone but a few miles along the trail beside the Marias when they began to flush various kinds of game: deer, elk, antelope, and an occasional buffalo. So quietly did they travel that Schultz was startled by coyotes and wolves sounding out almost beside him. At the first hint of dawn, they halted and Many-Tail-Feathers sent Bear Head on to kill an animal for them to eat during the day. The others waited a short time before moving slowly after him. When they heard his shot, they quickly joined him and helped butcher the deer, each selecting portions of the meat to his liking. Then, covering their tracks as skillfully as possible, they moved into a dense grove of timber and willow thickets by the river, where the driest wood was used to build an almost smokeless fire. When a fine bed of coals was ready, they broiled all their meat and ate some of it. Many-Tail-Feathers and the others were curious when Schultz insisted on sprinkling salt over his piece of meat. When he persuaded some of them to taste it on theirs, they expressed amazement that anyone could enjoy spoiling the good taste of broiled meat by putting that tastes-like-fire powder on it.

When they had finished eating, they eliminated all signs of the fire and Many-Tail-Feathers appointed Weasel Tail to climb to the edge of the plain and act as a lookout, alert to any sign of an enemy war party. While the rest of the party rested—smoking, softly talking, but mostly sleeping—Many-Tail-Feathers withdrew a short distance to smoke and make prayers for the success of their raid against the Cutthroats. He also prayed that while he slept he might have a prophetic dream of what might lie ahead of them. When the sun reached the zenith, Bear Head relieved Weasel Tail for the afternoon vigil.

At twilight Many-Tail-Feathers rejoined his party. He had had no vision of any kind, but the confidence he placed in his medicine made him certain that the gods would have warned him if there were danger ahead. After eating more of the broiled meat, the war party again set out along the trail next to the Marias.

Six days after they left Fort Conrad, they made camp in a grove of pines on the northern slope of the Bear Paw Mountains. As they drew closer to enemy country, not only Many-Tail-Feathers but every member of the party made daily prayers, as they rested, for a reassuring vision, but the gods failed them. Depressed by this, they sat around their small fire, silent and gloomy, as they broiled portions of meat from a yearling buffalo bull they had killed the day before. Following their usual routine for the day, they tried to sleep, but worry kept them awake most of the time. Had they lost the protection of the gods by some wrong they had committed, or was the gods' failure to send even a single one of them a vision a warning in itself of serious trouble ahead?

Schultz was appointed to take the morning watch. He found an excellent lookout point at the lower edge of the pines. A wide expanse of prairie spread out below him, and the air was crystal clear. Here and there he saw herds of buffalo and antelope grazing or resting peacefully, a sure sign that no enemy party was near. As usual, Many-Tail-Feathers had gone off alone in the hope of at last being granted a revealing dream. At noon Schultz returned and reported that he had seen no sign of the enemy. Little Otter took the afternoon watch.

Late that afternoon Schultz and the rest of the party were awakened and startled as Many-Tail-Feathers began to dance and sing the Wolf Song, a song of good luck for the hunter and the warrior. In a loud voice he announced that at last he had been truly favored by the gods in a vision. In it they were traveling across the plains when they were surprised by a large enemy party, which they attacked at once and killed many of the men in it. At that moment, Many-Tail-Feathers said, he awoke and began singing the Wolf Song. The fact that in his dream many of the enemy had been killed was an excellent omen; every member of the party was reassured. They cautiously moved down to the very edge of the timber to look out far across the plains and await the night, when they would continue on their way toward the camp of the Assiniboines.

Just as the sun was setting they saw far to the north a large herd of buffalo suddenly bunch together and dash off, a sign that the animals had been frightened, likely by a war party. Since they were traveling south, there seemed small chance that their trails would cross. To their amazement a raven, croaking loudly, came flying toward them from the east. Many-Tail-Feathers, a leader of the prestigious Raven Carriers Society of the Pikunis, was delighted when the raven, still croaking, circled over them and then flew back whence it had come. Almost immediately, however, it returned and again circled over them several times, croaking all the while, before it finally disappeared. Surely, Many-Tail-Feathers assured them, the raven, wisest of all the birds and true friend of warriors, had come to urge them to continue with their plan to attack the Assiniboine camp!

Sitting where they were, looking out over the wide sweep of prairie, they discussed just how they would carry out their plan to enter the Assiniboine camp at night, locate White Dog's lodge, and kill him. Then, taking advantage of the confusion that would arise, they would steal as many as they could of the Cutthroats' valuable buffalo-runner horses.

Then, well mounted, they would attempt to recapture all of
Lieutenant Beacom's horses and mules. During the discussion, Schultz began to realize what a dangerous enterprise
lay ahead. His companions apparently felt as he did, for
from that point on he noticed by the movement of their lips
that they were constantly making prayers for their success.
Taking Crow Woman's sacred buffalo stone in his hands,
Schultz, too, prayed silently to whatever gods might grant
him protection.

As soon as it became dark enough for them to proceed,
Many-Tail-Feathers reminded them that because they were
now out on the open plains and drawing ever closer to the
big Assiniboine camp they must be more vigilant than ever.
By dawn they had reached the wide, timbered valley of the
Milk River, which, unlike most of the rivers they knew, had
cut a wide, shallow path across the plains. As far as they
could see, buffalo and antelope were grazing peacefully—
again a sure sign that there were no war parties in the area.

Three mornings later they stopped to rest for the day
where the Milk River turns south to join the Big River (the
Missouri). So far, all had gone well. True to Many-Tail-
Feathers' medicine, they had not encountered a single sign
of the enemy. Red Plume had the morning watch, and
Many-Tail-Feathers admonished him to be particularly wary
as at any time they would be close to the enemy camp.

Later on that morning Schultz was awakened by the sun
shining directly on his face through an opening in the
branches. Going down to the river for a drink, he was startled
when Many-Tail-Feathers walked silently over the soft sand
toward him, his face dark with worry. He told Schultz that
during his sleep he had had a vision portending disaster.
He had seen many strange lodges dimly in the darkness and
from them he had heard the mournful wail of many
women. This, he said, was certain warning that there was serious trouble ahead. Schultz reminded him of the good vision he had had a short time before, but Many-Tail-Feathers
explained that the vision he had just experienced negated
the promise of the earlier one.

Shortly after the two of them had rejoined their companions, Red Plume dashed in to announce that he had seen a party of Assiniboines hunting buffalo. Much excited by this news, the Pikunis cautiously made their way into the thick fringe of sage and wild cherry just beyond the timber. There they got a clear view of the hunting party two or three miles away. Evidently the hunters had already made their kills, for they had dismounted and were starting to butcher the meat.

When they returned to their hiding place in the timber, there was complete agreement that what they had just seen indicated that the main camp of the Assiniboines was indeed close by. Many-Tail-Feathers announced that they would make their raid that very night. He stood watch and told the others to rest and get what sleep they could. In order to make an early start, they left a short time before the sun had set and quickly entered a long cottonwood grove bordering the river. It ended a short distance above an abrupt bend in the river, and they were forced to move into the open before they could reach the shelter of another cottonwood grove. Suddenly, below the bend, they could hear the voices of several men singing songs that were strange to them—undoubtedly war songs! Many-Tail-Feathers ordered his men to hide as best they could in a low thicket of sage and rose brush. He demanded that no matter how small the enemy war party proved to be, they must not fire a single shot unless discovered by it. To do so would spoil their chances of killing White Dog.

As Many-Tail-Feathers finished whispering his order to them, a single tall man wearing a white blanket capote and a fur cap walked quickly toward them from around the bend. He carried a Henry repeating rifle in the crook of his left arm. Many-Tail-Feathers recognized him at once, as did White Antelope and Little Otter. It was White Dog! In spite of the protests of his companions, Many-Tail-Feathers raised his rifle and fired. White Dog, badly wounded, fell to the ground. Many-Tail-Feathers shouted in triumph, shot again, and again wounded him. White Dog, in spite of his wounds, managed to fire three shots at them. Little Otter fell dead, and Schultz suffered a nasty wound in his upper left arm just below the shoulder.

As the rifle dropped from White Dog's hands, Schultz was
horrified to see Many-Tail-Feathers seize White Dog's hair,
cut his scalp at the base of his head and across his forehead,
and then yank free his entire scalp, braids and all. Not until
then did Many-Tail-Feathers put his tortured enemy out of
his misery. As he held his grisly trophy high in triumph, between fifteen and twenty of White Dog's followers dashed
up the riverbed toward them, shouting their war cries and
shooting as they came, killing Running Wolf. The Assiniboines, however, had only single-shot rifles and were
no match for Many-Tail-Feathers' party and its repeating
Henrys. When five of the Assiniboines had been killed, the
others turned and fled down the valley.

Many-Tail-Feathers took White Dog's rifle and cartridge
belts. Then, knowing that the Assiniboines would soon be
back in force, he ordered his followers quickly to take the
guns and personal belongings of Little Otter and Running
Wolf and get back to the shelter of the cottonwood grove.
White Antelope argued testily that they should take the
scalps and guns of the Assiniboines they had killed. When
Many-Tail-Feathers disagreed, White Antelope ignored him;
when the Pikunis started back up the valley, White Antelope
remained behind.

They were only halfway back to the grove when Schultz
became so faint from loss of blood that Many-Tail-Feathers
called a halt and bound up his wound as best he could with a
piece of his shirt. As he was doing so, they heard shots and
looked back to see White Antelope fall. In a flash some of
the Assiniboines were upon him and took his gun and scalp.

It was almost dark by the time they got back to the cottonwoods. Since the Assiniboines had not pursued them, they
rested for a while and counseled as to what they should do.
Feeling that the Assiniboines would expect them to spend
the rest of the night retreating up the valley, Many-Tail-
Feathers suggested that their best course would be to leave
the valley as soon as possible, cross the river, climb to the
plains, and travel north until daylight. Then, after a day's
good rest, they could safely travel on to their camp near Fort
Conrad.

Several of the party protested that they should not give up their plan to raid the main Assiniboine camp and at least capture some of the latter's good buffalo-runner horses, but Many-Tail-Feathers convinced them that they were now in no condition to risk such a raid. It was fortunate that they followed their leader's advice, for after crossing the river and climbing up a coulee that brought them to the edge of the plain, they heard the main band of the Assiniboines singing and shouting as they encircled the cottonwood grove where they expected the Pikuni enemy to be found.

Now very weak from loss of blood, Schultz found it difficult to keep up with his companions, but they took turns carrying his rifle and war sack and made no complaint at his slow pace. They were seventeen nights on the trail before they reached Fort Conrad. Many-Tail-Feathers alone returned with a sense of victory. Holding White Dog's scalp high in the air, he danced a victory dance and sang a victory song. As news of the death of Little Otter, Running Wolf, and White Antelope spread, songs and cries of grief dominated the camp. Lieutenant Beacom was bitterly disappointed when he learned that they had not even come within sight of his stolen horses and mules.

It was a weak and disillusioned Schultz who returned to the Pikuni camp. Despite the good and constant care of his almost-mothers, Earth Woman and Crow Woman, it was a long time before he could return to his couch in the office at Fort Conrad. Kipp did not have to say, "I told you so." [1]

---

[1] There are three versions of the story of Many-Tail-Feathers' revenge upon the arrogant White Dog, each written by Schultz. Two of them were published in his lifetime, while a third, substantially edited, was published fifteen years after his death.

The story of White Dog was first told by Schultz in 1923 on pages 223–54 of *Friends of My Life as an Indian*, with Many-Tail-Feathers himself as the narrator. None of the others in his party was named, and none was wounded or killed.

The second version of the story is the one reported in this chapter, with Schultz casting himself as the narrator as well as a grievously wounded participant. Three of the seven in the party reputedly were killed. The story appeared in the columns of the *Great Falls Tribune* on October 8 and 15, 1939 (Sunday editions), under the headline APIKUNI, 19, JOINS HIS FIRST WAR PARTY.

Version No. 3 comprised pages 3–25 of *Blackfeet and Buffalo*, published in 1962, fifteen years after the death of Schultz, with a footnote reading: "Adapted from the *Great Falls Tribune* (November 8 and 15, 1939)." This was a revised write-up of the 1939 version, with Schultz edited out as participant and narrator and his old friend Bear Head substituted in both capacities and as the asserted sufferer of the wound which Schultz, in the 1939 version, said he had received. In this version, however, only two of the party were killed.

To add to the confusion, research indicates that there are still other versions of who killed White Dog. And the *Blackfeet and Buffalo* version, although adapted from the 1939 *Tribune* story, fails to tell us by whom or why, and its accuracy is thus suspect.

Consequently, with all of the foregoing fully in mind, I have used the *Tribune* version of the story for the following reasons: (1) Its autobiographical character makes it appropriate for a story of the author's life; (2) It represents Schultz's own work, as distinguished from the rewrite by someone else appearing more than twenty years after first publication; and (3) When the material was sent by Schultz in 1940 to Houghton Mifflin Company for publication in book form, it was to be the opening chapter in a series relating his early adventures and to be entitled *Reminiscences*.

Incidentally, the White Dog story, with but one exception, was the last written for *Tribune* publication, or, for that matter, for anyone else, and as such should be preserved in a form more permanent than the columns of a Sunday newspaper, particularly since the other two versions of the story have been given permanence in book form.

CHAPTER 7

Hunters on Horseback

THE most spectacular big-game hunting the world has ever known undoubtedly was to be found on the Great Plains after the Civil War, and nowhere was it more spectacular or exciting than on the Montana prairies between the Missouri River and the Canadian border. For here lived the Pikuni Indians, the most powerful tribe of the Blackfoot Confederacy, and here were the plains where the buffalo roamed in seemingly endless profusion. It was a hunter's paradise, and no one dreamed that it would disappear in a few years.

For the Indians, it was much more than a sportsman's utopia; it was a way of life. Upon this seemingly stable state of affairs, the Montana tribes had created a buffalo-based economy. Nearly all of their necessities, from sustenance to shelter, were supplied by the great animals; and the beauty of it all was that they were nearly always available nearby in large numbers.

Although the supply proved adequate for the needs of the natives of the region, the coming of the white man disturbed Nature's balance. Soon the buffalo were being slaughtered by eastern whites for hides only and in some cases for sheer pleasure, until at last the end was in sight. Unfortunately, it was the end not only for the buffalo but also for the Indians, who had become totally dependent upon the buffalo. The white man conquered the Indian by eliminating his food supply.

Two things made hunting on the Great Plains unique while it lasted: the abundance of big game—buffalo, elk, antelope, deer, bear—and the fact that it was accomplished on horseback and usually at high rates of speed. On the western plains, the quarry often could be sighted by the hundred, and for the hunter a horse was as essential as a gun. The tribesmen of the plains were hunters on horseback, and young Schultz had now become one of them.

There came a time, after Schultz had become an associate of Joseph Kipp, when the buffalo herds decreased and Kipp detailed Schultz and his associate Eli Guardipee to hunt them for their hides. While camped on Armell Creek, they sighted a herd of buffalo grazing at the head of a long coulee putting into the creek. They set out to make a run on them, Eli on Jerry, Kipp's buffalo horse, the fastest, most-enduring, best-trained buffalo runner that any of them had ever known. Schultz was riding his own horse, Dick. Each hunter was equipped with a rimfire .44-caliber Henry repeating carbine: short, light, easy to aim and fire with one hand, the best of all weapons for running buffalo. In his memoirs, Schultz gave a vivid account of the action:

> We rode up the coulee keeping out of sight of the herd until at the head of the coulee we charged out and right in among them. They instantly ran, gathering compactly together, and we, choosing the cows we wanted, always those with rounded hips and rump, and so fat, turned our horses after them. And our horses were as eager for the chase and for the killings as were we. With ears set fiercely back they did their best to get us close to the left of the cow so we could put a single killing shot into their lungs or heart.
>
> The pace at which we were going seemed to us like the swiftness of lightning. Well we knew that at any moment our horses might step into a badger hole and we could go down to be trampled to death; that a hard-pressed bull might turn and gore us. It was that danger, that constant risk, that made the chase so exciting, so fascinating. Oh, how we loved it all: the thunderous pounding and rattling of thousands of hoofs, the sharp odor of the sage that they crushed, the accuracy of our shooting, the quick response of our trained horses to our directing hands.
>
> Always the run was over all too soon. Never was a horse that could keep up with a frightened buffalo herd for much more than a mile. When I had shot my sixth cow, my horse was all in, winded, and wet with white foaming sweat. I

brought him to a stand and sat watching Eli, still going on Jerry and frequently shooting. Then he, too, stopped, turned, came slowly back and, equally slow, I rode to meet him. "How many?" I asked.

Grinning he answered, "Eighteen. Eighteen cows with eighteen shots." Hard to believe, but there were the proofs blackly strewn upon the yellow grassed plain. To select, chase and kill eighteen cows in a run of a buffalo herd was something to talk about, to be remembered. I have never heard of anyone equaling the feat.[1]

While the Indians sought to avoid encounters with the Plains grizzly, of which there were many, sometimes they were come upon unexpectedly. In the summer of 1881, Schultz had frequent opportunities to go hunting with his friend Eli Guardipee. Sometimes they went on foot in the river bottoms or pine-clad breaks for deer; at other times they took off on their well-trained buffalo horses for the exciting run of a herd. On this particular day they decided they would like to have some antelope ribs for a change and rode out to hunt on the plain south of the trading post. Schultz had his fast buffalo horse and Guardipee a small, slow mare. They rode up parallel ridges, planning to get together on the rim of the plain.

Schultz reached the top just in time to see Guardipee riding wildly up through some timber with a large and obviously angry grizzly close behind him. Turning in the saddle, Guardipee was shooting back at the bear with no apparent effect. To Schultz's horror, the bear, with great leaps, was gaining. Schultz realized he was too far away to be of help— one more leap and the grizzly would be on the horse's back, tearing Guardipee to pieces. However, Eli fired one more shot, and to Schultz's infinite relief, the bear crumpled to the ground.

When Schultz rode up, Guardipee was off his horse, calmly examining the dead bear. Badly shaken by his friend's close call, Schultz managed to say, "What a narrow escape you had! I thought it was to be the end of you."

[1] *Blackfeet and Buffalo*, 54; first published in the *Great Falls Tribune* of December 10, 1935.

"*Sa! Matsikiwa*," Guardipee said in Blackfoot and then in English, "I knew that I could kill her when she came close." He then explained, as they prepared to skin the bear, that he had unexpectedly ridden into her two cubs and that when they began screaming with fright the grizzly took after him. She was an enormous animal, and they had difficulty removing the hide because of the layers of fat. It was far too heavy for them to carry back to Carroll, so Guardipee went back for it the next day with a team and wagon. In rendering out the fat, they collected ten gallons of bear oil, which was sold to a St. Louis druggist for seventy-five dollars.

Schultz had another interesting experience with a grizzly in the spring of 1883 after abandoning the trading post. Most of the Pikunis had trailed over to Milk River and the Sweetgrass country. However, a small band decided to head for the foot of the Rockies. Leaving the abandoned fort, they followed the Marias River to the Cut Bank River, then went up the latter to the pines at the head of the valley. Here was game in vast quantities; not many antelope, but elk, deer, mountain sheep, and moose were plentiful. As for bears, the whole country was torn up by them. Many of the hunters refused to molest a grizzly, regarding it as a sort of medicine or sacred animal, while some believed that it was really a human being. It was allowable for anyone to use the bear's claws for a necklace or other ornament, and some of the more adventurous wore a three- or four-row necklace of their own killing, of which they were very proud.

One morning with Heavy Breast, Schultz rode up the divide between the Cut Bank Valley and the Milk River, thinking to find mountain sheep plentiful there. They soon saw a band of bighorns, at which Heavy Breast took a shot and missed, while Schultz was able to kill two rams. While passing out of the pines, their horses loaded with meat, they saw, about five hundred yards away, a large grizzly industriously tearing up the sod on the bare hillside in search of a gopher. Schultz suggested that they kill the bear, to which Heavy Breast responded that it was Schultz's idea, not his. They turned into a deep coulee and followed it up, Heavy Breast praying all the while for success, expecting to come out of it near the spot where they had seen the bear. When they emerged, the grizzly was not fifty yards away. He saw them at once, sat up on his haunches, and wiggled his nose as he sniffed the air. They both fired and then, with a hair-raising roar, the bear rolled over, biting and clawing at his flank where a bullet had struck him, then sprang to his feet and charged the pair open-mouthed.

They turned their horses off to the north, for it was not a wise thing to turn back down the hill. Schultz fired a couple of shots at the bear without effect. The bear, meantime, had covered the ground with surprisingly long bounds and was already quite close to the heels of his companion's horse. As Schultz fired and missed again, Heavy Breast, his saddle and his sheep meat parted company with the fleeing pony; the cinch, an old, worn rawhide band, had broken. Down they came with a loud thud not two steps in front of the onrushing bear, which, with a loud *woof*, turned sharply about and fled back toward the timber, Schultz after him. With repeated firing, a lucky shot broke his backbone and a deliberately aimed bullet at the base of the brain finished him off. When it was all over, Schultz suddenly remembered how ridiculous Heavy Breast had appeared, soaring through the air on a horseless saddle. Schultz was convulsed with laughter at the thought, but his companion did not find it humorous at all.

The bear had a fine coat of fur which Schultz decided to have tanned. Heavy Breast took Schultz's horse in order to capture his own, which had run a mile or two away, and Schultz set to work on the carcass. It was a big bear and quite fat, the work tiring. When Heavy Breast returned with his animal, he sat down and smoked, declining to give Schultz any help. He explained that it was against his medicine to touch a bear.

When Schultz got the skin home and asked Nätahki to tan it for him, she begged off on grounds that to do so would be bad medicine. He finally persuaded her to do it by promising to buy her the prettiest shawl he could find and by agreeing to make a sacrifice to Sun. She went to work on the bearskin, and in four or five days Schultz had a large, soft rug with which to cover their couch. But there, it seemed, it could not remain if he cared to have visitors, for none of their friends would enter the lodge while it was inside. Schultz was finally obliged to store it under a couple of rawhides behind their home.

The Blackfeet, as we have seen, were hunters on horseback, hunters not only of buffalo and other big game but also of their human enemies. The young and middle-aged men of the tribe were constantly setting out for or returning from war in parties of a dozen to fifty or more. This was their recreation, to raid the surrounding tribes, to drive off their horses, and to take scalps if they could. The pursuit of game to these people was mere hard labor; the pursuit of man was their chief amusement, as well as their principal topic of conversation.

Schultz, interested in learning at first hand every aspect of Pikuni tribal life, had hoped that someday he would be invited to accompany such a war party. It was a day in 1878 or early 1879 that he learned that a plan for a raid against the Assiniboines was being formulated, and his friend Talks-with-the-Buffalo invited him to participate, saying, "You helped Wolverine steal a girl, and you might as well try your hand at stealing horses." "I'll go with you," said Schultz. "It is just what I have been longing to do."

When he told Kipp what he had in mind, Kipp protested strongly against it, saying, "You have no right to risk your life for a few cayuses," and his wife added, "Think how your people would mourn if anything happened to you." But Schultz had made up his mind, and he could be very stubborn when he chose. He explained that it was not the value of the horses or other loot that he might take; rather, it was the excitement and novelty of the adventure to which he was attracted.

The party was to consist of some thirty men and was organized under the leadership of Heavy Breast, an experienced warrior. As usual, they planned to steal as many horses as they could, for the more horses a man had, the greater was his prestige. Sometimes there would be a fight, and the Pikunis usually hoped one would ensue for the opportunity it would offer to gain further prestige by some act of heroism which would warrant the counting of coup.

Old Lone Elk, a medicine man of great power, was chosen

for the responsible position of praying in the sacred medicine sweat lodge with groups of Heavy Breast's party for
their success and safe return. When the medicine pipe was
passed around for each man to take a puff and offer a
prayer to Sun, Schultz prayed audibly like the rest to show
his sincerity.

Early one evening they rode off, each warrior with his colorful war costume and headdress carefully protected and
securely tied to his saddle. If time permitted, these would be
worn in a fight. Knowing the country well, they rode at
night and spent the day resting, concealed in a grove of
trees or a coulee.

One morning they found themselves close by a well-known
landmark east of the Little Rockies, a high butte, its summit
covered with trees, known as Hairy Cap. They went into
camp near a spring in a grassy spot surrounded by high
brush. Talks-with-the-Buffalo and Schultz were sent to the
summit of the butte to keep watch during the morning.
They followed a steep but well-worn game trail to the top.
Schultz was surprised to find there the remains of several
log and brush shelters, which had been built, Talks-with-the-
Buffalo told him, by sentinels or earlier war parties. Keeping a constant watch over the wide sweep of country visible
from their post, they ate pieces of meat they had brought
along. Then Talks-with-the-Buffalo produced his stone pipe
and they had a smoke. As Schultz began to feel drowsy after
their all-night shift, Talks-with-the-Buffalo told him to sleep
until it was time for him to take over the watch.

Schultz was suddenly awakened by a shout from his companion, who pointed out a war party of Indians, thought to
be either Assiniboines or Crees, driving a large herd of
horses in their direction. They dashed down and reported
to Heavy Breast, who immediately climbed a short distance
to a point from which he could watch the enemy's approach
while his party quickly put on their highly decorated war
attire and stripped the coverings from their war shields.
Schultz later confessed that he dreaded the moment of as-
sault and wished that he were safely at home with Kipp, realizing that he would be facing death in the fight that was
about to begin.

Satisfied as to the direction the enemy party was taking and the closeness of its approach, Heavy Breast led his party down a shallow coulee, out of sight of the enemy but cutting directly across the line of approach. When they could hear the hoofbeats of the enemy horses, he gave the command to attack. With wild cries the Pikunis charged out of the coulee into the herd of horses being driven ahead of the enemy party. The suddenness of the attack stampeded the horses and the fight was on. For a short time the enemy tried to make a stand, but since many were armed only with bows, they were no match for the well-armed Pikunis. Demoralized by the unexpected attack, they fled in all directions.

Once the fighting had begun, Schultz lost all sense of fear and found himself shooting with the rest of the party at the fleeing enemy. Seeing one of them, mounted on a fine pinto, riding wildly up the steep side of the butte, Schultz took after him. Finding himself being rapidly outdistanced, he began firing shot after shot at the man. Once in a while the man would shoot back, but all their shots went wild. Having reached the steep heights of the butte, the man turned his horse loose and ran into the timber. Dismounting in order to take better aim, Schultz fired three more shots. He saw where the bullets hit and not one was even close. He always felt that it was the worst shooting he had ever done. The pinto, meanwhile, had run out onto the plain, so Schultz was able to get some satisfaction by capturing it, a much better horse than his own.

By this time the fight was over and the Pikunis were jubilant. They had not lost a single man, although one young man had a bad cheek wound. They had killed nine of the enemy, identified as Crees, and had captured sixty-three horses. As they talked of their success, they took off their precious war clothes, repacked them, and began the long journey back to their camp near Fort Conrad.

Heavy Breast and his party took several days returning with the captured horses. When they approached the Pikuni camp, they paused to put on their war regalia for the purpose of staging a victorious entrance. As they rode triumphantly into camp, they were greeted with joyous acclaim. Those Pikunis who had lost loved ones in earlier encounters

with the Crees had painted their faces, hands, and moccasins black; with the nine scalps that had been taken held
high above them, the returning warriors danced in slow
steps throughout the camp, singing a mournful song.

In spite of his disapproval of Schultz's participation, Kipp
and his wife celebrated Schultz's safe return with a special
feast consisting of choice meats, bread, beans, three dried
apple pies, and a plum (raisin) duff for dinner, the two
latter courses a rare treat in that part of the country at that
time. Schultz was glad to get back to the fort. For a time he
stayed pretty close to the fireplace and his couch of buffalo
robes, doing nothing but sleeping, eating, and smoking; and
it seemed as if he would never get enough sleep.

In August, 1881, it was chokecherry-gathering time on
the plains, and the Indians were so busy laying in a supply
for winter use that they spent little time at Kipp's trading
post.[2] Schultz decided that with Kipp's approval he would
like to take a few days off to camp again with the Blackfeet.
He saddled his buffalo horse, tied on a slender roll of blankets, and in due course arrived at the Blackfoot camp on the
Musselshell River at the mouth of Crooked Creek. There he
was welcomed in the lodge of Three Bears, father of Schultz's
close friend Eagle Head, who like himself was twenty-two
years old. Soon Eagle Head's pretty sister, Flying Woman,
and his mother, Spear Woman, were setting food before
Schultz: a bowl of soup and a plate of rich berry pemmican.
Spear Woman, it seemed, had decided that her daughter
should have a new dress of antelope skins, for which six
skins would be needed. It was up to Eagle Head and Schultz
to furnish them, so they rode out from camp early one
morning, Eagle Head and Schultz to hunt and Eagle Head's
mother and sister to gather chokecherries.

They headed up the valley of the Musselshell and after
riding some five or six miles turned east into a wide, brushy
coulee. Reconnoitering a bit, Eagle Head discovered a large
band of antelope on the slope of a ridge about a mile away.
Between stretched a level plain, but close behind the ridge

[2] Adapted from story entitled "He Sang the Victory Song," first published in *The Open Road for Boys* in September, 1937, and later reprinted in
Blackfeet and Buffalo, 155.

where most of the animals were resting was another long coulee through which it would be possible for Eagle Head and Schultz to approach the band unseen. They left the women to pick chokecherries while they headed up the coulee toward the antelope. They told the women to come and help butcher the kills when they heard shooting.

The plan worked well so far as the approach was concerned, and they were able to kill eight antelope. As they proceeded with skinning the animals, the women did not put in an appearance. Eagle Head and Schultz finished the butchering and hurried back to the place where they had left the women, only to find they had disappeared. They discovered the abandoned chokecherry pouches and shortly found the trail of their horses heading up the valley but away from camp. Suspecting foul play, they circled about until they discovered what appeared to be the horse tracks of a war party. Just then Flying Woman, trembling with fear, emerged from a growth of willows to report that an enemy party of eight riders had surprised them.

Because Flying Woman's horse was a slow one, her mother made her get off and hide while she continued flight with both horses. She had recognized some Pikuni horses, which meant they had been stolen by the war party the preceding night. The two men took up the trail immediately and before long came within sight of the enemy, who were in hot pursuit of Spear Woman but about half a mile behind. Riding fast, Eagle Head and Schultz gained ground and opened fire, shooting as fast as they could work the levers of their Winchesters.

Almost at once one of the enemy pitched head foremost to the ground, and another's horse dropped, his rider landing upright on his feet. Then Eagle Head's horse fell, pinning him to the ground momentarily. One of the enemy continued to pursue Spear Woman while the others circled around Schultz and Eagle Head, shooting as they rode. Soon they succeeded in killing Schultz's horse, and the outlook became grim. Between shots, Schultz looked off at Spear Woman and her pursuer, who was gradually gaining on her. Seemingly it would be only a question of time until she was captured, but the two men continued to fire at the crawling warriors, who by this time had encircled them. Desperately, Schultz slipped his last four cartridges into the magazine of his rifle, thinking to himself that he would never get to use them all. Levering another cartridge into the barrel, he looked off at Spear Woman again and could hardly believe his eyes. "Eagle Head! Eagle Head!" he shouted. "See them! We survive!"

A little way beyond Spear Woman, forty or fifty riders had come up out of a coulee and were galloping toward her, waving their hands and shouting. At the sight of them, her pursuer turned abruptly and headed for his companions, who stopped circling Eagle Head and Schultz and drew together, yelling excitedly. The two horseless Indians sprang up behind two of their party and all headed away to the south. Then the Blackfeet came speeding past, yelling happily and noticeably gaining on the fleeing warriors.

At last came Spear Woman, both crying and laughing. Springing from her horse, she hugged and kissed Eagle Head and Schultz, both unharmed. Eagle Head proceeded to scalp the dead enemy, who turned out to be a Cutthroat (Assiniboine) Indian, and to take his weapons. Spear Woman looked happily on, singing and exclaiming again and again that her brave son had killed this enemy. So happy were they over the kill that Schultz refrained from saying that it might have been his bullet that tumbled the man from his horse.

In the meantime the tide had turned, both enemies and pursuers being out of sight beyond a low ridge of the plain. Presently, however, they heard distant shouting, and before long the Blackfeet returned, singing the victory song, waving scalps, and leading the horses that the Cutthroats had stolen from their herds during the night. All seven of the Indians were dead out there on the plain, and not one of the rescuers had been killed. Thus Schultz had a horse on which to ride home. They found Flying Woman where they had left her and gave her back her own horse to ride. And that evening the lodge of Three Bears and Eagle Head was crowded with visitors anxious to hear the story of the day's experiences.

CHAPTER 8

A Girl Called Nätahki

B Y the summer of 1879 young Schultz had spent two
years in the Northwest without developing a romantic interest.[1] There had been nothing in the record of
his early years at Boonville or Peekskill to suggest that he
ever had the slightest interest in the opposite sex. The same
was true of his time in Montana, even surrounded as he was
by a number of frontier liaisons without benefit of clergy between white men and Indian women, a not unusual practice
in those parts. Apparently, such an arrangement for himself
never entered his head until he came to know the Pikunis
well and to gain some familiarity with their language.

One evening, some two years after his arrival in Montana,
he was visiting the lodge of his good friend Talks-with-the-
Buffalo when another Pikuni friend, Weasel Tail dropped
in, accompanied by his woman. Schultz was somewhat taken
aback when Weasel Tail, after taking a few puffs on the pipe
before passing it on, asked Schultz abruptly: "Why don't you
take a woman?" Talks-with-the-Buffalo pointed out that he
was qualified by Pikuni custom to do so, having earned the
right to count two coups in the fight they had recently with
the Cree. Talks-with-the-Buffalo was referring to the time

[1]The story in this chapter about Schultz's first wife, whom he called
Nätahki, reflects their life together largely as he has told it in his book *My
Life as an Indian.*

She was born in 1865 and died in 1902, apparently of a heart condition.
Except for brief visits elsewhere in Montana, she spent her entire life in
the immediate area that is now the Blackfoot Reservation. This accounts
for the fact that little is known about her, apart from what Schultz had
told us.

74

Apikuni, Nätahki, and their ranch home. Courtesy James Willard Schultz Society Collection.

when, upon his invitation, Schultz had joined a party of thirty Pikunis under the leadership of Heavy Breast.

Women were a subject to which Schultz seemingly had given little or no consideration because when pressed for an answer he responded rather lamely that it was because "no one would have me." At that, Madame Weasel Tail, clapping her hand to her mouth, the Blackfoot way of expressing surprise or wonder, said:

> "*Kyai-yo*! What a reason! I well know that there isn't a girl in camp but would like to be his woman. Why, if it wasn't for this lazy one here"—giving Weasel Tail's hand an affectionate squeeze—"if he would only go away somewhere and never come back, I'd make you take me. I'd follow you around until you would have to do so."
>
> Said Weasel Tail, "It is the truth." "Yes, the truth," Talks-with-the-Buffalo and his woman joined in.[2]

Although Schultz turned the conversation into a different channel, he knew many white men who had done as Weasel Tail suggested and had taken Indian women to live with them, to all intents and purposes as their wives. The usual custom was to make the parents of the girl a gift of horses or other things of value. Frequently a deep and genuine affection developed between them, with the father showing great love for his children. Even so, the time often came when the man would move on, with no apparent feeling or remorse or any sense of responsibility for the woman or the children.

Schultz began to think more about the matter. He found it impossible to believe that his friend Sorrel Horse, whom he knew to be so deeply devoted to his woman, would ever leave her in such a way. He felt that it would be even more impossible for Kipp to do so. The latter's affection for Double-Strike Woman and for his adopted children was far too deep for him to ever think of deserting them. He noted, too, that his other white friends seemed content with their Indian women, and he reflected upon the Blackfoot saying that "happiness is not found without woman."

Schultz soon began to look a little more closely at the

[2] *My Life as an Indian*, 97–98.

young Pikuni women about the camp, wondering what each was really like. Since his arrival at Fort Benton, he had often been impressed by the beauty of the Blackfeet women. Many times pretty Pikuni girls had smiled at him; one or two had even spoken to him, and he had found himself wondering whether someday he should take one of them for his woman. On the other hand, he knew that when he reached majority, matters pertaining to his father's estate would make it necessary for him to return to Boonville. He knew, of course, that he did not intend to stay long in the West and that his eastern relatives and others there would be horrified at the mere thought of such an alliance. On weighing these various considerations, each against the other, he had, he thought, persuaded himself against it.

One day as he was sitting in the shade with Crow Woman, a friend of Kipp's mother, cleaning his rifle before going hunting, two Pikuni women walked by. The older of the two said a word of greeting to Crow Woman. Her companion was a young girl, possibly sixteen, rather tall and not exactly pretty, but handsome, with neatly braided hair that nearly reached the ground. For a moment her large, expressive eyes met his, then she looked shyly away. There was a dignity about her that Schultz found particularly appealing. He asked Crow Woman about her and learned that her name was *Mutsi-Awotan-Ahki*, or Fine Shield Woman, and that she was related to Kipp's mate, Double-Strike Woman.

Schultz went away on his hunt, but it didn't prove very interesting because he was thinking mostly about the girl. That evening he asked Kipp about her, learning that her father was dead and that her mother was highly thought of among the Pikunis; in fact, she was a medicine-lodge woman, a position of great respect and importance among the Blackfeet. To Kipp's surprise, and in spite of his own resolution, Schultz blurted out, "I'd like to have the girl. What do you think about it?"

Convinced that Schultz was serious, Kipp asked Double-Strike Woman to sound out the girl's mother about the matter. Nothing happened for a couple of days; then Kipp's woman told him that he could have the girl providing he would promise to be always good and kind to her. He readily agreed to that, at which Double-Strike Woman said she would make her some dresses similar to those worn by other women about the post. When he asked what he was to pay, in terms of horses or otherwise, the response was: "Her mother says there is to be no pay, only that you are to keep your promise to be good to her daughter."

This willingness to accept nothing but a promise for a daughter was unusual. Ordinarily, a number of horses would be paid as consideration, sometimes fifty or more. In some cases the father would specify the number of head to be paid; if not, the suitor gave as many as he could. Again it was not unusual for a father to ask some promising youth, good hunter and bold raider, to become his son-in-law. In that case he was the one to give horses, and even a lodge and household goods, with the girl.

As was the Blackfoot custom, Schultz and the girl had never spoken to each other or even been introduced. Their wedding involved no formality. One evening while Schultz and Sorrel Horse were visiting Kipp and his family, the girl, acting on her mother's instructions, entered the room shyly, her face covered with her shawl. It was a moment of embarrassment for Schultz as well as the girl. The good-natured joking they were subjected to by Kipp and Sorrel Horse intensified their discomfort until Kipp's mother, Earth Woman, put a stop to it. Suitable quarters had been arranged for the couple by Double-Strike Woman in the same row of log cabins where the Kipps themselves lived. Their mutual diffidence made their really getting to know each other difficult, particularly since the girl could speak no English and in spite of Schultz's growing facility in the oral and sign languages of the Blackfeet.

From the foregoing it is evident that when young Schultz took Nätahki for his woman, it was not just another frontier liaison based on mutual convenience. Rather, it was an unorthodox arrangement between a twenty-year-old white youth of New England background and a fifteen-year-old Indian girl who had never lived in anything but a tipi. There had been neither courtship nor personal acquaintance before their relationship began. Schultz had made no direct overtures to her family to gain her hand, and the girl herself may not even have been consulted about her wishes in the matter. Being without assets, Schultz was pleased, as well as surprised, that he was not asked to pay the usual or, in fact, any price for his Blackfoot bride.

No one ever said that Nätahki was beautiful or even pretty, but she was not without her virtues. From *My Life as an Indian* it is evident that she was diligent, obedient, and loyal. According to her son, Hart, she was a wise woman as well as a happy one, seeing beauty all around her and passing it on to others.[3] From a close friend of the family comes the word that she was "always happy and cheerful, and enjoyed a good joke."[4] As far as Schultz was concerned, having in mind the setting of which he was so fond, she was the perfect wife. As for Nätahki, she must have been pleased, in view of the chronic shortage of available males, to have a man all to herself, and she must have considered herself exceedingly fortunate to have been chosen by one who was young, white, personable, and a good provider.

The Blackfoot world was a male-dominated as well as a polygamous society, with the women occupying a subservient position. They were taught from infancy to look up to their men as heroes and to serve them as slaves. To their lot fell the drudgery and unpleasant chores of living, and they accepted them without complaint. In this regard, Nätahki was a role model, sometimes embarrassing Schultz in the zeal with which she performed her often onerous duties. His slightest wish was her command, but she, in turn, was bewildered by the consideration and respect with which he, by reason of his upbringing in a civilized society, accorded her and other members of her sex and race.

Mutsi-Awotan-Ahki was industrious in the care of Schultz's clothes and their quarters. Earlier he had purchased a shield, a war bonnet, and other articles deemed proper for a war-

[3] Paul Dyck, "The Return of Lone Wolf," *Montana: The Magazine of Western History*, Winter, 1972, 21.
[4] Jessica Donaldson Schultz, "Adventuresome, Amazing Apikuni," *Montana: The Magazine of Western History*, Autumn, 1960, 7.

rior and held sacred by the Blackfeet. These, his medicine things, she always hung on a tripod with the utmost care and respect. In all such ways she was an excellent wife, but he constantly wondered what she really thought of him. She seldom spoke except to answer his direct questions, yet he often saw her chatting and laughing with the other women.

This barrier between them was suddenly and rather dramatically swept away. One day while he was at the Pikuni camp he learned that a marauding party against the Crows was being organized. Weasel Tail and Talks-with-the-Buffalo were going and invited him to go with them. He agreed and went back to his quarters to get things ready. To his amazement, the girl wanted to know where he was going—the first question she had ever asked him. When he told her, her shyness evaporated. In a flood of words she reprimanded him, a white man, for planning to go with a party of Indians to steal horses and probably kill innocent people.

Schultz was dumbfounded. He protested that he had already promised to go. She broke into tears, seized his arm, and, declaring her love for him, pleaded with him not to go. Then, suddenly feeling that she had gone too far, she fell silent, the tears still big in her eyes. Deeply touched by her unexpected revelation, Schultz put his arm around her and made her sit down beside him. He agreed not to go with the war party and urged her not to withdraw into herself when they were together. They must be free, he said, to talk and laugh together, free to show their love for each other. He found himself calling her Nätahki, an affectionate nickname derived from the Blackfoot *a-nat-ah-ki*, meaning "cute or pretty girl."

Thus the great love of his life began, and many pages of his first book were eloquent with the warmth and the depth of the affection that developed between them. In the preface to *My Life as an Indian*, entitled "Principal Characters," she was described as "a Blackfoot Indian girl who becomes the wife of the AUTHOR: a cheerful and sweet-tempered woman about whom the interest of the story centres. The book's finest character."

Apart from what Schultz himself has written about Nä-

tahki, we know little else about her. One exception, however, is to be found in the fact that she was given official
mention in the records of the Census of 1880 for Choteau
County, Montana, in which she was listed as a member of
the Kipp household and specifically as "Good Shield, female
Indian servant." Schultz was shown as "Schultz, James W.,
21, cattle dealer." No mention of the fact that she had become his woman was made in the official record, possibly because he did not want the fact that their relationship was
without benefit of clergy to be thus documented officially.

The year 1880 brought not only the federal census but
the age of majority for Schultz. As his twenty-first birthday
drew near, he received many letters from his family, urging
him to return to New York. They reminded him that there
would be papers to sign and other business to attend to, but
after living with Nätahki for a full year he found it difficult
even to consider a return to Boonville. When he talked it
over with Kipp and Sorrel Horse, explaining his need to return to Boonville and possibly to remain there, they laughed
at his assurance that he would never return to Montana.
When he told Nätahki of his impending departure, she began to sob brokenheartedly, even though he did not dare
admit to her that he might not return.

When the *Helena*, last steamboat of the season, left Fort
Benton in August, 1880, Schultz was on board after a tear-
ful parting with Nätahki. The long journey by boat to Bismarck, Dakota Territory, and by train to Boonville brought
him to the old hometown on the evening of September 1,
1880, only a few days after his twenty-first birthday.[5]

Boonville was just as he remembered it: a pretty town with
comfortable homes and carefully tended gardens, each
piece of property well fenced. But he found it difficult to explain his love of frontier life to his family and friends, who
were advising him day by day to change his ways and settle
down. Only his mother was able finally to understand that
he could no longer bear the thought of living in a town or

---

[5] His arrival was chronicled by the *Boonville Herald* of September 2, 1880
(information supplied by Joe Conway to *The Piegan Storyteller*, Vol. VII,
No. 3, 16–17).

city. He was unable to mention Nätahki to anyone but his Uncle Jeff, with whom he visited at Lyon Falls and who gave him his blessing to return to Montana.

In two days Schultz was in St. Louis, where he bought a trunk and filled it with gifts for Nätahki; then he took the train to Corrine, Wyoming, and the stage to Fort Benton, where he was happily reunited with Nätahki and his friends. Soon his trunks were brought over. Handing the key to one of them to Nätahki, he told her that the contents were all hers, some of them to be shared with Double-Strike Woman and Crow Woman. Schultz always looked back upon that morning as one of the pleasantest of his life.

With friends they traveled to the Indian camp where Nätahki's mother was living, visiting with her and their many other Indian friends. That evening he dropped in at a number of lodges, including that of Chief Big Lake. When he finally got back to his own lodge, Nätahki was waiting for him. They talked for some time before going to sleep. Schultz watched the shadows from the dying fire dance across the lodge skins. There was soft laughter somewhere in the camp, and far, far away he heard faintly the wild coloraturas of the coyotes. Half asleep, he murmured in Blackfoot, "Thrice blessed I am by propitious gods."

The following day, the Pikuni chiefs held a council and decided that the band should move out to the foot of the Bear Paw Mountains. There they found vast numbers of elk, deer, and bighorn sheep. Wolverine and Schultz between them killed four fat ewes, but they could have slaughtered twenty had they been so inclined. Soon thereafter the Pikunis were able to repel a sneak attack by a Crow horse-stealing party, repulsing the enemy without loss. Schultz participated and returned unharmed, although a Crow bullet creased Weasel Tail's thigh. Rather than pursue the enemy, since there was a shortage of ammunition, it was decided to push on to Fort Benton.

When they reached Fort Benton a few days later, they found it full of traders, trappers, bullwhackers, muleskinners, and Indians. When Schultz and Kipp paid a visit to the Overland Hotel, they saw a man whom Schultz, from his appearance, took to be a preacher. In response to Schultz's inquiry on the subject, he stated that he was a minister of the Methodist Episcopal Church and had been preaching in the mountains for the past year but would soon be returning to the States. Schultz then asked him if he would be willing to perform a marriage if the other party would consent. For some time it had been on Schultz's mind to have his relationship with Nätahki legalized by a formal marriage ceremony when and if it were possible. With Kipp acting as interpreter, the knot was tied, despite some misgivings on Nätahki's part about the fact that the minister wore no black robe. Nevertheless, she was overjoyed at this unexpected confirmation of her status as a wife, making her one of the few women, possibly the only Indian woman in that vicinity, to enjoy the luxury of a formal marriage.

CHAPTER 9

Winter Trading Post on the Judith

RUMORS had reached Fort Conrad that the buffalo herds seemed to be diminishing, and this gave Kipp grave concern. According to Blackfoot tradition, there had been times in the past when the great herds had seemed to disappear, but the medicine men had made fervent supplication to Sun for their return and they had never failed to come back. To both white men and red who remembered herds covering the plains from horizon to horizon, it seemed incredible that the buffalo might be facing extinction.

During the summer of 1879 several prominent Pikuni chiefs met with Kipp to discuss plans for hunting and trading during the coming winter. A Pikuni war party, returning from a raid on the Crows, brought reassuring reports of large buffalo herds from the Judith to the Yellowstone. This information convinced the chiefs that Kipp should build a trading post on the Judith. The tribe would winter there, they promised, and would trade only with him. At Kipp's suggestion the chiefs also agreed that at this post no whiskey would be used in trade—a virtually unheard of development in those days.

Kipp's bull train was making so much money freighting along the Whoop-Up Trail that he decided not to use it in operating the proposed post on the Judith. In late August, Kipp, Schultz and a small party left Fort Conrad with five wagons, each drawn by a four-horse team, to establish the post. In addition to Kipp and Schultz, the party consisted of Frank Pearson; Crow Woman and her adopted daughter,

Flag Woman, as cooks; and four men to help as teamsters. All the other women were to remain for the winter at Fort Conrad, which was left in charge of Hiram Upham, one of Kipp's most trusted employees. However, Frank Pearson's wife put up such a protest at being separated from him that she was finally allowed to go along. Schultz comforted Nä-tahki by promising that he would return to Fort Conrad for short visits whenever he could during the months to come. Trade goods and all necessary supplies were purchased at Fort Benton. These proved to be more than Kipp's five wagons could hold, so he had to hire another wagon and team for the trip to the Judith.

Some days later when they arrived at Arrow Creek, a tributary of the Judith, they were reassured when they caught sight of several large herds of buffalo, for which Crow Woman instantly gave thanks to the gods. As the party approached the confluence of Sage Creek and the Judith River, where Kipp had decided to build his new trading post, they saw still more herds of buffalo, as well as bands of antelope, and when they crossed the river to make temporary camp in a grove of cottonwoods, they frightened away a large number of deer and elk.

While they were busy making camp, Schultz, with willow pole and line and a hook baited with grasshoppers, found time to catch two good-sized panfuls of fine trout, the first he had caught in Montana. After cleaning and frying them, he found to his surprise that Kipp was the only one who would even think of eating them. It was then that he discovered that no member of the Blackfoot tribe would touch one, let alone eat it, for they believed that all fish were the property of the dreaded Water People, the *Suyi Tupi*.

The following morning they started cutting logs for the buildings they would need. By early October they had two cabins finished. The main one was to serve as a trade room and storehouse; the other, smaller cabin had three rooms: one for Kipp and Schultz, the second for the kitchen to be occupied by Crow Woman and her daughter, and the third for Pearson and his wife. When the teamsters were there, they slept in the storehouse.

Shortly after the cabins were finished, the Pikunis began to arrive and were soon followed by a party of Bloods. By the time all the Pikunis had arrived and had set up their camp, it formed a huge circle of more than four hundred lodges in an area where they would have considerable protection from the fierce, cold north winds. According to custom, all the lodges were made of freshly tanned cow-buffalo hides, products of the past summer's hunt. Schultz noted that at the back of each lodge near the top, painted in red and black, was the symbol of a butterfly, the bringer of good dreams. He also observed that many lodges were decorated with paintings of animals and symbols of the sun, moon, and stars and that the lodges of the chiefs and of the medicine men bore decorations that served to identify their owners. Schultz was pleased to see that among the lodges were those of his friends Red Eagle, Little Dog, Lone Elk, and White Calf, the head chief of the Pikunis.

With the Pikunis had come a man who for many years was to play a significant role in the life of James Willard Schultz. This was Eli Guardipee, whose family was prominent in the early history of the Northwest. The Pikunis had named him *Isinamakan*, or Takes Gun Ahead, and evidently he was well named for Schultz once wrote of him: "He was the most successful hunter and the surest shot I ever knew." Eli Guardipee was just a year older than Schultz, slim and tall, highly intelligent, and both brave and kind. Within a short time the two of them developed a close friendship that lasted throughout their lives.

Not until November would the buffalo fur reach prime condition, so during the interval Guardipee and Schultz frequently hunted together for antelope, deer, and elk to help supply the trading post and the Pikuni camp with meat. On one such trip Guardipee found the bodies of two bull elk, their antlers so interlocked that they had starved to death. Schultz was sure that his longtime naturalist friend C. Hart Merriam would be interested in them, so he shipped the two heads to Merriam from Fort Benton. Merriam, in turn, gave them to the Smithsonian Institution.

The new post daily bought from the Pikunis a hundred or

more hides, a dollar's worth of trade goods being paid for each hide. A tin pint cup was the post's only measuring device. Tea and coffee were sold at fifty cents a cup, sugar at twenty-five, flour at three cups for fifty cents. Tobacco was sold at two dollars for a guessed-at pound and cartridges for two dollars a box. Other standard goods—trade cloth (both red and blue), calico, gingham, needles, thread, baking powder, Chinese vermilion, axes, knives, pots, and frying pans—were traded at 100 per cent profit over their cost at Fort Benton.

Schultz visited the Pikuni camp nearly every night and was soon known to nearly everyone in the camp. The All Friends Warrior Society welcomed him to its meetings, where he became familiar with its traditions of warfare, its songs, and its dances. He had so many invitations to meals that he seldom ate supper at the trading post. Although not a gambler by nature, he joined in many of the games, seldom finding himself a match for the Pikunis. The Pikuni children invited him to join them in their games. The day after the first snowstorm, he came upon some youngsters using a variety of pans to slide down a small hill. Great was their delight when they persuaded Schultz to join them. At the height of their fun, some mothers, having missed their cooking utensils and visibly annoyed, came rushing over after them. They thought Schultz had suggested to their children that the pans be put to such use, and there was a moment of considerable embarrassment for him until the youngsters managed to exonerate him.

By late November the fur of the buffalo had become prime and the harvest of hides got under way. When the men went hunting, a few of the Pikuni women took turns going with them to help with the skinning and butchering of those suitable for eating. As many tongues as possible were brought back to camp. The women who remained in camp were busy with the back-breaking labor of fleshing and tanning the heavily furred hides, making them into soft robes; for each they received five dollars' worth of trade goods.

The constant hunting served to drive the buffalo farther and farther away to the east and south. This made it neces-

sary for the hunters and their female helpers to travel farther and farther from camp in spite of intense cold and
deep snow. Many suffered crippling frostbite, and one person was frozen to death.

During the winter, Kipp's wagons made several trips to
Fort Benton with loads of buffalo robes and the pelts of
various other animals. Entrusted by Kipp with business
to attend to at Fort Conrad, Schultz was able to keep his
promise and have an occasional visit with Nätahki. Her joy
at seeing him always touched him deeply, and, much as he
enjoyed life there, made him loath to return to the post on
the Judith.

When spring came and the buffalo-hunting season was
over, Kipp reckoned that they had taken in trade one thousand eight hundred buffalo robes; three thousand deer, antelope, and elk hides; and a goodly number of pelts from
such smaller animals as wolves and foxes. Kipp considered
that winter of 1879–80 only a fairly profitable one, and the
persistent stories about the diminishing buffalo herds continued to give him great concern.

For Schultz it had proved a particularly fruitful winter.
He had learned more and more about the varied and often
complex religious rites of the Blackfoot tribes. Many of the
rites were concerned with the unwrapping of sacred medicine bundles consisting of an assortment of objects considered sacred as the symbols of certain supernatural powers.
On one occasion Schultz was invited to attend the ceremonial unwrapping of several of these.

The Beaver Bundles, of which there were but a very few
among the Blackfoot tribes, were considered to be the oldest
and most important of all. Their owners were known as
Beaver Men and were looked upon as persons of importance. There were a number of traditions regarding the
introduction of the Beaver Bundle medicine among the
Blackfoot tribes. These, in a general way, were concerned
with the close relationship that in days long past had developed between certain Blackfoot individuals and the vener-
able Chief of all Beavers and his son. It was this chief who
instructed a Blackfoot friend how to construct a Beaver

Bundle and taught him the songs and dances that were part of the ritual that must be followed for its unwrapping.

Knowing its importance, Schultz was particularly pleased when he was invited by one of the owners of a Beaver Bundle to participate in its opening. He arrived at the lodge at dawn, knowing that it was a daylong ceremony. He learned some of the innumerable songs that were sung as one animal skin after another was unwrapped from the large bundle placed before the Beaver Man and his associates. Dances imitative of each animal were performed during the songs, some of which were very amusing.

Schultz was persuaded to join the group of dancers when a coyote skin was taken from the bundle. As this group danced it imitated the antics of coyotes; when its members began to bark and howl as they danced, the spectators howled and barked with them. To the amusement of everyone present, one of the dancers stopped in front of a dignified old chief and lifted his leg as if to urinate. The stars were beginning to come out before the ceremony was concluded and Schultz, feeling a strange refreshment of the spirit and a deep sense of community with his hosts, walked slowly back to the post.

Every detail of the rite attending the unwrapping of the Beaver Bundle was soon preserved in one of Schultz's notebooks. Traditional stories, accounts of customs, and even the games that were new to him all became a part of that mass of Blackfoot material that he was accumulating so painstakingly. Good reporter that he was, nothing was considered too trivial to warrant his attention. More and more notebooks were filled.

In sharing a room with Kipp that winter, Schultz learned a great deal about Kipp's eventful life, including some years he had spent in the army. Their friendship deepened to such a degree that from then on he looked upon Kipp more as an older brother than as a friend and employer. Throughout the winter their small trading post and even the large Pikuni camp were pervaded by an atmosphere of tranquility. Many times the only sound heard during the day would be that of children playing happily together.

The peace and contentment that had prevailed came
to an abrupt end one afternoon in March, 1880, when the
Pikuni camp was suddenly thrown into noisy confusion.
Kipp and Schultz hurried there to find a Lieutenant Crouse
and a dozen mounted infantrymen from Fort Benton. They
learned from Crouse that the Pikunis were to be moved, by
force if necessary, far to the north, where, on Badger Creek,
an agency had been established on orders of the Commissioner of Indian Affairs. With Kipp acting as interpreter,
the lieutenant explained to the Indians that this was being
done because a Colonel Henry Brooks, who had a cattle
ranch a short distance to the north, had complained that the
Pikunis had been killing his cattle. The Pikuni chiefs vehemently denied this, claiming that they had seen many of
Brooks's cattle, evidently strays, grazing with buffalo beside
the Musselshell River, a considerable distance away.

Lieutenant Crouse insisted that the lands where the Pikunis were now camped no longer belonged to the Blackfoot tribes. Chief White Calf immediately protested that the
lieutenant was mistaken. He stated positively that he and
several other Pikuni chiefs had been present twenty-five
years earlier when a treaty between the United States government and the Blackfoot tribes was agreed upon and
signed by the representatives of both parties. This treaty,
White Calf insisted, made secure to the Blackfoot tribes all
the lands from "the Red Coat's Country south to the Musselshell River, and from the Backbone of the World east to the
Milk River."

Kipp translated what White Calf had said. Lieutenant
Crouse was nonplussed. "Surely they have been told," he
said, "that since that treaty was signed, the United States has
opened for settlement all the lands between the Missouri
and the Yellowstone rivers, and also has thrown open the
lands north from the Missouri to the Marias." Kipp assured
him that the Pikunis knew nothing of this and added, "And
I won't tell them, for God knows what might then happen."

During these conversations a large crowd had gathered,
including the powerful All Friends Warrior Society. When
word spread that the Pikunis were to be driven from what

they considered their own lands, there were angry shouts of protest. It appeared to Schultz that violence would break out at any moment. Crouse pleaded with Kipp for advice. Kipp told him bluntly that there was nothing for him to do but to tell the Pikunis that he had to obey orders and that they would have to move. Kipp then added that as soon as he had finished translating the lieutenant's statement he would talk with the Pikunis and try to persuade them that they should comply with Crouse's orders.

Sometime before this, Kipp had told Schultz of how in 1869 he had joined the army as a scout at Fort Shaw and that he had been with Colonel Eugene Baker when, despite Kipp's protests, Baker had given the order that led to the brutal and unnecessary massacre of Heavy Runner's band of Pikunis. Schultz hoped that Kipp's army experience would enable him to cope successfully with this confrontation between Crouse and the Pikunis. Kipp, however, knew only too well how futile it would be for them to resist the order of Lieutenant Crouse. If the Pikunis did resist, the lieutenant would be bound to attempt to force them to obey and the fight would be on. Crouse and his handful of men would be wiped out in a matter of minutes, but in the end the army's retaliation undoubtedly would decimate the tribe. All this he tried to make clear to the Pikunis.

At first they listened quietly, but then such pandemonium resulted that Kipp was given no chance to continue. There were shouts of "This is our country, we will not leave it!" and "Get your guns and we will kill these dog-faced soldiers." By shouts and signs, Kipp finally was able to quell the furious mob. Addressing the leading chiefs, he reminded them of what the army had done to Heavy Runner's band on the Marias just ten years before when, without cause, the soldiers attacked the sleeping camp and killed men, women, and children. Few escaped. He impressed upon them that if they did not do as Lieutenant Crouse commanded, hundreds upon hundreds of soldiers would come with their big-mouthed guns and slaughter the Pikunis as they slaughtered Heavy Runner's band. Such was Kipp's prestige among the Pikunis that Head Chief White Calf and then Chief Little

Dog reluctantly agreed to persuade their people that they must do as Kipp had requested and follow the army's orders.

Later, White Calf went to the trade room to ask Kipp and Schultz if it were really true that their treaty with the United States had been broken as the lieutenant had said. First making him promise that he would make no trouble at the time, Kipp told him the bitter truth. White Calf was stunned. "Oh what thieves, what liars are the white men!" he groaned. As Schultz has written, there was no laughter and no singing in the Pikuni camp that night or for many a night thereafter.

Preparations for the long trek north began the next morning. There were still many buffalo hides that had not been tanned, and these had to be packed so that they could be carried on the horse-drawn travois with the buffalo-hide coverings for lodges and other baggage. In three days the slow and sorrowful journey began. Schultz and Kipp and all those who had been with them at their post on the Judith went with the Pikunis. The Indians' horses were by this time worn out by the constant, long, hard riding they had been subjected to during the winter months. Added to this, the grazing had been unusually poor. Such was their condition that more than two hundred of them died before the Pikunis reached Fort Benton, and another two hundred before they arrived at Fort Conrad.

The Pikunis made camp at Fort Conrad. Their sadly jaded horses at last had a chance to graze. The women set to work on the untanned buffalo hides, and the men went hunting deer and antelope to keep the camp supplied with food. The hides of these and the tanned buffalo robes were traded at Fort Conrad, mostly for food to supplement the meat the hunters were able to procure.

By this time, whatever news had been withheld from the Pikunis by Kipp and White Calf had become common knowledge. Sadly they faced the fact that all the land between the Missouri and the Yellowstone, as well as those from the Missouri to the Marias, was no longer theirs, this in spite of the "Treaty with the Blackfoot Nation." This treaty, Schultz learned, had been negotiated by a delegation of Blackfoot chiefs, including Sees-from-Afar, head chief of the Bloods, and Lame Bull and Little Dog of the Pikunis. It was ratified by the Senate on April 16, 1856. Ten days later, President Franklin Pierce approved it.

For the first time Schultz became aware of how fully the Indians were at the mercy of the United States government and its military forces. It was sad knowledge indeed for a white man who was already deeply involved with and devoted to the Blackfeet.

CHAPTER 10

Last Winter Trading Post at Carroll

THE handwriting was rather plainly on the wall. Kipp was now convinced that the end of the buffalo herds was near and wondered whether it would be worthwhile to plan for another winter trading post. He made many inquiries to determine whether any large herds remained and if so just where they were; the results assured him that there were sizable herds to be found in a large area near the confluence of the Musselshell and Missouri rivers. Kipp discussed the matter with the Pikuni chiefs and they readily promised that if he did decide to build a winter trading post in that area they would go there for their winter hunt and again do their trading with him. Then Kipp rode north to visit the chiefs of the Bloods and the Siksikas, and they, too, agreed to make their winter hunts there and trade with him.

After conferences with Charles Conrad and others of the I. G. Baker Company in Fort Benton, Kipp decided to build what might well be his last trading post at Carroll on the Missouri River a short distance above its junction with the Musselshell. The town was named for Matthew Carroll, who with Colonel C. A. Broadwater had attempted to develop a freight line from that location to Helena.

Early in June, 1880, with Long John Forgy in charge of the bull train as usual, Kipp left Fort Conrad for Fort Benton to purchase trade goods and other supplies for the winter trading post at Carroll. When the purchases had been made and loaded, Forgy and the bull train started on the long haul to Carroll and Kipp returned to Fort Conrad

to complete with Schultz the necessary preparations to establish the new post. It was decided that trustworthy Hiram
Upham would remain behind to take charge of Fort Conrad. Again both Nätahki and Double-Strike Woman would
stay at Fort Conrad, as their husbands considered the country they were going into too hazardous to risk taking them
along. This time, Frank Pearson's wife agreed to remain
behind.

On June 10, 1880, the party that was to man the new trading post left Fort Conrad with three four-horse teams to
pick up additional supplies at Fort Benton. Kipp, Schultz,
and Eli Guardipee headed this party, and with them were
Earth Woman, Crow Woman, and Crow Woman's adopted
daughter, Flag Woman. Charles Rose (Yellow Fish), Frank
Pearson (Horns), and Comes-with-Rattles were the drivers.

At Fort Benton, the wagons drew up at the I. G. Baker
Company warehouse to load additional trade goods and
supplies. As soon as the wagons were loaded, Kipp sent
them on their way to Carroll. He, Schultz, and Guardipee
did not accompany the wagons, as it had been planned that
they would go to Carroll by steamboat. After a few days in
Fort Benton visiting old friends, the three men embarked
on the I. G. Baker Company steamboat *Red Cloud*. As Schultz
stepped aboard, he could not quite believe that it had been
only a little more than three years since he arrived at Fort
Benton by leaping to the levee from the boat. What a life he
had led since the day Kipp had taken him in hand.

The captain, Charles Williams, welcomed them cordially.
It was early in the morning when they left Fort Benton. As
soon as they reached the mouth of Arrow Creek several
miles below Benton, they began to see buffalo; from then
on, buffalo were constantly in sight. The men's spirits rose.
After all, the winter trade might not be as poor as they had
feared.

Captain Williams extended to Schultz, Kipp, and Guardipee what was considered a great honor by inviting them to
sit with him on the upper deck as they entered the most
spectacular part of the river, which Schultz usually referred
to as the Grand Canyon of the Missouri. Guardipee, as

usual, had his rifle by his side. As they were passing the
mouth of Eagle Creek, they moved rapidly by a high cliff
from which a large bighorn ram was looking down at the
passing boat. Guardipee raised his rifle, but Schultz protested, "You can't hit it. It's a good 250 yards away, and the
motion of the boat . . . ." Guardipee paid no attention to
him but raised his rifle and fired. The ram leaped into the
air, plunging down the face of the cliff into the water. Instantly Captain Williams jumped to the wheel and guided
the *Red Cloud* so that members of the crew could get hold of
the bighorn and hoist it to the deck; that evening the passengers of the *Red Cloud* feasted on choice bighorn steaks.
By then Schultz was thoroughly convinced that Guardipee
was the finest rifleman he had ever known.

Arriving at Carroll the *Red Cloud* tied up beside a cut bank
that rose twenty feet from the river. There Carroll and
Broadwater had in earlier days cut a wide, gently sloping
trail leading to a sagebrush-covered flat with a large grove
of cottonwoods at the lower end. Long John Forgy and his
bullwhackers were already hard at work there, cutting logs
for the trading post. Nothing remained of the Carroll-
Broadwater buildings, but at the extreme end of the flat was
a small log store whose customers were wood hawks: the
men whose job it was to supply firewood for the steamboats.

Mail now reached Schultz more frequently because steamboats often stopped at Carroll and the captain would have
a packet of letters and papers for him. Sometimes there
would be letters from C. Hart Merriam, who now was a
practicing physician and surgeon at Locust Grove, New
York, Merriam's boyhood home. The letters sometimes contained news about the slaughter of the buffalo, expressed
concern about it, and asked for Schultz's comments.

By the first of September the trading post was finished.
The low, earth-roofed main building, one hundred forty
feet long, had a partitioned-off section at one end for the
trade room. In one corner Kipp and Schultz had their bed,
and beside it they placed their imposing Wells Fargo safe.
Back of the counters in the trade room were shelves filled
with groceries and dry goods. The other portion of the

main building served as a warehouse for the six thousand dollars' worth of trade goods Kipp had purchased at Fort Benton.

Directly back of the main building was a smaller one for the kitchen and dining room and quarters for the cook and other employees. Off to one side was a small cabin in which were stored sixty barrels of "good Blue-ribbon whiskey" which had been shipped from St. Louis. In anticipation of a visit by a United States marshal, they decided not to have the whiskey in the trade room, for should he find it there he might put them out of business. A man named Hewie lived in this small cabin and was held responsible for it; when an Indian wanted whiskey as a part of his purchase, he was given a chit to present to Hewie. There was also a small smokehouse for the smoking of buffalo tongues.

North and south of Carroll the plains were dark with buffalo. Every day herds came down to the bottomlands to drink at the river, then return to the plains to graze. By the time the trading post was ready for business, it was mating season. From far off, like distant thunder, came the deep, guttural moaning of the bulls. At this season some of the herds would dash down on the run, plunge into the river, swim across, and climb to the prairies on the other side.

Schultz had managed to build a skiff, and one day he suggested to Kipp that when a herd was swimming they attempt to catch some calves and raise them. Kipp put an end to that suggestion by asking Schultz where they would get the necessary milk. It is interesting to note, however, that the same year, according to Schultz, two ranchers in the Flathead Indian country acquired some buffalo calves. These became the nucleus of the herd which the Canadian government bought in 1906 for forty thousand dollars to establish its Wainwright herd in Alberta.[1]

The first members of the Blackfoot Confederacy to arrive at Carroll were the Siksikas. Schultz spotted their mile-long

---

[1] There is considerable disagreement among old-timers about who was responsible for catching and raising the calves which eventually were used to start the Wainwright herd. See David A. Dary, *The Buffalo Book.*

procession as it began moving down from the plains across
the river to the bottomlands of the Missouri. He quickly
launched his skiff and rowed across to greet them just as their
leaders were dismounting on the sandy shore. They were an
impressive looking group: well armed, neatly clothed, and
of great dignity. Leaving his boat, Schultz walked up and
spoke to them in Blackfoot: "I am a messenger from Raven
Quiver. He asks chief Crow Big Feet[2] to come and smoke
and eat with him."

"At this," Schultz has written, "the most keenly, intelli-
gently featured Indian I have ever known—not tall, not
heavy, but of a wonderfully dignified appearance"—stepped
forward. Taking Schultz's hand, he said, "You speak our language well, young white man. I am eager to visit my close
friend, Raven Quiver. Let us go."

At this point, according to Schultz, a slender, bewhiskered
white man wearing buckskin trousers and a blanket capote
stepped up to him and said, "We are in great danger. The
Assiniboines, great numbers of them, are on their way to
wipe us out."

Crow Big Feet interrupted him abruptly: "You, Three
Persons, close your mouth. Should the Cutthroats come to
fight us, we shall, as we have ever done, make them cry."
With this he signed to Schultz, "Let us cross."

Two other chiefs of the tribe followed Crow Big Feet into
the skiff and Schultz quickly rowed them across to the place
where Kipp was awaiting them. He and Crow Big Feet embraced and rubbed cheeks, and after the other chiefs had
exchanged greetings with Kipp, they all walked up to the
post for the smoke and feast that awaited them.

All afternoon the Siksikas were busy fording the river and
making camp back of the post. Later they moved on to the
Musselshell, but before they did so Crow Big Feet had several serious talks with Kipp and Schultz about the condition
of the buffalo. Kipp finally convinced the chief that they
were indeed going fast, that in a year or two they would be
gone.

[2] This was the name used by Schultz. The correct name of the chief was
Crowfoot.

Suddenly the chief blurted out to Kipp, "When they, our real food, are gone, what then for us?"

"You will have to take to the white man's ways. Raise grains and white horns [cattle] for food."

"*Haiya, haiya*," Crow Big Feet sorrowfully exclaimed, "what a nothing existence that will be! Better that, when our buffalo pass, we pass too!"

After Crow Big Feet had left, Schultz asked Kipp about the strange white man the chief had called Three Persons. In evident distaste, Kipp told him, "Oh, that fellow. He came to this country as a missionary, but got into a scrape over a woman and his church repudiated him. He still hangs around three gods—God, the Son and the Holy Ghost. That is why, in derision, they have named him 'Three Persons.'"[3]

While the Siksikas were still in camp at Carroll, the Bloods, or Kainahs, arrived. Under Chief Running Rabbit there were about one thousand of them, and the post began a thriving trade with them and the Siksikas. Because they had many friends among the Indians, Schultz and Kipp eagerly awaited their arrival, but to their great surprise and serious concern Louis Riel leader of the historic rebellion of Canadian métis (mixed bloods), also arrived with a hundred families of Red River French-Cree métis. At about the same time, Chief Big Bear arrived with a thousand Crees and Kipp had a problem. The Pikunis and the Crees were bitter enemies, and it seemed unlikely that the Pikunis would winter anywhere near Carroll as long as the Crees were there, not to mention Riel and his métis.

Immediately after the Crees arrived, men of the All Friends Warrior Society of both the Siksikas and the Bloods began to paint and arm themselves, certain they could now exterminate the Crees. Kipp knew only too well that if war should break out, it undoubtedly would ruin trading that winter. Although chances of averting such a catastrophe seemed slim, he called a council of the leading chiefs of the

[3]This is the way Schultz told it. Jean L'Heureux (Three Persons) was actually a Canadian who had been studying for the ministry in Quebec when he was expelled and came west, where he passed himself off as a priest. He was not in a scrape with a woman because he was a homosexual.

Siksikas, the Bloods, and the Crees. They arrived quickly, a good omen, for evidently the chiefs, too, desired peace. Big Bear, head chief of the Crees, at first appeared to Schultz to be a poorly clothed, dumpy, unintelligent-looking man in contrast to the chiefs of the Blackfoot tribes. Nevertheless, Big Bear proved to possess great strength of character.

As the chiefs were seated, each was served a drink of the post's good whiskey. Then a long-stemmed stone pipe was handed to Crow Big Feet to light. After a few puffs he passed it on to make the rounds, and, another good omen, no one refused to smoke. Food was served, and they ate as they talked. As is usual at such councils, they spoke of many unimportant matters not relevant to the subject they all knew was the reason for Kipp's calling them together. There was another round of whiskey, the big pipe was refilled, and again all smoked. As the pipe continued to be passed, Kipp addressed them, as Schultz has reported: "My friends, you are camped here in the midst of the last of the buffalo herds. Soon there will be no more. That you may live well upon them as long as they last, I urge that you camp and hunt in peace with one another. I speak, too, for your women and children. Well you know that your fighting makes widows and orphans of them."

As Kipp spoke, all could hear the young hotheads in the Blackfoot camps singing their war songs and shouting for war. When Kipp finished speaking, Crow Big Feet of the Siksikas was the first to speak. "I am for peace between us and your Crees, Big Bear. What say you?" Big Bear replied, "We knew that you all were here, but we had to come or starve, for there was no place else to go. I am all for peace. You are many, we are but few. I ask that you have pity on us." Running Rabbit of the Bloods immediately suggested, "Hear them, out there, shouting and singing their get-ready-to-fight songs. Let us quiet them. At once, go!" he urged.

Without another word the chiefs rose. With Kipp and Schultz following, they first visited the Siksika camp, where Crow Big Feet ordered his warriors to stop all plans for fighting the Crees. If any of them disobeyed, they would have to fight him, he declared. At the camp of the Bloods,

Running Rabbit issued similar instructions to his warriors, who somewhat reluctantly agreed to obey. As Big Bear and the Blackfoot tribal chiefs approached the Cree camp, the people ran forward, fearful and anxious to know the decision of the chiefs. When Big Bear told them there was to be peace, they broke into smiles and returned to their camp singing and laughing.

In all three camps, Siksika, Blood and Cree, were many young warriors still eager to fight, but the promises of their chiefs held and there was peace among them. All three tribes made separate camps on the plains south of the Missouri; all three came to the post at Carroll to trade their buffalo robes.

Riel's métis followers roamed the prairies back of Carroll in their homemade carts; the wooden axles of their two big wheels could be heard for miles, frightening the very game they sought. A few eager families built cabins in the bottomlands below Carroll. Schultz and Kipp found the men to be good hunters and trappers and their women excellent tanners of buffalo robes. Their trade was appreciated but, according to Schultz, they were not liked, largely because of their freely used phrase *sacre Americaines* ("damned Americans").

As he remembered the French he had learned in Peekskill and sometimes had used at St. Louis, the dialect spoken by the Red River métis stirred Schultz to unreasonable antagonism. One day he could stand it no longer and leaped over the counter, hitting one of them such a smashing blow in the face that the man went sprawling to the floor. With respect to Riel, however, it was a different story, especially as far as Kipp was concerned, and he and Riel became rather close friends. Schultz appreciated the opportunity Riel offered for good conversation with a man of education. Frequently they spoke together in French, and Riel was as proficient in it as he was in the patois of his métis. Like Kipp, Schultz appreciated Riel's dislike for the word *breed* and the contempt that led to its use in describing mixed bloods. His dedication to the cause of the Canadian métis won their admiration.

Riel's exaggerated courtly manners amused Kipp and annoyed Schultz. Often when he was still thirty or forty yards away, Schultz has written, Riel would bow, doff his big hat with a wide sweep of his arm, and, still bowing, advance toward them with showers of flowery compliments.

Kipp had allowed Riel to have an open account at the post, and when Riel left with his followers to help the métis in Saskatchewan, the account was, as Schultz put it, still open—to the extent of seven hundred dollars. Kipp took the loss philosophically and even found something amusing to say about it: "I figure that each of those majestic bows and wonderful compliments was worth a dollar and we certainly received more than seven hundred of them—so I think we have broken about even." Schultz did not agree, but both he and Kipp were sorry when Riel's attempt to help the métis in Saskatchewan failed and he was hanged at Regina. It is interesting to note that when Pierre Trudeau became Prime Minister of Canada, one of his first official acts was to go to Regina to dedicate a statue to Louis Riel. The spirits of Schultz and Kipp no doubt approved.

Crow Big Feet and his Blood warriors were urged by Riel to join him in the Saskatchewan rebellion, but this the chief always refused to do. Crow Big Feet and his people always maintained a friendly relationship with the Canadian government. Today there stands on a hill above the Bow River a bronze marker where once stood the lodge in which the old chief died.

Although there were occasions when disagreements developed among members of the three tribes, the peace that Kipp had so diplomatically brought about held. Several times during the winter, groups from all three tribes camped close by the post at Carroll to trade and relax for a few days from the arduous task of hunting. For a well-tanned robe they were paid five dollars in brass tokens. Often as many as ten robes would be brought in by a single family; with the brass tokens the women would purchase such necessities as sugar, flour, tea, and baking powder, plus cloth for dresses, beads, needles, and thread. The men bought cartridges, tobacco, and sometimes a drink of whiskey. Although many of the men did not drink, including Crow Big Feet, enough of

them did so that their camps were lively with singing, dancing, and storytelling.

Schultz and Eli Guardipee took turns with Kipp in spending a few days visiting the Siksika or Blood camps to hunt
with them. While visiting with the Siksikas, Kipp joined
them in a buffalo hunt in which one of the young men killed
a large spotted cow. Its head and its tail were pure white,
along its belly was a white stripe, and on its flanks were large
white spots. The young man skinned it carefully and presented it to his father, old Spotted Eagle, who promised
Kipp that he should have it as soon as it was tanned. However, one of the Sun priests objected to this on grounds that
all white buffalo belonged to Sun. Therefore, in the coming
summer, when the Okan, the most important of all Siksika
ceremonies, was held, this hide must be tied to the main post
of Sun's lodge and thus presented to him.

Spotted Eagle protested that the hide was not that of a
white buffalo but only that of a spotted one and therefore
Sun would not desire it. This satisfied the Sun priest. In a
few weeks Schultz and Kipp were advised that Spotted Eagle
and his family were on their way to give Kipp the spotted
robe. The two men hurried to the trade room and assembled a pile of presents for the old man: a sack of sugar, five
hundred cartridges, fifty pounds of flour, two blankets, a
Winchester carbine, five pounds of tobacco, a gallon keg of
whiskey, and trinkets for the women.

Spotted Eagle, followed by his son and his two wives, entered the trade room with the robe over his arm. The robe
had been beautifully tanned and on its back Spotted Eagle
had painted some of the important exploits of his life: pic-
tographs of the enemies he had killed in battle, the horses
he had captured, his encounters with grizzly bears. When
Kipp pointed to the pile of presents, Spotted Eagle put his
hand over his mouth in amazement. "How generous is my
friend, Raven Quiver," he said, as he and his family began
examining the gifts. He then ordered his wives to roll up the
keg of whiskey in the blankets. After they left, Kipp told
Schultz that such a uniquely spotted robe was certainly valuable, worth perhaps a hundred dollars.

That summer while Kipp was in Fort Benton, the *Red Cloud*, on its way to St. Louis, tied up at the Carroll landing. Captain Williams had mail for Schultz and brought his passengers to the post to see the robe. A man from Montreal asked Schultz how much it was worth and when Schultz replied, "A hundred dollars," the man handed him two fifty-dollar bills. The *Red Cloud* had no sooner departed than Schultz began to worry that maybe he should not have sold it. When Kipp returned and saw that the robe was gone, he roared at Schultz, "Where's that spotted robe?" When Schultz told him, Kipp moaned, "At Benton Charles Conrad told me we ought to get at least five hundred for it."

The first steamboat of the season had brought several of the leading dealers from St. Louis and Boston up to Fort Benton. On her return trip she stopped at Carroll so they could bid on Kipp's buffalo robes, which at this time numbered 4,111. Schultz and Kipp were delighted that their good friend Charles Conrad came, too, representing the I. G. Baker Company office in St. Louis.

Every day for a week they sat with pencil and paper, examining each robe as it was shown. First the fur and then the inside, to check the tanning, were inspected. Each robe then was graded as No. 1 or No. 2. When all the robes had been examined and graded, each firm handed in its bid for the entire lot of 4,111. John Goewey, representing a Boston firm, submitted the highest bid, $7.11 per robe, and handed Kipp a check for $29,229.11. He also purchased all the post's other hides. Charles Conrad's successful bid on more than one thousand smoked buffalo tongues was forty cents each, and a trader from Standing Rock Agency (for the Sioux) bought several thousand pounds of dried buffalo meat and pemmican.

After the bidding was over and the dealers had left, everyone at the post had a busy time getting the robes and other purchases ready for shipment. The bulky robes presented a problem because space was valuable on steamboats. To solve this, they constructed a press of heavy planks in which the folded robes could be placed and then, by means of a large lever, compressed tightly together. Each bale was bound tightly with strips of rawhide and the bales were stacked, ready for the *Red Cloud* to pick up.

The winter of 1880–81, in spite of the buffalo slaughter throughout the Great Plains, was a remunerative one for Kipp, and he felt sure that the coming winter would be equally good. For Schultz, it had been an interesting and exciting winter, but he had not gained as much information about the Blackfoot tribes as he had during his earlier seasons with them. Nevertheless, he gave little consideration to the letters that continued to come from Boonville, urging him to return. This was still the life he wanted to live. Often during the seemingly endless winter nights Kipp would talk of his life with Double-Strike Woman and Schultz would think of Nätahki—if only she could be there with him at Carroll!

By the summer of 1881 the three tribes were hunting only for cow-buffalo hides for their women to tan for new lodge skins, for clothing, and for other purposes, as well as for meat.

From one of the steamboats from St. Louis there landed one day at Carroll a missionary who came, he said, to look after the souls of heathen, both red and white. Schultz chose to call him Sacred Talker and was somewhat annoyed when the ever generous Kipp invited the missionary to live with them. Schultz suggested that Hewie's liquor house would have been just the place for him, but unfortunately it had burned down. Kipp had an even better idea. He proposed that, as the smell of smoke might serve as a constant reminder of the hereafter and as the smokehouse had a bed and other conveniences, it should prove an ideal abode for Sacred Talker, whereupon the latter was moved into the smokehouse and more than made himself at home in it.

For reasons unknown, Kipp and Schultz no longer feared a visit from a United States marshal, so the liquor was now stored in the warehouse and sold at the post. One day while Kipp was away at Fort Benton, having left Schultz in charge at Carroll, there rode up to the post, leading a pack horse, a member of Big Nose George's gang of notorious horse thieves and killers. Their camp was somewhere out in the badlands; nobody seemed to know just where. Neither Schultz nor Kipp had ever seen Big Nose George himself,[4] but the latter frequently sent one of his men in for supplies. They were unwelcome customers, and Kipp, Schultz, and their employees feared that someday the gang of murderous desperados would descend on Carroll.

As the gang member entered, carrying a rifle and wearing a six-shooter on each hip, he handed Schultz a list of supplies he needed and announced that he wanted a drink. Schultz led him into the warehouse and drew a good-sized glass of whiskey. He downed that one and two more before Schultz began to put up his list of whiskey, groceries, and cartridges, all of which he skillfully packed into his canvas saddlebags and lashed to his pack horse. He then returned and had another round of whiskey.

Schultz walked with him to the door. As they stepped out, a young Cree and his wife, an exceptionally beautiful young woman, were walking by. The desperado turned to Schultz and said, "Watch me kill that damned Injun!" As he spoke he drew one of his six-shooters and fired. The Cree, shot through the kidneys, screamed and fell writhing to the ground. The killer leaped into the saddle and, leading his pack horse, was quickly on his way. The Cree's wife seized a knife and ran after him, but it was a hopeless chase. Sacred Talker helped Schultz carry the dying man to his lodge, where they did what little there was for them to do: Sacred Talker prayed and Schultz plied him with whiskey to dull his agony, which, fortunately, did not last long.

Schultz sent a note about the killing to the commander of a company of mounted infantry camped nearby. The reply was, "I have nothing to do with civil cases. If you want the man arrested send for the sheriff at Fort Benton." This, of course, was impossible at the time.

[4] Big Nose George, it seems, soon fell into disfavor with law enforcement officials in Montana because of his road-agent activities during the early 1880's. He was captured by authorities near Miles City and taken to Rawlins, Wyoming, where indignant citizens removed him from the jail and hanged him to a telephone pole. See Frederick G. Renner, *Charles M. Russell*, 163 (Painting No. 140).

Joseph Kipp in 1889. Courtesy James Willard Schultz Society Collection.

The killing of the Cree brought about some strange re-
percussions. His beautiful widow was at once desired by
many of the men. One of them was a Kipp employee whose
Indian name was Long Whip, but she would have nothing to
do with him. Instead, to the surprise of Schultz and Kipp,
she chose to live with Sacred Talker.

Kipp had returned from Fort Benton with a large stock of
a variety of goods for the coming winter's trade. Whiskey,
another sixty barrels of it, would come upriver later from St.
Louis.

A short time after Kipp returned, one of the leading Cree
medicine men had a dream that indicated the Crees should
establish a camp some distance from Carroll. Being farther
from the Bloods and Blackfeet tribes would lessen the opportunities for trouble. Big Bear and his subordinate chiefs
decided that they would move their camp down the Missouri to the mouth of the Musselshell, provided that Kipp
and Schultz would establish a branch post there for their
convenience. If they would not do this, then the chiefs would
plan to go farther away and make camp in the country of
the Assiniboines. Reluctantly, Schultz and Kipp complied
and arranged for a French-Canadian Cree employee, Archie
Amiott, to take a tent, stove, and other necessities, as well
as a thousand dollars' worth of trade goods, to establish a
branch post where the Crees planned to camp.

The hopes that Kipp and Schultz had for one more successful winter trade suffered a severe blow when the Bloods
and the Siksikas surprised them by announcing that their
people had determined to return to their reservations in
Canada. By treaty, Queen Victoria's government had agreed
to pay five dollars per annum to every member of these two
tribes. Two such payments now were due them, and they
were eager to collect.

Crow Big Feet and Running Rabbit joined Schultz and
Kipp in urging the Indians to remain for what would probably be their last opportunity for a truly rewarding buffalo
hunt. They met with little success, although thirty lodges of
the Bloods finally decided to remain. It was a sad day at Carroll as everyone at the post watched all the Siksikas and most

of the Bloods begin their long trek, leaving only the Crees, Riel's métis and a handful of the Bloods for the winter trade.

Making everything worse was the fact that word got around about the successful trade of the past winter and that several herds of buffalo still remained in the area. Unaware that the Siksikas and most of the Bloods had returned to Canada, several other traders established posts, either at Carroll or very close by. These would provide most unwelcome competition for what little trade there would be. Schultz and Kipp were convinced that the winter of 1881–82 would be their last trading for buffalo robes.

On one of his trips to Fort Benton, Kipp learned that the hide hunters and sportsmen brought to the plains to the east and south by the new railroads had so decimated the buffalo that a new business had sprung up. Equipped with two-wheeled carts, buffalo hunters were scouring the plains to send trainloads of buffalo bones and horns to eastern cities. According to one, the horns were used to make such items as buttons, knife handles, and combs; the bones were used to manufacture a carbon for refining sugar; glue was made from the hoofs.

Kipp suggested that if things got too bad at Carroll they would buy some of the two-wheeled carts from Riel's métis and go into the bone-collecting business themselves. They probably could ship their take down to St. Louis, where, Kipp understood, there was a good market for them. Bone buyers at Dodge City were paying nine dollars a ton for bones and fifteen dollars a ton for hoofs and horns. It was not an enterprise that appealed to either Schultz or Kipp, and Guardipee spat with contempt at the very thought of it. Schultz realized that Kipp was not really serious about this, and *he* certainly had not come to the Blackfoot country to collect bones!

The Northern Pacific Railroad was steadily edging farther and farther west and by 1881 was following the valley of the Yellowstone. From there, white hide hunters armed with new high-powered Sharp's rifles were killing buffalo by the thousand. To the east, the Assiniboines and the Sioux were taking their full share, and the Gros Ventres and the Pikunis were hunting them hard to the north. Fortunately for the post at Carroll, Riel and Big Bear were constantly urging their people to do more and more hunting so as to have more and more well-tanned robes to trade for the rifles and cartridges to use when they joined the métis in Saskatchewan.

There were times when, in defiance of their chiefs, the Crees would camp near the post at Carroll and trade their robes for whiskey instead of guns and ammunition. Schultz took a certain amount of pride in the fact that the whiskey he was selling to the Indians was good whiskey, the very same that they themselves drank. It was a far cry indeed from the diluted and weirdly fortified stuff that only too commonly was sold to the Indians. According to historian Arthur Woodward, a recognized authority on such matters, it was common practice to dilute the whiskey liberally with water and then, to add color and zest, throw in some chewing tobacco, a generous dusting of cayenne, and some gunpowder. On occasion, a small rattlesnake was dropped in to add still more zest to the concoction.

Schultz was amazed that even when a thousand Indians, both men and women, would be drinking, singing, and dancing around their many camp fires there was so little unpleasantness. During the entire winter of 1881–82, there was only one nasty incident.

One morning while Crow Woman was standing on a buffalo hide, chipping it clean for tanning, a drunken Cree came by, seized her, and started off with her. Seeing what was happening, Schultz dashed after him and hit him, knocking him off his feet. Although Schultz injured his own hand badly, the blow seemed to have little or no effect on the Cree, who dropped Crow Woman and started after Schultz with a heavy stick. There was nothing for Schultz to do but run, and run he did. Fortunately, at that moment Kipp, who was in the trade room, happened to look out the window. Seeing what was going on, he grabbed a bottle of beer and hit the Cree over the head with it, knocking him out. After a short time the Cree came to, staggered off to his lodge, and was not seen again.

By March, 1882, they had traded off the last of their blankets, so Schultz and John Hudson, a trustworthy English-Cree employee, each of them with a horse and sled, food, bedding, and their rifles, started out for the T. C. Power and Brothers trading post at the mouth of the Judith. Following every twist and bend of the frozen Missouri, they saw a few but very small herds of buffalo until they passed the mouth of Cow Creek, and from then on there was not a solitary buffalo.

By nightfall of their second day out, they had arrived at the trading post, only to find that its manager, "Diamond R." Brown, had gone to Fort Benton. His wife and daughter made them welcome to stay for the three days until his return. Brown, it seems, was very downcast, for although both the Gros Ventres and the Pikunis had promised to trade with him that winter, neither tribe showed up because, he surmised, there were too few buffalo.[5]

As soon as Schultz and his companion had loaded their sleds with bales of blankets, they set out for Carroll. Again they saw no buffalo until they approached the mouth of Cow Creek, when a herd dashed down the creek bottom in a way that buffalo rarely move unless pursued by their No. 1 enemy, man. As the buffalo were running swiftly across the snow-covered frozen river, Schultz and Hudson saw a large band of Indians riding in pursuit. Certain that they were a band of Assiniboines who, under Chief Mountain, reportedly had been killing trappers and woodcutters in that part of the country, they became alarmed. Hudson wanted to make a dash for it down the frozen river, but Schultz felt sure it was too late for them to do so. Instead, lashing their horses, they tried to gain safety in an old cabin which was

[5] Schultz has related this incident in two of his books. That reported herein is based upon the version in *Blackfeet and Buffalo*, 57–59, in which John Hudson, an English-Cree, was stated to have been his companion. In a much earlier book, *My Life as an Indian*, 391–92, he stated that his companion was Nätahki, his wife. This was pure fiction, of course, because Nätahki was never at Carroll during the trading years. Furthermore, the incident took place in March, 1882, a date when she had just given birth to her son at Birch Creek.

not far away. However, a number of the Indians on their fast
buffalo horses had left the main group and would soon be
able to cut them off from it.

"Well," said Hudson, "if we are going to die, we'll die fighting!" Schultz agreed. They got down behind their sleds and,
rifles cocked, awaited the Indians, who, quirting their horses
furiously, were almost upon them. Schultz was just about to
raise his rifle when the leader reined up his horse and
shouted, "*Ha! Apikuni unook! Kitsikipah anom?*" ("Ha! Far-
Off White Robe himself! What do you here?") The men
proved to be Schultz's Pikuni friend Red Bird's Tail, and with
him were Little Plume, Running Crane, and many more of
Schultz's good Pikuni friends.

After exchanging news, Schultz explained that they were
on their way to spend the night at the old cabin, but Red
Bird's Tail would hear nothing of that and insisted that
Schultz and Hudson must go with them to their nearby
camp. As they approached the Pikuni camp, men, women,
and children ran out to meet them. Red Bird's Tail insisted
that they stay in his lodge, and after a fine meal many old
friends dropped in to sit with them around the fire.

The Pikunis had been wintering along the foot of the Bear
Paw Mountains, and all agreed that buffalo were becoming
scarce. Schultz tried to persuade them to go downriver and
camp at or near Carroll, but this they would not do because
their enemies the Crees were there. The Pikunis were certain
that meeting them would lead to a fight and although they
were more than anxious to fight the Crees it must be as a
war party, with no women and children involved.

Schultz told them that he and Raven Quiver knew that the
only country where herds of buffalo were still to be found
lay between the Missouri and the Yellowstone. But old Three
Bears protested and told how long ago the bad god Red Old
Man had hidden all the buffalo in a great mountain cave so
that all the people would starve. But the beneficent god
White Old Man found the buffalo and turned them free on
the plains again. Now, he said, their enemies, the white men,
have hidden the great herds in the hope that all Indians will
starve to death. Old Three Bears, however, was certain that

eventually Sun would take pity on his people and would find the buffalo and turn them free upon the plains once more.

Just before they reached the mouth of Cow Creek, Schultz saw a single yearling buffalo, which he shot. Its fur was rather unusual, being very dark and beaverlike in texture. He had Hudson skin it carefully so as to remove its juvenile horns and small hoofs. Crow Woman tanned it with care and later, as Merriam suggested in a letter, he sent it to the Smithsonian Institution.

The fifty blankets from the T. C. Power trading post were gone in three days. In return they secured in trade a goodly number of well-tanned buffalo robes and from Riel's métis a quantity of dried meat and pemmican.

During the summer, Schultz had a surprise one day when there walked into the post from the railroad on the Yellowstone a giant of a young man who, in Schultz's boyhood days in the Adirondacks, had been his guide. He was not only footsore from his long walk but also was sore from having sat down on a bed of cactus. Kipp, with his usual generosity, made him welcome and gave him a job in the warehouse and trade room. He was promptly named *Mansksi Stumik*, or Young Bull, by the Indians, who soon noticed that he considered himself quite a man with the women.

Living at Carroll at this time was a burly, bad-tempered chap by the name of Burns who spent much time away with a team and wagon, trading with the métis and the Crees. His wife, Susette, was a most attractive French-Canadian Cree, and Young Bull lost no time in getting acquainted with her. One evening when Burns was away, Young Bull was spending a pleasant evening with Susie when they heard a team drive up. Burns had returned unexpectedly. Sure that he would kill them both if he found them together, Susie had Young Bull hide under the bed. There he lay while Susie and Burns ate dinner and then went to bed. Expecting to be discovered at any moment, Young Bull hardly dared to breathe. Burns lay in bed until late in the morning; Young Bull remained hidden under the bed. Not until Burns finally got up and had Susie make him a good breakfast did he leave to take care of his horses. Finally Young Bull had his

long-awaited chance to escape. Since his bed at the post had
not been slept in, he had not appeared for breakfast, and
was late for work, he was questioned by Kipp and Schultz.
To their amusement he gave a full account of his evening's
adventure. In fact, the story got around Carroll and both he
and Susie were in for a good deal of joshing. Strange to say,
Burns never seemed to have heard anything about it.

When the ice had been cleared from the Missouri that
spring of 1882, and when the steamboats again began to
make the long trip up from St. Louis, with them came the
fur buyers. John Goewey of Boston once more was the highest bidder for the post's 2,130 tanned robes at $7.35 each,
and Charles Conrad bid in its thousands of pounds of dried
meat and pemmican, as well as several thousand deer, antelope, and elk hides.

In July, 1882, the post at Carroll was abandoned. Kipp
and Schultz took the *Helena* to Fort Benton. Long John
Forgy with the bull train and the four-horse teams with the
other employees and such baggage and furnishings as were
deemed valuable were to meet them before going on to Fort
Conrad.

CHAPTER 11

Back at Conrad and on the Ranch

H ARD as it was for Kipp to give up trading with the Indians for buffalo robes, he now realized that the railroad would soon reach Helena and then even the days of his highly profitable bull train would be numbered. The night before leaving Carroll, Schultz had asked Kipp, "What will we do now, what *can* we do now that trade in buffalo robes has ended?" Kipp replied sorrowfully, "Huh! Go back to Fort Conrad and a nothing life!"

In spite of Kipp's forebodings about the future at Fort Conrad, for Schultz it proved to be a life worth living. However, it was some time after their return to the fort in the latter part of July, 1882, before Kipp and Schultz, as well as the employees who had accompanied them to their various winter trading posts, became accustomed to the fact that they would be living there the year round.

Fortunately, quarters at the fort were commodious. Kipp's immediate family, besides himself and Double-Strike Woman, included their own three children, Mary, James, and George, as well as their adopted children, Bill and Maggie Fitz-patrick; and the two inseparables: Kipp's mother, Earth Woman, and her old companion, Crow Woman. Others in the Kipp retinue, besides Schultz and Nätahki, as a sort of extended family, brought the number of Fort Conrad residents to more than twenty. These included Hiram D. Upham, his wife, and their daughter, Rosa; Eli Guardipee and his wife; Crow Woman's adopted daughter, Flag Woman; and three long-time Pikuni Kipp followers named Red Eyes, Takes-Gun-at-Night and Comes-with-Rattles. All of the men's wives were of the Pikuni tribe.

During the winter of 1881–82, Schultz learned that Nätahki was pregnant. Because of his great affection for her,
he had yearned to have a child as a living link between them.
He knew that to Pikuni women childbirth seemed a rather
simple thing, and he hoped it would be so with Nätahki.
When he spoke with Kipp about it and showed some concern, Kipp reassured him by pointing out that with Nätahki's
own mother, as well as Earth Woman, Crow Woman, and
Kipp's Pikuni wife, all experienced women who were devoted to her, on hand to help, Nätahki would be well taken
care of.

When Schultz talked to Nätahki about her pregnancy, she
showed him the wide adjustable belt of rawhide that her
mother had made for her to wear as her time approached.
Her mother made Nätahki put it on to show how it could be
adjusted so as to be comfortable as she went about her usual
household duties. Came the day at last, and the baby, a boy,
was born without difficulty or incident in the early part of
1882.[1] Since Schultz at that time was working with Kipp at
the latter's winter trading post at Carroll, he was unable to
be present when the child was born. Nätahki was staying
with her mother on Birch Creek near the Joseph Kipp trading post at Robare Crossing, Montana.[2]

The Pikunis at that time were camped on Badger Creek,
fifty miles or so west of Fort Conrad. For generations their
way of life and their culture had been based upon the
buffalo. The horse had supplanted the dog as a beast of
burden, and in more recent years the rifle had virtually
taken the place of the bow and arrow. Deprived of the
buffalo, they now had little choice but to hunt nearby wild
game: deer, elk, antelope. After months of intensive hunting in relative proximity to their camps, the effect began to
be felt. Any kind of meat, their basic food, became harder
and harder to get. Several Pikunis, particularly those who

---

[1]The date of birth was February 18, 1882. See Paul Dyck, "Lone Wolf
Returns to the Soil of His Indian Forebears," *Montana Post* Vol. 8, No. 4
(November–December, 1970), issued by the Montana Historical Society;
reprinted in *The Piegan Storyteller*, Vol. III, No. 2, 2.
[2]Dyck, "The Return of Lone Wolf," 20.

were close friends of Kipp and Schultz, moved and set up their lodges close to Fort Conrad.

With the disappearance of the buffalo and the increasing scarcity of other large game came various changes in the Fort Conrad area which were further proof to Schultz and Kipp that their old way of life was gradually but surely being eroded away by "progress." Already a few settlers were establishing ranches, both above and below them, in the valley of the Marias. Now, more and more bull trains and four-horse teams were needed to supply the fast-growing settlements along the Whoop-Up Trail, all the way from Fort Benton to Fort Macleod in Canada. The I. G. Baker Company had established the Benton, Macleod and Calgary Stage Company, which carried mail, express packages, and passengers in an open wagon drawn by four mules. Mail and express had considerable priority because they were more remunerative than the passengers.

The store, dining room, bar, and sleeping quarters were bringing in substantial revenue, and soon a post office was established at Fort Conrad, an innovation that brought gratification to Schultz in certain respects. Now his copies of the *New York Tribune*, with its news of concerts and opera, were only a few weeks rather than many months old when they arrived. Single copies of *Forest and Stream*, to which he was an early subscriber, came with regularity, not in bundles containing the issues of several months. But the more frequent mails also brought letters from Boonville; these continued to worry him with their insistence that he return home and assume the responsibilities his family felt he should be taking upon himself.

The initial mail service from Fort Benton to Fort McLeod was biweekly. With its inception, Schultz, "by special arrangement" with United States postal officials, was entrusted to add a gallon keg of whiskey to each of the mail-bags destined for Colonel James F. Macleod and Captain William Winder of the Northwest Mounted Police at Fort Macleod, which was in Canada's bone-dry Northwest Territories. It must have amused Kipp that in a way Schultz was following an example Kipp had set some years earlier when he became all too well known for the amount of whiskey he had managed to smuggle into Canada. Kipp, however, had not enjoyed the cooperation of U.S. officials that Schultz had.

As the winter of 1882–83 approached, traffic along the Whoop-Up Trail began to taper off until, in midwinter, it was virtually nil except for the biweekly mail stage to Fort Macleod. As Kipp had feared, life for him after returning to Fort Conrad became a nothing kind of existence. For one who had traded with the Indians at Fort Standoff, Fort Kipp, Judith-Sage, and Carroll, it is easy to understand that when he returned to Fort Conrad life might have become less than exciting. The days of trading for buffalo robes at huge Indian camps were over and Fort Conrad presented no challenge or opportunity for substantial income, so, in 1884, taking Hiram Upham with him, Kipp paid the trader at the Indian agency three hundred dollars for his stock and built a store and saloon on Birch Creek, just off the reservation and on the agency–Choteau–Sun River stage and freight road.

To make these acquisitions, Kipp left Schultz in charge of Fort Conrad and visited there only occasionally. Ultimately, the period of Kipp ownership (1878–86) would last only eight years. Ever since his return from Carroll in 1882 he had gradually lost interest in Fort Conrad. As a result, when his old friend James McDevitt was looking for a location for headquarters for a cattle ranch, Kipp was glad to sell. Schultz, on the other hand, had spent more time at Fort Conrad than any other member of Kipp's staff.

By the time that Fort Conrad was sold in 1886, Schultz had established a personal as well as a working relationship with the St. Mary country, about sixty or seventy miles to the northwest. At first, commencing in 1883, he merely went there with friends to hunt and fish, but he began his long and interesting career as guide and outfitter for the region in 1885 and by 1886 had Joe Kipp helping him. Of course, this was strictly a seasonal type of occupation, since the time his eastern clients preferred to visit the area was usually

September. In the ten or eleven other months of the year, he needed a place to live and a means of subsistence.

During the year 1884, Schultz got what he called an "insane idea" that he wanted to be a sheepman. Locating some fine springs and hay ground about twelve miles above Fort Conrad, he built a house and some sheds and put up huge stacks of hay. He was not, however, to enjoy his spread for long. Cattlemen, apparently irate because Schultz had taken possession of the only good springs for miles around, burned house, hay, and ranch buildings to the ground.[3]

Schultz then began to think about cattle ranching. During his first trip with George Bird Grinnell in the autumn of 1885, he questioned Grinnell about his experience with cattle in the West. Grinnell agreed with Schultz about the damage sheep can inflict on good rangeland by overgrazing; as a result, Schultz was not particularly bitter toward the cattlemen who had burned him out. In *My Life as an Indian* he stated that he was glad of it for then no one could ever accuse him of having a hand in the devastation of the once lovely plains of Montana.[4]

With Fort Conrad and the sheep ranch behind them, Schultz and Nätahki decided to build a house on property to which she was entitled as her allotment from the reservation lands. They selected a site in Two Medicine Valley about five miles north of the agency on Badger Creek. It was in an open, grassy valley where they felt certain that cattle would thrive. They spent several days selecting a spot for the cabin they would build and finally settled on one that delighted them both with the fine view it offered of snow-capped mountains. To construct a house, outbuildings, and corrals, Schultz had to cut lodgepole pines of just the right size in a

---

[3] *My Life as an Indian*, 415. According to the FORT BENTON PRESS for June 10, 1885, "James W. Schultz of the Marias has met with quite a loss. His sheep sheds, fifteen tons of hay, a mowing machine, plow and a valuable dog were destroyed by fire on Tuesday last. Mr. Schultz was away and has no idea how it happened. He is of the opinion that it was set on fire."

[4] P. 416.

wooded area convenient to the homesite, yet with the Rockies in plain sight not far away.

Schultz was to be a part-time rancher for the next seventeen years. Fortunately, he had the help of several Pikuni friends who had had experience with cattle. They advised him in purchasing the nucleus for his herd, as well as taking the responsibility for caring for it while he was spending time as a guide for explorers and hunting parties in the mountains. His principal assistant was his brother-in-law, Last Rider, whom he left in charge during his absences. As his son, Hart, became old enough to help around the ranch, the boy's services were used also.

Hart has told us about one such absence in the late 1880's which took Schultz to the Sweetgrass Hills in north-central Montana in search of gold. It seems that a man named Baker, who had a pretty good outfit, a wagon, and all the tools, talked him into going along on a prospecting trip. Schultz took with him his wife and his son, then seven or eight years old. Also going along was her brother New Robe, who planned to hunt while they were in camp.

One day Baker and Schultz went panning for gold along a creek and young Hart was allowed to accompany them. Hart sat down beside Baker to watch him use his pan. After dipping it in the stream to pick up sand and gravel, he shook the pan and let the water run out. Occasionally he picked out a small yellow stone and put it with others beside him. Hart wondered why he selected only yellow ones, since they did not look as interesting to him as the multicolored ones he had picked out. Hart asked about this, but Baker could not understand his Pikuni talk, so presently Hart picked up the yellow stones and threw them back into the creek. Baker became very upset at this, yelled at Hart's father, and it looked for a while like there might be a fight, but Baker finally calmed down. Needless to say, Hart had to stay in camp with his mother and uncle thereafter while his father and Baker were out in the hills doing their prospecting.

One day while the two men were out of camp, a war party of Cree horse raiders rode up on a height overlooking the camp and saw the Schultz group's grazing horses. After surveying the situation, they raced down the hill, unhobbled the horses, and drove them away. Although New Robe, Hart, and his mother saw this happen, they could do nothing but report the incident to Baker and Schultz when the latter returned. After some thought had been given to the problem, it was decided that New Robe should return to the camp of his brother, Boy Chief, and get him to come and help. While the Indians took off on the trail of the Crees, Schultz stayed in camp and Baker continued prospecting.

The two brothers were gone many days.[5] Then one evening the camp occupants saw dust rising in the distance and before long New Robe and Boy Chief came into camp trailing a good bunch of horses, including the stolen ponies. Their story was a thrilling one. They had found the Cree camp at a time when the Crees were holding their Medicine Lodge ceremony. While the Crees were thus off guard, the two Pikunis slipped in and got the horses. On discovering the bold theft, four Cree warriors took after them, forcing them to make a stand. After Boy Chief had killed two with his repeating rifle, the other two fled, making it easy for Boy Chief to scalp the dead warriors. Of course the Sweetgrass country now was no longer safe for them, so the Schultzes and New Robe decided to pull out and return to their camp on the Two Medicine.

For Schultz, the romantic years of trading with the Indians at their winter camps had ended with the disappearance of the buffalo from the Great Plains. Finally, also, his nine-year affiliation with Joe Kipp came to an end. Thrust upon his own resources, he began very slowly and gradually to build himself the career that was to bring him success as a guide and outfitter and, ultimately, renown in the art of letters.

The period from Schultz's return to Fort Conrad to the end of his ranching days in Two Medicine Valley spanned approximately twenty years. The contents of this chapter fall considerably short of encompassing the activities and

---

[5]Story based on Dyck, "The Return of Lone Wolf," 22–23.

interests suggested in its title. Each of them was too important in Schultz's life to be explored fully in a single chapter; rather, each topic deserves examination at some length and has been given such treatment.

During this tremendously interesting twenty-year period, there were many changes in Schultz's lifestyle. Among other things, he ended his career as a rancher and as a guide in the St. Mary country. The two decades saw the end of Schultz's happy years with his Pikuni sweetheart and the growing up of his son Hart. In hindsight, it is apparent that the period brought to an abrupt end the first half of Schultz's unusual life.

To provide an adequate picture of Schultz's activities during this segment of his career, each has been made the subject of one or more chapters herein. His many visits to what was to become Glacier National Park are described in Chapters 12 to 18, 20 and 23, all but the last of which deal with visits between 1883 and 1903. The "starvation winter" of the Blackfeet people during the early part of Schultz's Fort Conrad years and the role he played in it are a part of Chapter 29, entitled "Champion of Indian Causes."

CHAPTER 12

Early Outings at Lake St. Mary

THE early acclaim of the St. Mary region was largely attributable to the activities of a young man named Schultz. Thither, once its magnificent vistas had met his unbelieving gaze, he brought his family, his friends, and, as time went on, a host of enthusiastic and well-to-do eastern sportsmen. To no small degree it was his sponsorship that served to bring the area to national attention, and before he was thirty his clientele as a master guide included international visitors of distinction. As a matter of fact, who knows whether or when Glacier would have become a national park had there been no James Willard Schultz?

The mysterious St. Mary Lakes, sheltered in a remote valley between the Hudson Bay Divide and the Continental Divide, lay somewhat off the ancient route known as the Old North Trail. But whether it was the spectacular location or the beauty of these sister lakes, lying half-within, half-without the main range of the Rockies, early travelers who came upon them seemed to feel that the lakes should be given an appropriate name, and so it was that the lakes came to have not one but many names.

The first visitors, of course, were the Indians, and the Blackfeet, because of the semi-enclosed character of their narrow valley, called them "Lakes Inside."[1] The Blackfeet, however, were followers of the buffalo, a plains animal, and therefore spent little time at the lakes. After all, the magnificent St. Mary trout provided no attraction to people whose

---

[1] George Bird Grinnell chose to translate the Indian name "Walled-In Lakes."

diet excluded fish; and the elusive sheep and goats of the
mountains were of little interest to a people who preferred
to do their hunting on horseback rather than on foot.

When early white men came to the lakes, they, too, gave
them names. When James F. Doty, a lieutenant of Governor
Isaac Stevens, visited the lakes in June, 1854, he gave them
individual names, calling the upper body of water Bow Lake
because of its shape and the lower one Chief Mountain Lake
because of its proximity to the mountain of the same name.
Doty had no idea, of course, that only nine years earlier the
lakes had been christened by Hugh Monroe in the presence
of a worshipful group of Kutenai[2] Indians and before a
huge cross of logs and that they had been given the name *St.
Mary* to honor the mission by that name recently established
west of the Rockies by Father DeSmet. Thus because of Doty
the lakes were known to many whites in the vicinity as the
Chief Mountain lakes.

Nevertheless, Schultz, not long after his arrival in Montana, became aware of the name St. Mary and the existence
of the lakes, possibly learning of them from Monroe himself, for in his *Forest and Stream* article of October 14, 1880,
he wrote:

> After the rainy season I intend going up to Chief Mountain
> and St. Mary's lake on a hunting expedition. As it is impos-
> sible to get among the game with a wagon I shall take an In-
> dian along named Enucki-yu. He is an A No. 1 Indian; has a
> large new lodge, plenty of horses to pack the plunder; and
> last, but not least, three strong women to do all the work.
> The expenses of the trip would be nothing, and good saddle
> horses can be bought for $20.[3]

Schultz had also been told that on the rocky summits
above the lakes dwelled strange animals which the Indians
called "white big heads," the description of which was unlike
that of any animal theretofore encountered by him. In talk-

---

[2]The name has been variously spelled *Kutenai, Kootenai, Kootenay,
Kutenay.* The spelling in Canada is usually *Kootenay,* while in this country it
is more often *Kutenai.*

[3]*Forest and Stream,* Vol. XV, 137, No. 11, October 14, 1880, 205–206.

ing with Schultz about the subject, an old-timer named John
Healy claimed to have seen the creature and thought it was
an ibex because it looked like pictures of an ibex he had seen
as a boy. This was a circumstance that intrigued Schultz,
since he had always understood the ibex to be a species of
ruminant found only in Europe.

THE 1883 VISIT

Not until the autumn of 1883 did the opportunity for
Schultz to visit the St. Mary Lakes arise. It was in October of
that year that two of his friends, Sol Abbott and Henry
Powell, came to Fort Conrad and invited him to accompany
them on a hunting trip to Chief Mountain. Others in the
party were to be Charles Carter, a trapper, and three
employees of Major Young, the Indian agent: Charlie
Phemmister, Jim Rutherford, and Oliver Sandoval.

Schultz, of course, was delighted to go and, after obtaining Kipp's permission, packed his bedroll, clothing, and a
share of the provisions, then double-checked his rifle, shotgun, and ammunition. They headed north in two wagons
along the unfamiliar route and soon caught their first close
view of the Rocky Mountains, rising impressively above the
plains. When Schultz asked if the peaks had names, he was
told that only the farthest ahead, standing out as if leading
all the rest, had a name. This was *Ninastoko*, the Chief Mountain of all the Plains Indians, a name which he felt was very
appropriate.

Only Oliver Sandoval, among the group, had been to the
Chief Mountain area previously, and he knew of a way to
reach the lakes by wagon. The route, after leaving the Cut
Bank Valley, led northwest across the Milk River to Duck
Lake, where they camped the second night. With an early
start the next morning, they were soon, as Schultz described
it, "looking at a scene so tremendous, so beautiful that I felt
I could gaze at it forever. Straight down from us was the
lower one of the two lakes; close above it, the other and
longer one, from whose shores the mountains rose in gran-

Going-to-the-Sun Mountain and Upper St. Mary Lake. Courtesy Kabel.

deur to great heights. It was no wonder that the Blackfeet
had named them the 'Lakes Inside.'"[4]

The wagons of the party were the first ever upon this
branch of the Old North Trail. As they followed it, they
found it almost impassable for the wagons, but by noon they
had managed to reach the foot of the lower lake. In a stream
just below the outlet of the lake, Schultz, using hook and
line on a willow pole, soon caught enough trout for both
breakfast and supper. He found that they were of three va-
rieties: mackinaw, native, and another that he later learned
was the Dolly Varden.

Next morning, they found a ford below the foot of the
lake, where they picketed the horses and headed on foot toward a long, bare, flat-topped mountain to the west where
Sandoval had heard there was a lick used by all of the big-
game animals. After some arduous climbing, they reached
timberline and came unexpectedly upon the lick, a shallow
basin of mud encrusted with alkali, with a trickle of water
running through it. Deeply worn game trails radiated out
from it in various directions. After watching for a time, they
were rewarded by seeing seven large white animals appear
in a single file. Schultz described them thus:

> Like the buffalo, they had humped backs, low hindquarters,
> chin whiskers, and long, wavy fringes of hair down to the
> knees of the forelegs, reminding one of a girl's pantalettes in
> the wind. But there their resemblance to the buffalo ceased,
> for their heads were long and narrow, their faces dishlike,
> of mournful, silly expression, and their round, tapering,
> sharp-pointed horns curved upward and backward instead
> of outward—deadly scimitars they would be in a fight.[5]

Taking careful aim, Schultz and one of his companions
fired. Two of the animals fell dead. The others gave a jump
and, after staring at their dead brethren, disappeared up
the mountainside with long leaps. Particular care was taken
in skinning the two animals, and the men started down the

[4] *Blackfeet and Buffalo*, 72; first published in the *Great Falls Tribune*, November 18, 1936.
[5] *Idem.*, 74.

mountain with bundles of the skins and some of the meat. On the way they saw a solitary white animal sitting on its haunches like a dog and gazing out at the scene before it. They decided to call the creatures goats.

After Schultz and Abbott had returned to their wagon and rested a while, they were joined by the other members of the group. They brought with them the meat of a bighorn ram that Sandoval had killed behind the flat-topped mountain. They said they had seen a number of elk, a band of goats, and three grizzlies but had not attempted to kill any of them because of the difficulty in getting out the meat. Thereafter for five days, they hunted close to camp and, having killed all the elk and deer they wanted, were ready to leave, even though they had not visited the upper lake. On the morning of their departure, Schultz wakened long before his companions and climbed to a good viewpoint just as the sun struck the summit ridge of Flat Top Mountain. He sat down and looked long and longingly at the vast panorama before him. How little of it they managed to get into!

Schultz promised himself that he would return and investigate all of it—climb every mountain, explore every valley, fish every stream and lake, and hunt all over it. It was a promise that he kept. Throughout his life, no other place was to become so closely identified with James Willard Schultz as the Lakes Inside, or St. Mary Lakes, and Flat Top Mountain was only the first of many peaks in Glacier National Park that Schultz would name.

THE 1884 VISIT

Schultz paid his second visit to St. Mary Lakes in the autumn of 1884. His companions on this trip, according to his article "To Chief Mountain," which appeared in *Forest and Stream* on December 10, 1885,[6] were Jim, Charlie, and an Indian named Man-Who-First-Took-His-Gun-and-Ran-Ahead but who, for convenience, was called Seip. They de-

[6]P. 362.

parted from Kipp & Upham's store on Birch Creek on the twenty-fourth of October, 1884. Their outfit consisted of a four-horse team and wagon, a two-horse team and wagon, boat, tent, stove, lantern, bedding, and grub. They had "a big fishing outfit, including a gill-net," for they hoped to catch a barrel of whitefish for winter use. Their arsenal consisted of four magazine rifles and Schultz's 12-gauge breechloader.

The party followed the 1883 route and again camped at Duck Lake, where, despite a high wind, Schultz shot a number of high-flying ducks. On the afternoon of the twenty-eighth, they reached the St. Mary River and camped in full view of Chief Mountain, which Schultz described as "the grandest mountain I ever saw" and estimated the height from its base to its summit to be at least seven thousand feet. They were not alone for long. On the twenty-ninth there arrived an outfit from the agency, consisting of three men and two small boys. On the thirty-first, two four-horse outfits rolled in, one belonging to a beaver trapper known as Medicine Beaver, the other to Ben S., a prospector who had with him two young men named Dick and John. With the members of the latter two groups, Schultz and his companions packed up and moved to a point near the head of the lower lake, where they made camp.

On November 2 a party of North Piegan Indians under Chief Yellow Fish arrived and made camp near the foot of the upper lake. They were in search of game, a fact bemoaned by Schultz, who commented that "an Indian is insatiable. When he sees a band of game, he is not satisfied with making one killing, but will keep following it and shooting as long as possible. This gives the game a tremendous scare and they get out of the country as soon as possible."

The fishing at the lakes was engaged in with great success by the visitors. When the agency party left for home, they took with them fifty lake and red-throated trout, the largest of the lake trout weighing perhaps twenty-five pounds. During their stay, the Schultz party caught ninety-two whitefish, which when weighed at home, tipped the scales at two-hundred-thirty-two pounds. "Lake trout are so large and plentiful that it is no pleasure to fish," Schultz wrote.

Within a week of each other, separate groups of hunters made treks up the Swiftcurrent Valley. On October 30, Jim and two of the agency men headed up the valley after bighorn and returned the same day, reporting plenty of game. On November 5, Ben, Jim, and Medicine Beaver went sheep hunting up the same valley, returning the following day with "three fine bucks." They penetrated as far as Swiftcurrent Lake and reported the scenery to be grand, "sheep plenty, and the lakes teem with trout." Undoubtedly they saw Grinnell Glacier but were not up on glaciers and did not recognize one when they saw it. They were hunting sheep, not glaciers. These three were the first white men known to have explored much of Swiftcurrent Valley.[7]

Later Schultz joined Medicine Beaver, Ben, and Jim for a sheep hunt in the valley of Upper Lake St. Mary, taking saddle horses and a pack horse and crossing the inlet where Yellow Fish and his followers were camped. They followed old trails to a point near the head of the lake. There the party divided, and Schultz and Jim, after a long, hard climb, got above timberline to a point where they were stopped abruptly by a canyon of great depth. Of the scene here spread out before them, Schultz wrote:

> Below us several thousand feet lay the lake—an immense canyon filled with water, save at its head and foot no shore. Around us mountains of great height. Beyond the head of the lake is a long, wide, densely timbered valley and on the upper left hand side of this valley is a mountain, the top of which is a true glacier. With the glasses it appeared to be at least three hundred feet thick. . . . We were unable to determine the length of the glacier, as intervening mountains obstructed a view of either end.

In the meantime their companions, Ben and Medicine Beaver, had gone around behind the mountain, seeing a small, high-up, walled-in lake and seven goats, none within shooting distance. To that day's unsuccessful hunt and the

---

[7]Schultz and Grinnell first visited the Swiftcurrent Valley in the fall of 1885 and explored Grinnell Glacier in 1887. Hence this trio of hunters preceded them by a full year.

episode of the seven goats, Goat Lake and Goat Mountain owe their names. As the record now stands, Schultz and Jim were the first white men to see the valley of the Upper St. Mary River and the glacier at its source, and Schultz was the first to put in writing and into print a description of them.

After twenty-one days of hunting and fishing, the weather turned cold, and Schultz and his party headed for home. He summed up their outing in these words:

> All in all, we had a pleasant trip, plenty of fish and game for camp use and, above all a sojourn among the pines and lakes so like those of our boyhood days [referring to the Adirondacks]. As a resort for sportsmen the Chief Mountain country cannot be excelled. The scenery is grand, game plenty, the fishing unexcelled.[8]

On the basis of Schultz's reports concerning his 1883 and 1884 visits to St. Mary Lakes, it becomes apparent that the area was serving as an objective for quite a few other people. During Schultz's thirty-day sojourn in 1884, five parties visited the area. In addition to the camp of North Piegan Indians, there came a prospecting group of three men, a lone trapper, a party of three men and two small boys from the agency, and Schultz's own group of four.

In other words, the area was already known to, and occasionally visited by quite a few people, most of them hunters. These included Blackfeet, Kutenais, white men, and half bloods of the Upper Marias, unlearned and rustling for a living. Some of them followed game trails to the head cirques and learned the geography of the region long before it was known to the outside world. No one kept track of the visits, and had it not been for Schultz and his penchant for wildlife, adventure, and writing, the story of Mr. Bird, Oliver, Jim, Ben, Charlie, and Medicine Beaver and their sheep hunts and incidental explorations, which make up some of the earliest history of the valleys of the Swiftcurrent and Upper St. Mary, would not have come down to us.

---

[8]"To Chief Mountain," p. 362.

CHAPTER 13

Exploring with Grinnell

O F the half-dozen people who exerted an important influence upon the career of James Willard Schultz, none played a greater role than George Bird Grinnell, editor, publisher, writer, explorer, ethnologist, and outdoorsman. He was the first to recognize Schultz as an unique personality, as well as a perceptive and talented writer. He provided Schultz with an outlet for his early articles and stories and later sponsored Schultz's first book, the western classic *My Life as an Indian*. Together with Schultz, he explored the St. Mary and Swiftcurrent regions, eventually being generally credited with having more than anyone else to do with their becoming parts of a national park.

Grinnell's 1885 visit to St. Mary Lakes launched both Schultz's career as a mountain guide and a long series of similar visits by eastern sportsmen, yet it was only the first of many collaborations by Grinnell and Schultz. The two most important of these took place in 1887 and 1891, and it was in the latter year that the exploratory phases of the visits ended with the investigation and naming of Blackfoot Glacier.[1] Grinnell had prepared a map of the region in 1887, but it had to be updated in 1891 to reflect the additional features to which names were given in the latter year.

---

[1] Although Grinnell continued to make visits to the St. Mary area, usually with Schultz as a guide, no record of them remains. It is known, however, that Grinnell, accompanied by his wife, did make a final visit in 1926 to Glacier National Park and to the glacier which bears his name.

Mount Grinnell and Swiftcurrent Lake and Falls. Courtesy Great Northern Railway.

Grinnell Glacier. Courtesy Great Northern Railway.

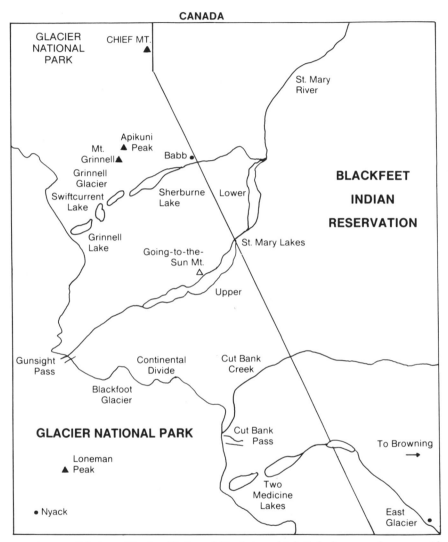

Areas of future Glacier National Park in which Schultz served as a guide. Map by author.

THE 1885 VISIT

Grinnell's attention was first attracted to the St. Mary Lakes by Schultz's article describing his 1884 visit, entitled "To Chief Mountain."[2] As a result, Schultz received a letter from Grinnell saying that he would like to visit the St. Mary country. He asked if Schultz would take him there the following September and intimated that he would like to collect some specimens of big game. Although Schultz was steadily employed at Fort Conrad, Joe Kipp granted him leave of absence, and the necessary trip arrangements were made. The plan was that Grinnell, after traveling by train to Helena, would take the stage to the Piegan agency, where Schultz would meet him with the necessary equipment and provisions.

Grinnell wrote of the trip in a fifteen-installment story entitled "To the Walled-In Lakes," the first part of which appeared in *Forest and Stream* the following December:

It was in the early days of September that we left the Piegan Agency for the Walled-In Lakes. So the Piegans have named the bodies of water which form the source of the St. Mary River.

Our party was not a large one. It consisted of Appekunny, Yellow Fish and the writer. J. W. Schultz (Appekunny) is well known to the readers of *Forest and Stream* as the author of the extremely interesting and scientifically valuable series of papers on "Life Among the Blackfeet," published in *Forest and Stream* a year or two ago. Yellow Fish—also known as Rose— is a French half-breed, but one who has always lived with his mother's people. He is thus in manners, education and feeling a thorough Indian, and can speak only a very few words of English.

We were starting a short trip to the St. Mary Lakes which are distant less than one hundred miles from the agency. Our wagon held a fourteen-foot skiff for use in case the one left on the lakes by Appekunny the previous autumn had been stolen or destroyed. A boat is a necessity on these large

[2]Since the article bore the date January, 1885, it probably reached *Forest and Stream* in February but for unknown reasons was not published until December. See Vol. XXV, December 10, 1885, 362–63.

lakes, where much of the fishing must be done in deep water. A 10×10 wall tent and sheet-iron cook stove, with our bedding and provisions, completed the load in the wagon. Our arms comprised a rifle apiece, and Mr. Schultz also had a shotgun with which, at various times during the trip, he did remarkably good execution. I had a light split bamboo fly-rod.[3]

They picked up two saddle horses at Cut Bank Creek and after three days reached the summit of the Hudson Bay Divide; a short time later they were able to pitch their camp at a pleasant spot near the head of the lower lake. For the next two days Grinnell, first with Yellow Fish and later with both men, rode and climbed over the area above the lower end of the upper lake. They saw signs of sheep but no sheep or other large game.

Evidently, game was scarce because eight lodges of Kutenai[4] Indians had been camped below the St. Mary River for fifty days, during which time they had killed forty mountain sheep; two bears, one a grizzly; a moose; a few elk; and plenty of beaver. Grinnell made arrangements to hunt with two of the Kutenais on a mountain trail above the lower end of the upper lake. He fell behind and, stopping to rest, caught a glimpse of a sheep about three hundred yards away. When it had approached within one hundred fifty yards, he was able to get a hasty shot at it and with that lucky shot dropped it. With much difficulty he managed to get the carcass back to the place where they had left the horses and rode triumphantly into camp with his kill. He wrote of it:

> That night in camp I told the story of the day to my companions, and after I had ended it Appekunny said: "That mountain shall be called Singleshot Mountain from this day forth, in memory of your single shot."

The following morning they moved camp to a point near the foot of the lower lake, where they paid a friendly visit to the Kutenai camp and fished for a day or two with a white

[3] Vol. XXV, December 10, 1885, 382.
[4] Grinnell spelled it *Kootenay*.

man named Dick King. Then, leaving their equipment in the care of King, they departed on a two-day excursion on horseback to the Swiftcurrent Lakes. They found the way into the valley to be merely a hunters' trail, although it showed considerable recent use, apparently by the Kutenais. Two or three miles into the valley they saw where some Canadians the previous year had cut a large quantity of timber, which, during the high water in spring, they floated down to the St. Mary River and across the international border.

The group continued past a series of lakes (now Sherburne Reservoir) until it reached Swiftcurrent Falls, which they had heard described in glowing terms as being one hundred feet high and of great beauty. Grinnell described their reaction as follows:

> We were greatly disappointed in them. They consist of a series of broken cascades, each about twenty-five feet high, the stream itself being about twenty feet wide and flowing between vertical walls of rock. The lake itself, walled in as it is by lofty mountains, is very beautiful.

As they proceeded up the valley, the glacier became visible. They estimated the thickness of its ice at several hundred feet and described it as being "broken in two by falling over a tremendous cliff, the height of which is greater than the thickness of the ice, so that the face of the rock is visible." After Grinnell and Apikuni[5] had spent a full day exploring the difficult terrain of the upper Swiftcurrent Valley, they returned to camp.

Being out of meat, the three men went hunting for game the following morning, but without success, and found it necessary to return to base camp at the lower lake. The following day they rode toward Chief Mountain to get a closer view and for an hour or two sat on the hills "admiring the majesty of this Western Matterhorn." They began the return trip to the agency the next morning and reached it without incident. That night they spread their blankets in the trader's store, enjoying the hospitality of Joe Kipp.

[5]Grinnell spelled it *Appekunny.*

On the following morning they asked old Red Eagle, a relative of Apikuni's wife and the most potent of the Pikuni medicine men, if he would perform the Bear Pipe ceremony for them, first sending him some tea, bread, and tobacco, together with a large bag of dried serviceberries. After he had agreed to do so and preparations had been completed, they repaired to Red Eagle's lodge, where a number of Indians were already seated, and the ceremony, described in detail by Grinnell, was performed by the blind Red Eagle, with special prayers for Apikuni and for Joe Kipp, their wives and children.

The next morning while they were in Kipp's store, Four Bears, the camp orator, came in to chat. On learning who Grinnell was, he offered to give him a name. Facing Grinnell toward the sun, Four Bears began to pray to Sun, saying that for years his own name had been *Pinutoyi Istsimokan,* or Fisher Hat (meaning a "hat made from the skin of a fisher"). "Now I am getting old and before long I shall die," he said. "I do not longer need this name, and now I give it to this my son. Pity him. Give him long life. Keep him from all dangers of every kind."[6] When the ceremony was over, Grinnell gave Four Bears a plug of tobacco, which he accepted very pleasantly. A few days later, Grinnell bade good-bye to Schultz and started for the East.

It was on this 1885 trip to the St. Mary country that other names besides Singleshot were bestowed on natural features. Grinnell and Schultz agreed that the mountain beyond Singleshot should be called Yellow Fish Mountain and that the stream beyond the latter should bear the name of Yellow Fish Creek. For many years they were so called, but to Schultz's disgust, when the United States Geological Survey's first map of the region was published in 1912, they had been renamed Whitefish Mountain and Roes Creek, respectively.

Also during this trip, Grinnell and Schultz decided to give an English name to a mountain Yellow Fish had pointed out

_____

[6]The reader who is familiar with the Schultz version of this christening (see *Blackfeet and Buffalo,* 83–85), written more than fifty years after the incident, will recognize the total dissimilarity between it and Grinnell's account, written only a few weeks after it happened.

to them when they were on Flat Top Mountain. Schultz, in *Signposts of Adventure*, translated the long Blackfoot name as "Mountain-from-Which-the-Water-Goes-to-the-Behind-Direction-and-to-the-South-Direction"[7] but called it simply Divide Mountain, the name it retains today. It is the high, sharp-crested peak at the long ridge running between the streams flowing to the Missouri and the Saskatchewan. In other words, it is the dividing ridge between the waters of the Atlantic and Arctic oceans.

THE 1887 VISIT

In the annals of the St. Mary country, the year 1887 was a memorable one.[8] It was not, of course, because it marked the return of George Bird Grinnell after he had been unable to come west in 1886; rather, it was because 1887 was the historic year when a glacier in the future national park was first visited and explored by white men. One of those men was James Willard Schultz in his role as companion and guide for Grinnell. The year 1887 was also the one in which pilgrims to the St. Mary region first availed themselves of a new approach to the area from the north, taking advantage of the recent completion of a transcontinental rail line by the Canadian Pacific. Consequently, for the first time a sportsman from the West Coast and one from the eastern seaboard reached the St. Mary Lakes via that route.

Grinnell had asked a friend to join him for at least part of the time he planned to spend in Montana; the friend was George H. Gould, a resident of Santa Barbara, California. In the series of articles Grinnell wrote for *Forest and Stream*

---

[7] P. 98.

[8] This story of the 1887 visit is based on the account prepared by Grinnell for publication in *Forest and Stream.* It was entitled "The Rock Climbers," and the first installment appeared on December 29, 1887 (Vol. XXX, 442). Some fifty years later, Schultz wrote a short report of the trip, apparently from memory (*Blackfeet and Buffalo,* 99–102), in which he stated that it had taken place in 1886. As will readily be observed by anyone having an opportunity to make a comparison, there is little similarity between the two stories.

about the 1887 expedition, he never referred to Gould by
that name but always as "H. G. Dulog" or "the Rhymer," the
former being an anagram for G. H. Gould. In these articles
he used a pseudonym, Yo, and referred to Lieutenant John
H. Beacom of the United States Army, who spent a few days
with the party, as "Lieutenant B." As always, Schultz was referred to as Appekunny.

Grinnell and Gould had taken advantage of the new Canadian rail facilities by scheduling their respective depar-
tures from the eastern and western seaboards so as to arrive
on the same day at Lethbridge, Canada, where they would
be met by Schultz with his outfit and transported back to
Lower Lake St. Mary. While this wagon journey from Lethbridge to the lower lake required about five days, it was
probably no more time consuming than that from Helena to
the lakes by way of the Blackfoot agency. It did, of course,
require Schultz to make the long trip from his home on the
reservation to Lethbridge in order to meet them.

Because it required more than ten days to go to Lethbridge and back to the lakes, Schultz managed this part of
the journey alone. For the rest of the trip an assistant was
necessary, and the services of Jack Monroe, who happened
to be at a whiskey trader's camp at nearby Pike Lake, were
procured. With his help they were able to get Schultz's boat
from its winter storage spot to the lake and load it for a trip
to the head of the lower lake.

Gould's time at the lakes was limited, but he was a semi-
invalid and not an active hunter. In spite of bad weather,
Grinnell was able to kill two mountain goats and a panther
which stole one of the hams they had hung in a tree near
their camp. When at last Gould's time was up, he and Jack
Monroe packed his things on a mule, and after hearty hand-
clasps they rode away, Monroe escorting Gould back to
Lethbridge.

When Monroe returned from Lethbridge, the party broke
camp and moved to the foot of the lower lake in preparation
for a trip up the Swiftcurrent Valley—the real purpose of
the trip. In the meantime, they encountered Lieutenant
Beacom, an acquaintance of Schultz who happened to visit

the area, and invited him to join them on their trip to the Swiftcurrent. For this part of their journey they took only enough equipment and supplies for one week, all stowed on two small pack mules. Early one morning—it was now late October or early November—the four men rode up the Swiftcurrent trail: Grinnell, now thirty-seven years old, and Schultz, Monroe, and Beacom, all in their late twenties or early thirties.

After camping the first night below Swiftcurrent Falls, they set out to explore potential routes to what is now Grinnell Glacier. Proceeding along the west shore of Swiftcurrent Lake, they followed an old Indian trail to the head of what is now Lake Josephine, where the trail was blocked by an avalanche of logs. They returned to camp, Grinnell and Beacom as they had come, Schultz and Monroe via a used Kutenai trail which led them back easily and quickly, probably along the eastern or southeastern side of the two lakes.

The next morning, after bidding Beacom good-bye, they packed provisions and bedding on the two mules and departed before daylight. Soon they stood on the shore of a milky-blue lake, circular in form and about a mile in diameter (present-day Grinnell Lake). Behind it was a wall of sheer black rock over which flowed a stream of white foam from the glacier above. They estimated the basin in which the glacier lay to be two miles deep and three or more wide. It consisted of two principal masses, the upper of which, somewhat smaller than the lower, rested on a ledge which ran far back among the peaks. The whole glacier occupied not less than three thousand feet vertically on the mountainside. They guessed the thickness of the ice to be about seven hundred feet in the lower mass and eight hundred feet in the upper.

A long, hard climb brought them to the surface of the lower section of the glacier, where they spent a full day exploring the ice field. Late in the day they stumbled upon a magnificent bighorn ram, which Grinnell brought down with a well-directed shot from a distance of two hundred yards. From a hunter's standpoint, that constituted a perfect ending to a perfect day. Heavily loaded with parts of the ram, they returned to camp for the night. It took all of the next day for Schultz and Monroe to bring down the rest of the animal while Grinnell remained in camp updating his notes.

On the following day they returned to their camp below Swiftcurrent Falls, where they stopped to gather up and repack the articles left there, then continued down the valley to the foot of Lower St. Mary Lake. After repacking the wagon for the return trip, they drove to Cut Bank Creek, where they camped for a week. There were plenty of goats and sheep in the area, but it snowed every day and the wind blew incessantly, so they got no game. By this time it was mid-November and they began to think it was time to be moving out of the mountains.

On the sixteenth of November, Schultz and Grinnell headed north by wagon to Lethbridge, where the latter would take the Canadian Pacific east. After crossing the border, they were overtaken by the Mounted Police on an erroneous tip that they were whiskey smugglers. A quick search showed nothing illegal, and they were allowed to proceed. Grinnell returned home by way of Montreal to write "The Rock Climbers" for *Forest and Stream*,[9] and Apikuni returned to the reservation to become reacquainted with his Pikuni son and wife.

It was on this trip that the name *Appekunny* was given to a mountain and waterfall in the Swiftcurrent Valley situated opposite the party's main camp below Swiftcurrent Falls. In his story of the 1887 expedition, Grinnell refers to "the much-used campground, under the frowning face of Appekunny's Mountain."[10] It is undisputed that Appekunny (now Apikuni) Mountain and Falls were named for Schultz by Lieutenant Beacom. There is, however, some controversy with respect to the naming of Grinnell Glacier, Mountain, and Lake. Schultz has asserted that it was he who was re-

[9] A series of articles entitled "The Rock Climbers" commenced in *Forest and Stream* on December 29, 1887.

[10] "The Rock Climbers," *Forest and Stream*, Vol. XXX, March 22, 1888, 163.

sponsible.[11] There is other evidence pointing to the fact that the names of the glacier and mountain, at least, were conferred by Lieutenant Beacom.[12] Other than Grinnell Lake, none of the other lakes in the Swiftcurrent Valley were given formal names then. The present Swiftcurrent Lake was usually referred to as the Fifth Lake, and the present Lake Josephine was the Sixth Lake. Had anyone previously reached Grinnell Lake, it presumably would have been referred to as the Seventh Lake.

The other principal peaks in the valley were named by Grinnell himself: Mount Gould, for his friend from Santa Barbara, George H. Gould; Mount Allen, for Cornelia Seward Allen, sister of William H. Seward III; and Mount Wilbur, for E. R. Wilbur, Grinnell's associate on the editorial staff of *Forest and Stream.*

[11] *Blackfeet and Buffalo*, 94.

[12] Lieutenant Beacom is said to have recorded in his journal of the day he saw them the fact that he had given Grinnell's name to both the glacier and the mountain. Some support is lent to this by a statement from Grinnell, writing in the issue of *Forest and Stream* dated May 24, 1888, in reference to a map which he prepared of the St. Mary–Swiftcurrent region: "To this map details were added by Lieutenant J. H. Beacom, U.S.A., who took compass bearings during the few days he spent at the lakes in October and November, 1887, when in my company he penetrated to within a few miles of the glacier which he named for me." It may be, of course, that among the details added to the map by Beacom were the names he had heard Schultz give to the glacier and the mountain. Beacom never saw Grinnell Lake and viewed the glacier only from a distance.

CHAPTER 14

Hunting with Celebrities

THE articles by George Bird Grinnell which had appeared in *Forest and Stream* following his 1885 visit to the St. Mary country[1] came to the attention of many people and made it known that a new type of game was plentiful in that area, to wit, the white goat of the Northern Rockies. Among these were the Baring brothers of London, England, who had been hunting that same year in the Yellowstone country and were intrigued by the prospect of an encounter with this rare species of big game. They undertook to make the necessary arrangements through Charles Conrad, one of the partners in I. G. Baker Company, merchants of Fort Benton.

Conrad, in turn, had close ties with Joe Kipp and his associate, James Willard Schultz, so he promptly called on them and handed them a letter from Cecil Baring stating that he and his two uncles wished to do some hunting for bighorn sheep and Rocky Mountain goats especially. Conrad explained that the Barings were important English bankers and that Cecil Baring was in charge of the firm's New York office. The letter mentioned that the year before Jack Bean of Bozeman had outfitted and guided the group on a deer and elk hunt in the Yellowstone country and would be with the group again this autumn. It went into considerable detail about the outfit they would require and clearly demonstrated that these men were far from being tenderfeet. After study-

---

[1] Fifteen articles under the pen name Yo appeared in *Forest and Stream*, beginning with the issue of December 10, 1885.

ing the letter carefully, Schultz and Kipp agreed to take care of the Barings, and Conrad wrote Cecil Baring in New York to that effect.

The firm of Baring Brothers & Co., Limited, was indeed an important one. The owners' history as merchant bankers goes back more than two hundred years, during which time they had served as bankers and financial advisers to many of the crowned heads of Europe.

The Barings became the first merchant bankers to realize that beyond the Atlantic there was a land of unlimited possibilities. Young Alexander Baring came to Boston in 1795 and in February, 1796, negotiated with William Bingham, reputedly the richest man in America, the purchase of one and a quarter million acres in the state of Maine. Two years later he married Bingham's daughter, Anne Louise, who brought with her a dowry of nine hundred thousand dollars.

Before long the Barings had become, in effect, bankers to the United States government. They provided financing of a million dollars for the use of the American minister negotiating with the Barbary powers in the closing years of the eighteenth century. When the United States agreed upon the Louisiana Purchase with Napoleon, the Jefferson administration called upon the Barings to finance the deal. In doing so, a Baring acted as go-between with both the French and British governments.

The Barings made loans to the states of Maryland and Massachusetts in the 1830's and began to finance American railroads in the 1840's. It was a Baring, Lord Aberdeen, who negotiated the settlement of a northeast boundary dispute with Daniel Webster, then secretary of state. They were financial agents for the Russian government and helped to finance the Trans-Siberian Railway. They made large loans to South American countries. It was once said that "there are six great powers in Europe: England, France, Russia, Austria, Prussia and the Baring Brothers."[2]

Barings have distinguished themselves through holding high British diplomatic posts and signing state treaties.

[2] Joseph Wechsler, *The Merchant Bankers*, 76.

They now hold five peerages: Ashburton, Northbrook, Rev-
elstoke, Cromer, and Howick. It was George R. S. Baring,
the third Earl of Cromer, who served as governor of the
Bank of England as recently as 1966. Today the firm prefers
to limit its activities for the most part to conventional banking services. However, it still commands a respected position
in international banking circles, with headquarters at 8,
Bishopgate, London E.C. 2.[3]

On September 1, 1886,[4] the *Fort Benton River Press* announced the arrival of the Baring party:

> The River Press acknowledges the pleasure of a call from
> Col. Robert Baring and Mr. Thomas Baring of the cele-
> brated banking house of Baring Bros. & Co., London. They
> are accompanied by a nephew, Cecil Baring and are traveling
> for pleasure and information. This is not their first trip to
> America for the same purpose. They have on former occa-
> sions visited the Yellowstone Park, portions of the Rocky,
> Coeur d'Alene and Sierra Nevada ranges, California, and
> other interesting portions of the western continent. This,
> however, is their first visit to the great northwest.
>
> Their party fully equipped with everything to make life on
> the plains and in the mountains comfortable will leave in the
> morning. They go from here along the eastern base of the
> Rockies north to St. Mary's lake, where they will camp for a
> season and enjoy the superb fishing, and then follow along to
> the Canadian Pacific railroad over which, if time allows, they
> may take a run toward the western coast, and return by rail
> through Canada, home.

The Baring party was met at the Fort Benton levee by
Schultz, Kipp, and Charles Bristol, who was to be the cook,
along with a large wagon partly filled with camping equipment and supplies. The party consisted of Sir Thomas
Baring and Colonel Robert Baring, forty-nine and fifty-one
years old, respectively, the latter very much a British officer,
and Cecil Baring, age twenty-four. With them was Jack Bean

---

[3] *Idem*, 76–127.
[4] As shown in Schultz's *Forest and Stream* article of December 30, 1886, on
which the foregoing is based, the Barings' visit took place in 1886, not in
1889, as later reported by the same author in *Blackfeet and Buffalo*, 110.

of Bozeman, mentioned in Cecil Baring's letter to Charles Conrad.

Among the Barings' gear was a large canvas folding boat and a forty-five-pound bear trap. From their London wine cellar they had brought a case of champagne and half a dozen quarts of 1834 whiskey. It had been stipulated that they would not want any saddle horses, making it evident that they would do all their hunting on foot.

On making their first St. Mary camp at the foot of the lower lake, they held council and decided to head up the Swiftcurrent Valley the next morning. It was a dark, windy day, although they managed to reach Swiftcurrent Falls, where they camped for the night. The next day brought no success at either hunting or fishing, and when the third morning broke dark and chilly, they decided to return to the lower lake.

Back at their main camp, Schultz and Cecil Baring went hunting on Flat Top Mountain to obtain a supply of fresh meat. Cecil killed a ram with his first shot, and the two men lugged the massive head and hindquarters back to camp, where it was the signal for celebration with a drink of the 1834 whiskey. A few days later they decided to move their camp to a pleasant spot on the upper lake where a small stream flowed down between Going-to-the-Sun and Goat mountains. It was a beautiful day as they rowed up the lake, and the Barings were thrilled to see a band of Rocky Mountain goats high up on Red Eagle Mountain. The scenery evoked repeated exclamations of surprise and excitement, Colonel Baring saying: "I have been in the Alps of Switzerland, the Himalayas of India, but in neither of those ranges have I seen any setting of lakes and mountains that compare with this before us."[5]

They made camp at the foot of Going-to-the-Sun Mountain and in the morning were led by Schultz and Jack Bean up an old game trail along the mountain. They had not gone more than a mile when they spotted a large male goat

[5] *Blackfeet and Buffalo*, 114; reprinted from *Great Falls Tribune*, November 8, 1836.

that was brought down by a timely shot from Sir Thomas Baring. A few days later, Cecil Baring killed a billy that became trapped on a ledge. On each of these occasions, Governor Baring poured a drink of 1834 whiskey in honor of the excellent marksmanship.

Colonel Baring was the only member of the party who so far had had no luck in hunting, so Kipp and Bean suggested that Schultz take him out for a day in the hope of rectifying the deficiency. They crossed the lake to a spot where a small stream flowed down to the lake between Red Eagle and Little Chief mountains. After a short but hard climb to the point where the stream ended in a steep-sided, almost-circular basin, they sighted a band of fifteen or more goats directly across the basin. There were males, females, and kids of various ages. Schultz estimated that they could not possibly get close enough for Colonel Baring to risk a shot, so they sat down among some stunted pines and waited in the hope that some of the animals would move closer to them.

After an hour or so, they were surprised when another band of goats appeared above the basin and made its way down to the first band. At their approach, the females of the other band began walking forward very stiffly and shaking their heads. Then the females of the first band did likewise, and soon Schultz and the colonel were treated to a regular circus as the animals of both bands engaged in a variety of battles, high leaps, and fierce buttings. Presently they quieted down and started to move toward the place where Schultz and Baring were waiting.

When the leaders of the band were about one hundred fifty yards away, the colonel began to shoot. Surprised, the entire band stopped. At his second shot they began to run, and he continued shooting without effect. His last shot spattered against the rocks directly in front of the retreating band. Suddenly the band turned and ran back toward the hunters. As it drew closer, Schultz handed his companion his own Winchester. When the goats were only fifty feet or so away, the colonel succeeded in killing a mature female, whereupon the rest of the band scattered.

Schultz skinned the hard-won trophy and the two men started back to camp. About halfway down to the lake, Schultz stepped on an old log, out of which a cloud of hornets came swarming. The colonel was right behind, and in a moment the hornets were upon him, repeatedly stinging his hands and face, which immediately began to swell and become painful. At the lake he got some relief by bathing them in cold water.

In the meantime, Schultz, borrowing the colonel's field glasses, had sighted four splendid bighorn rams on the face of Goat Mountain across the lake. He asked the colonel whether he felt well enough to go after them, and the latter signified his willingness. They crossed the lake and, after reconnoitering, sighted the rams again. Three were lying down, but the fourth, a magnificent specimen, was standing watch. With the utmost caution, Schultz led them to within one hundred fifty yards of the ram, then signaled the colonel to take careful aim with the Winchester. When the colonel fired, the ram leaped high in the air and fell dead. Thus in less than half a day the colonel had bagged a sheep as well as a goat. Baring examined the dead ram with no visible sign of satisfaction over his success, but he finally managed a smile and agreed with Schultz that it was indeed a perfect animal. It was dark when they reached camp. The colonel drank champagne, Schultz sipped whiskey, and Kipp and Jack Bean prepared the two heads for shipping and mounting.

The Barings so enjoyed their outing that they returned in a later year. Unfortunately, all we know about the second trip is that they visited the Schultz ranch and met Nätahki. They were responsible for sending other English parties to Schultz to outfit and guide in what is now Glacier National Park. When the time came for them to leave, the Barings presented Schultz with their folding boat and the mighty forty-five-pound bear trap.

In 1927, Cecil Baring came to Glacier Park for a last outing there, bringing his son Rupert with him. Schultz had the pleasure of meeting them and introducing young Rupert to some of the Pikunis. Later, Cecil became Lord Cecil Baring;

after his death, his son Lord Rupert Baring wrote to Schultz
that he hoped to visit Glacier Park and to meet him again.

The Barings' visit has left an indelible impression upon
the maps of Glacier National Park. Schultz tells us:

> That evening just before supper, Governor Baring
> broached another bottle of the '34 for us. I raised my cup
> and said: "Let us drink to Baring Creek, Baring Basin, Bar-
> ing Glacier. And may they be so lettered on the maps of the
> future."[6]

A glance at the latest United States Geological Survey map
of Glacier shows that Baring Creek has survived. Although
Baring Basin has never appeared on any map and Baring
Glacier has unaccountably become Sexton Glacier, in lieu
thereof the Geological Survey has given us Baring Falls. Let
all who may wonder hereafter about the origin of these
names remember that they were conferred in the year 1886
by none other than James Willard Schultz, by whom these
various natural features were discovered.

[6] *Blackfeet and Buffalo*, 117.

CHAPTER 15

The Trojan Hunters

ONE of the most fascinating chapters in the history of early visitations to the St. Mary country has to be that of the four citizens of Troy, New York, who found their way to the Northwest in the 1880's to hunt bighorn sheep and grizzly bears. Not only were they one of the first three groups of eastern hunters to visit the area, they were the first to write and publish the story of their adventures in book form. The Iliad that one of the four Trojans wrote after their return was entitled *Sport Among the Rockies*.[1] The Homer who wrote it was John M. Francis, manager of the *Troy Times*.

These modern Trojans were not geologists, botanists, geographers, or mapmakers. They went on no serious mission, explored no new territory, gave no names, and made no effort "to accomplish impracticable or hitherto unperformed feats of mountain climbing." They were simply soft, flabby, prominent citizens and tired businessmen of the modern Troy headed for the wilds of the Montana Rockies on a short vacation jaunt, forerunners of the countless throngs who today ride or hike the trails of the St. Mary country in what is now Glacier National Park.

The reason their adventures now become a part of our story is that they were so fortunate as to have James Willard Schultz as a guide—one of three, in fact. That worthy ne-

[1]The book was published in 1889 by its author, the press work being done by the *Troy Times* job-printing establishment.

glected to include any word about their visit in his published works or reminiscences, possibly because he felt that a story about such undistinguished visitors was not worthy of being reported.

The book actually represented a compilation of twenty-five letters written for publication in the *Troy Times* by Francis, who signed himself "Scribe." It comprised one hundred thirty-four double-columned pages of fine print filled with good-humored but informative prose and illustrated with forty-eight photographs by the author. The background of the carefully planned safari was set forth in the opening paragraph of the first letter, which said:

> There were four of us. Four Trojans. We started August 14 for the far Northwest on a hunting and fishing trip. One of us was a doctor; one was an artist; the third was a merchant; the fourth was a newspaper man. . . . We were all fired with ambition to kill large game, catch big fish and face ferocious Indians. That ambition was gratified to a greater or less extent, depending upon the experience and expectations of each gentleman.

After making elaborate preparations, the four Trojans left nearby Albany on the afternoon of August 14, 1888, and arrived in Great Falls, Montana, a day or two before their scheduled departure from that point on the nineteenth. On the afternoon of the latter date they crossed the Missouri River to the point where their outfit awaited them. Its personnel consisted of three guides, a cook, and a herder. The guides were Joe Kipp and J. W. Schultz of Piegan, Blackfoot Agency, and Bill Weaver of Fort Benton; the cook was Charles Bristol of Fort Benton; and the herder was Frank Upham of Birch Creek. All were men of experience. With them were sixteen horses, two pack mules, two prairie schooners, two eight-by-ten canvas wall tents, and a sheet-iron cookstove. The Trojans had brought a canvas boat in three sections. They felt it safe to say that no hunting party ever started for the mountains of northwestern Mon-

The Four Trojans. From Sport Among the Rockies (*1889*). *Courtesy Yale University, Beinecke Rare Book and Manuscript Library.*

tana better prepared than they were for comfort and convenience.

Unexplained by the author was the source of their information about a safari of this kind or their choice of those in charge of it. However, the available facts permit the drawing of certain reasonable inferences as to the manner in which they became aware of the possibilities of such a trip. Knowing that one or more of them had been subscribers to *Forest and Stream* for the two or three preceding years, it is not difficult to surmise that they would have read Grinnell's article about his 1885 trip to the St. Mary country, as well as that of Schultz covering his 1886 trip with the Barings. From the fact that the guides and cook with the 1886 expedition were the same as those arranged for by the Trojans in 1888, it may reasonably be assumed that they had read Schultz's 1886 article, had liked what they read, and in effect had arranged to be furnished with an outfit and outing of a similar kind. A third guide was added because of the size of the Trojan party.

The Scribe was very much interested in the background and experience of the crew and devoted two letters in their entirety to this subject. He was particularly taken with Joe Kipp, his personality and wide experience, and devoted nearly two thousand words to an outline of his career and a list of the exploits of this colorful frontiersman whose mother had been the daughter of a Mandan chief. The others were disposed of in a single letter, and the sketch of Schultz was as follows:

APPECANI [*sic*]

Our other guide, J. W. Shultz [*sic*], is about thirty-two years old. He came from New York state some years ago, having received a good education at one of our best institutions of learning. Always possessing a fondness for outdoor life and for hunting and fishing, he sought the extreme northwestern part of Montana in which to gratify his inclination to that life. Marrying an Indian girl and acquiring the red man's language, he settled down to a semi-civilized life, and now lives happily in the vicinity of the Blackfoot agency.

AN INTERESTING CHILD

He has a little boy about six or seven years old, of whom he is very fond, and who seems to be a bright and engaging child. While we were in camp at the Two Medicine Creek the little fellow visited us, accompanied by an Indian attendant, and he was proudly introduced by Shultz [*sic*], who seemed to idolize the boy. The father announced his determination to us to send his son to the states to be educated, and declared he did not desire him to follow his footsteps and reside permanently among the Indians. Shultz called by the Piegans and by the white men as well, Appecani ("Big Wolf Skin"), and many of our readers will recognize in that name the author of numerous interesting communications that have appeared from time to time in the *Forest and Stream*, touching the fauna, together with their life and habits, of northern Montana.

A MAN OF INTELLIGENCE

He is a remarkably intelligent man, and one is surprised to find so much intelligence and education away up there, almost out of the world and certainly far beyond the limits of civilization, but Appecani, as we all came to call him, and he seemed to prefer to have us call him by this name, seems contented with his lot; certainly he is placed in a position where he can gratify to the fullest his fondness for hunting and fishing. His mother is still living in New York state, near Boonville, and judging from the photographs we saw of her, she is a most refined and estimable lady. We learned, too, that an old school chum of his is now one of our most promising young lawyers in Troy.

A WELL-POSTED GUIDE

Appecani's knowledge of the St. Mary's country showed that he had traveled a great deal through that region and was well posted concerning the mountains and lakes. He did all he could to afford us fine hunting and fishing. Always polite and affable, Appecani worked hard for our interests throughout our mountain trip.

Schultz (seated, in shirtsleeves), with guides and crew for the Four Tro-
jans. From Sport Among the Rockies. *Courtesy Yale University,*
Beinecke Rare Book and Manuscript Library.

The Trojan party headed north across the plains, camping the first night at Sun River, on the second at Spring
Creek five miles beyond Choteau, on the third at Dupuyer,
where there were only four houses, and on the fourth day
rode down the hill into the Indian village of Piegan, where
the Blackfoot agency was located. Here they went directly
to Joe Kipp's trading post and later enjoyed dinner at his
home. Afterward they called on Major Baldwin, agent at the
Blackfoot agency, where they were cordially received and
welcomed.

Resuming travel the next afternoon, the party camped at a point in Two Medicine Valley not far from Schultz's cabin. At about 9 P.M. Major Baldwin and his wife rode in, and all sat down to a sumptuous supper served on an improvised table made of two broad planks supported by a couple of cracker boxes. The meal was followed by cigars and the exchange of a variety of stories about frontier life.

Early the next morning, Schultz's boy, a youngster whose age they guessed at seven or eight, visited them in the company of an Indian attendant. Wrote Scribe:

> Our guide's home was only a mile from our camp, and the bright little fellow came to see the pale-face visitors. White men were curiosities in their way to him, and he evidently wanted to give us a critical examination. He was dressed like our children, but the Indian blood was plainly in his veins, and in looks he resembled his Blackfoot mother much more than his father. Those sharp black eyes of his followed us closely as we moved about camp, and obtained "points," beyond question, to be subsequently divulged to his mother and his playmates. All efforts to talk with him were fruitless; he didn't seem to understand a word of English.

On their sixth day out they followed Cut Bank Creek for twenty miles and camped in an open glade. They continued the next day up the Cut Bank trail to an elevation of six thousand five hundred feet, camping close to the cold and swift-running waters of the creek at a point where they would remain for several days. For hunting purposes they divided into three parties, each moving in a different direction. When they recounted their experiences that evening, they found that among them they had caught sight of more than thirty bighorns, had killed three, and had wounded two others. However, sooner or later, each member of the Trojan party was to bag at least one bighorn, some more than one, and they were delighted with the results.

One of the party's objectives in coming to the Rockies was to glimpse and if possible to shoot a grizzly bear. The Scribe and Joe Kipp set out to do just that, hanging a portion of a sheep's carcass on the limb of a tree a few feet above the

ground in an open area where fresh grizzly signs had been
found and settling down to wait for a bear. About 5 P.M. a
grizzly appeared, and at the appropriate moment the Scribe
pumped a bullet into the bear's right shoulder from seventy-
five yards away. Screaming with rage and pain, the animal
started for the hunters. The Scribe's second bullet struck the
bear close to the heart, but on it came. The third shot evidently reached a vital spot, but with a supreme effort the
grizzly lifted itself to an upright position and staggered in
their direction. When it had approached within fifty feet,
the Scribe pulled the trigger again, and with one last tremendous cry the bear dropped to the ground, dead. It weighed
about four hundred pounds and its pelt became a prized
trophy.

While the party was camped near the head of Cut Bank
Canyon, the Scribe and Joe Kipp spent a day riding to the
summit of Cut Bank Pass, and the Scribe devoted an entire
chapter in the book (the fourteenth letter) to a description
of the experience. When, at last, the summit was attained,
the Scribe burst into superlatives over the views toward the
Pacific side of the Continental Divide:

> What views! What scenery! Words cannot describe the
> grand, sublime outlook on all sides. . . . All this was a revela-
> tion to the Scribe, and made an everlasting impression upon
> him—the mammoth mountains, the jagged peaks, the snow-
> drifts, the little lakes, the streams, the vast pine forests with
> their sombre hue and the great pasture fields of a lighter and
> more brilliant shade of green that looked so attractive in the
> valleys below. He had seen some of the finest views in the
> Alps of Switzerland; he had been over the Marshall pass in
> Colorado, but never before was he so struck with the solemn
> grandeur, the impressive magnificence and the wondrous
> beauty of Nature.

After their return to camp and a few more days in this
hunter's paradise, provisions began to run low and it was
necessary to return to the base camp. The coffee there had
never tasted so good, and the cook outdid himself in preparing a royal supper consisting of "light and snow-white warm

biscuits, potatoes saute, grilled bacon, fried apples 'smothered with onions,' corn and tomatoes, pears and peaches, mountain mutton," together with trout and grouse bagged or caught that day in the neighborhood.

It was some forty or fifty miles through rough country to St. Mary Lakes, but the Trojans had heard so many Münchhausen tales about them from Schultz and Joe that they were anxious to see them. It was nearly 5 P.M. on a long day when they reached the summit of the Hudson Divide, some one thousand two hundred feet above Lower St. Mary Lake. Visible on their left far up the valley, the larger Upper St. Mary Lake nestled between stupendous mountains that rose almost perpendicularly four thousand or five thousand feet above the water. The Trojans decided that this region was "beyond all question the Switzerland of America."

The party found a campsite on Upper St. Mary Lake within one hundred feet of the shore and opposite Singleshot Mountain. Here the Trojans experienced much success with rod and gun. The fishermen frequently returned from river and lake excursions with more fish than one man could comfortably carry. The merchant, sometimes referred to as "the Commodore," left camp one morning determined to shoot a grizzly. He and Schultz took a quantity of large fish to a small clearing where grizzly signs had been seen. Tying some of them to the branch of a low tree, they retired to a position a short distance away. In about two hours a grizzly appeared, providing an excellent target for a good shot. It took two shots from the Trojan's rifle to finish the enraged animal, which weighed about five hundred pounds.

For his part, the doctor announced that he had set his heart on bagging an elk. In company with guide Bill Weaver, he left camp one afternoon, laden with sufficient food and gear to stay away a night or two if necessary. After being ferried across the lake, the two men made their way to a big alkali lick some four or five miles into the mountains. No animals appeared that evening, but at dawn the next day, while Weaver was still asleep, the doctor saw a magnificent bull elk approaching the lick. He took careful aim and fired when his quarry was not more than one hundred feet away, putting a bullet directly through the big animal's heart. Estimating its weight at six hundred pounds, they soon stripped off the head and pelt and with these trophies struggled back to join their companions at the lake.

Came the day, however, when it was necessary to break camp at Upper St. Mary Lake and start homeward, although with regret. They traveled a few miles north of the lower lake in order to strike the regular beaten track from Fort Macleod to the Blackfoot agency. On the second day they were able to reach the Cut Bank River, a trek of some forty or fifty miles. There they camped within a few hundred yards of the ranch of Cut Bank John, an industrious young Blackfoot who, with his wife and young son, was prospering at this location. The following day they were able by noon to reach the Blackfoot agency, where again they were welcomed and entertained by the Baldwins.

After an overnight stay, the Trojans continued to Great Falls, where they said good-bye to their faithful guides and boarded the train for Helena. At that point the quartet broke up, the artist and merchant to return directly to Troy while the Scribe and the doctor "did" a one hundred fifty-mile trip through Yellowstone National Park, thereby deferring for about a fortnight their departure for home. Their adventure had been a thrilling one and included the Scribe's bagging a large bull elk near Yellowstone Park.[2] He concluded his final letter with these words:

[2]Since the Trojans were only the third party of eastern sportsmen to be conducted through the St. Mary country by Schultz, one wonders why no word from him about the safari ever appeared in the columns of *Forest and Stream* or elsewhere. Conceivably it could have been that the Trojans did not represent people of distinction, as had been the case with Grinnell and the Barings.

However, in a letter to Alexander Legget dated June 30, 1927, Schultz had this to say: "I did have a copy of Charles S. Francis' book, but after glancing at it, tossed it into the fire, as from beginning to end, there was not a word of truth in it. He and his friends killed not so much as a grouse, on the whole trip, and their conduct was such that Kipp, Weaver and I were more than glad when the trip ended."

It was with sincere regret that a dissolution of this sportsman copartnership became necessary. In the days to come we will live over again and again the pleasures of the trip. The few disagreeable features will fade from memory, many happy "occasions" will come to mind and we shall all of us feel that our excursion to the great Northwest in the fall of 1888 was not in vain.

CHAPTER 16

More Outings at the St. Mary Lakes

THE WINTER OF 1887–88 was a difficult one for Schultz and his family. They were snowed in most of the time, and it was only with the utmost difficulty that they were able to travel even the short distance from their place on Two Medicine River to the agency for supplies. By January even the agency store had run out of tobacco, that most-sought-after of all trade goods. This was such a blow to Schultz that old Red Eagle, the uncle of Nätahki, took pity on him and from time to time gave him a little from his sacred Elk-Tongue-Pipe Bundle. To make matters worse, young Hart Schultz became ill, and of course no medical aid was available. Nätahki asked her uncle to pray for the boy. After painting the youngster's face with his red paint, sacred to Sun, the old medicine man spent hours in prayers and songs for Hart's recovery. In a short time the boy began to feel better and soon was well.

When the spring of 1888 finally arrived, Schultz decided the time had come when he should take his wife and son to see his beloved Lakes Inside country. Having loaded their camping equipment and food supplies on their wagon, Schultz took the reins and they were off. They made camp in an opening among the pines near the shore of Upper St. Mary Lake. After Nätahki overcame her fear of the water and the dreaded Water People, they spent much time rowing about the lake to enjoy the spectacular wall of snow-capped peaks that encircled them, and the constantly shifting perspectives thus afforded them.

One day Nätahki reminded Schultz that he had recently

named a mountain and a glacier, or "big ice" as she called it, for his friend Grinnell. Then she announced that she would like to name her favorite mountain *Mekotsipitan Istuki*, or Red Eagle Mountain. When Schultz inquired her reason, she reminded him of how Red Eagle's prayers had made Hart well and of Red Eagle's generosity with his sacred tobacco, thereby keeping Schultz from going crazy. Thus reminded, Schultz readily agreed, and that is still the mountain's name.

One day, to their great surprise, a party consisting of thirty lodges of Kutenai Indians from British Columbia rode in and made camp close to them. They and the Blackfoot tribes had long been friendly, and their chiefs, Back-in-Sight and Bear Hat, as well as several of their people, spoke Blackfoot. So Nätahki, Schultz, and little Hart were welcome visitors in the Kutenai camp. Schultz was surprised when at day's end Back-in-Sight called his people to evening prayers by ringing a little bell. When they had all gathered around him, he led them in prayers which the Black robes (Jesuit missionaries) had taught them.

One evening a young Kutenai invited Schultz to go with him to hunt bighorn. The latter gladly accepted, and the following morning they rode up a trail to an area beneath the cliffs of Red Eagle Mountain. On signal from the Kutenai, they dismounted and moved cautiously to a point overlooking a draw of mud and a trickle of water where three bighorn rams were drinking and eating some of the mud. Schultz killed one of them and the Indian killed the other two. Schultz arrived home that night loaded with red meat and excited about the events of the day. When he told Nätahki of the fine stream that led to the attractive lake at the very foot of the mountain she had so recently asked him to name Red Eagle, she promptly insisted that both the lake and the stream should bear Red Eagle's name. To this Schultz agreed, and the names are still to be found on the topographic maps of Glacier National Park.

The Kutenai party remained encamped near the Schultzes on Upper St. Mary Lake for about two weeks then moved north for more hunting and trapping, finally to return to their reservation in British Columbia by way of one of the Canadian passes across the Continental Divide. The Schultzes stayed on a few more days before carefully caching their boat and returning during the month of August to home base on the Two Medicine.

After Schultz completed a guiding assignment in September, 1888,[1] he decided to build a cabin at his favorite campground near the foot of Upper St. Mary Lake. This was to be in association with his friend Jack Monroe, who had collaborated in the handling of the Grinnell-Gould expedition of 1887 and was a white man with competence as a guide. After several trips to Browning to assemble the necessary hardware and furnishings, they and their wives, with two wagons piled high with supplies and equipment, headed for the building site.

When they arrived at Upper St. Mary Lake, Schultz and Monroe got busy felling aspen logs, and in surprisingly short order the cabin was completed and the wives took over the work of moving in. This was the first cabin at the lakes, and Nätahki was particularly pleased with the large, brand-new cookstove and a fine set of pots and pans. Their first meal in the new cabin was quite an event for all four of them.

In November, to Schultz's delight, they were joined by their friends Tail-Feathers-Coming-Over-the-Hill and Ancient Man, who came to visit and to do some hunting with Schultz and Monroe. Every morning after getting out of bed the two Pikunis would run down to the river, throw off their blankets, and plunge into the icy waters. They insisted that this was good for them as well as being their custom, hardening them so that they were able to stand the cold when they had to butcher the game they had killed, even in the coldest weather. When Monroe undertook to do the same, he nearly perished with pneumonia.

When the winter of 1887–88 had really set in, the lakes

---

[1] This was the expedition of the four businessmen from Troy, New York. See Chapter 15.

were thickly frozen over and covered with snow. Schultz and
Monroe built a sled and fashioned a harness so that it could
be drawn by one of the horses. This made it easier to trans-
port their day-to-day meat supply. With one of the horses
hitched to the sled, they would ride up the lake to the foot of
Goat Mountain or Red Eagle Mountain, where, during the
winter, the bighorn ranged lower than they did in summer.
After shooting all the animals they needed, the pair would
load them on the sled and in short order be back at the cabin
before the kill was so frozen as to make skinning and butchering difficult.

It was during this winter that Schultz and Tail-Feathers-
Coming-Over-the-Hill killed a bighorn ram on Red Eagle
Mountain. When they finished butchering it, they built a
small fire and sat down beside it for a leisurely smoke. As
they took turns puffing on Tail-Feathers' long-stemmed
black stone pipe, Schultz noticed that his friend was gazing
constantly at a particularly beautiful mountain across the
lake. Finally he commented to Schultz:

> How very high it is, its summit far up into the blue. Of all the
> mountains that I have ever seen I think it is the most beau-
> tiful. Were I younger and were it summertime, how I would
> like to climb up and lie on its summit, and fast, and pray Sun
> for a vision.

Schultz, too, had admired that particular peak and had considered it the finest in the area. Often he had tried to think
of a name for it that would be fitting, and now Tail-Feathers
had given him an idea. The mountain should have some relationship to Sun, the most important of all the gods of the
Blackfoot tribe. After pondering the matter for a while,
Schultz turned to Tail-Feathers and said: "We will name that
mountain. Let us call it Going-to-the-Sun Mountain." With
which suggestion Tail-Feathers was in complete accord, saying, "Good. That is a powerful, sacred name; it could not
have a better one!"

In the years that followed, Schultz was amused and sometimes annoyed at the tales—and even a long poem—written

about Going-to-the-Sun Mountain in which the authors solemnly stated that the name was based on an ancient Blackfoot legend. So fitting was the name, however, that to this day Going-to-the-Sun Mountain is one of the best-remembered and most-photographed peaks within the boundaries of what is now Glacier National Park.

CHAPTER 17

Grinnell Returns to Map the Region

Ｉｎ the fall of 1891, George Bird Grinnell returned to Montana, having advised Schultz earlier that his party would include two young friends. One of these was William H. Seward III, grandson of President Lincoln's secretary of state; the other was Henry L. Stimson, later to serve as secretary of war under the two Roosevelts and as secretary of state under Herbert Hoover.[1] Grinnell had preceded his friends to Montana by a day or two, since they were coming west via the unfinished Great Northern Railway, traveling the last one hundred fifty miles by work train. For the trip, Schultz had arranged to have assisting him his friend William Jackson, and it is interesting to read the description of them in Stimson's memoirs, written many years later:

> One of them was a famous character. He was a quarter-breed Blackfoot Indian known as Billy Jackson who had served as one of Custer's scouts in the battle of the Little Bighorn far away to the south of us, and his tale of how he escaped with his life from that disaster was a thrilling story when told over our campfire. The other was a white man by the name of Schultz who had married into the Blackfoot tribe. Neither of them was a mountaineer, and their experience in these mountains had been very slight.[2]

[1] The visit of Grinnell, Stimson, and Seward, as shown by Stimson's book entitled *My Vacations*, 43, and Grinnell's article entitled "The Crown of the Continent," *Century*, September, 1901, 664, took place in 1891, despite the report by Schultz in *Blackfeet and Buffalo* that the date was 1888.
[2] *My Vacations*, 46.

According to Schultz, he and Jackson met the Grinnell party at the Blackfoot agency on September 3 and arrived at the Schultz-Monroe cabin on Upper St. Mary Lake on the fifth. As Stimson has told it:[3]

> From the railway we traveled by horse and wagon northward over the prairie some sixty or seventy miles to the Upper St. Mary's Lake—a beautiful sheet of water some twelve miles in length, stretching from the edge of the prairie into a fringe of steeply rising mountains.[4]

No detailed report of the trip was published in *Forest and Stream*, but it did form the basis for an article, entitled "The Crown of the Continent," which appeared in *Century* magazine in 1901. It was written by Grinnell immediately after he returned from the trip, but he wrote afterward: "They wanted it to grow and held it for nine years before printing." The principal purpose of the trip was to explore the Upper St. Mary Valley.

On the morning after their arrival at Upper St. Mary Lake, all five men were soon in the saddle and on the trail, together with their pack animals. They followed an ancient game trail on the west side of the lake, finding travel difficult. When they sat around the fire after the evening meal was over, Grinnell took a good look at Jackson and said he was sure they had met somewhere before. Jackson smiled and reminded him that they had both been with Custer on the Black Hills Expedition of 1874, for which Grinnell had served as a naturalist and Jackson as one of the Indian scouts. This led Schultz to suggest that Jackson tell them of his experiences with Custer during the tragic campaign of 1876 and how he managed to escape at the Battle of the Little Bighorn. Grinnell listened with great interest to this first-hand account.

For three days the trail led through exceedingly rugged terrain, including one area where, years before, an ava-

---

[3] *Idem*, 46–47.
[4] It is probable that after Grinnell came by rail to Helena and by stage to the agency, they traveled by horse and wagon to meet their friends at the railroad.

William Jackson (far right) and Hugh Monroe. Courtesy Montana Historical Society.

lanche had swept down the valley, leveling huge trees like jackstraws. Another all-day struggle brought the party to a spot within a few hundred yards of the foot of the glacier they were seeking. The next morning it took a scramble of only an hour or so to reach the foot. They had no trouble finding a route to the top of the glacier and spent most of the day exploring it. They estimated its length to be three miles and its widest part a mile and a half. They calculated the depth of the ice to be several hundred feet. In the 1920's, it was estimated to cover five square miles.

That evening around the lodge fire there was considerable discussion of what the glacier should be named. Jackson suggested Pikuni Glacier, but Schultz thought its name ought to be Kutenai. Grinnell was of the opinion that it should be

Blackfoot Glacier, since that would honor all three tribes of the Blackfoot Nation: the Pikunis, the Kainahs (Bloods), and the Siksikas, or Blackfeet proper. This name met with immediate approval.

The next morning, at Schultz's suggestion, Grinnell, Jackson, and Schultz set forth to locate the summit of the range. Two or three miles southwest of their camp they noted on the skyline a large V-shaped notch which looked promising. As they approached it they found unmistakable evidence of an old trail with cuttings on many of the stunted trees to mark it; the trail led directly to the notch. As they passed through it, a sweeping view of the west side of the range lay spread before them. When they returned to camp, Grinnell pointed out the notch's similarity to the rear sight of a rifle and noted the tip of a mountain that could be seen through it as if it were the front sight of a rifle. When he called attention to this, there was general agreement on the names Gunsight Pass and Mount Gunsight, and it followed that the lake on which they were camping should be Gunsight Lake—all names that they still bear.

Grinnell says they spent several days at this camp before returning to the outlet of the upper lake.[5] There they spent a few more days hunting on Flat Top and Singleshot and enjoying the fine fishing available virtually at their front door.[6]

[5] Although Schultz wrote in *Blackfeet and Buffalo*, 123, that Grinnell had remarked to him in 1885 how fine it would be if the St. Mary country could someday be set aside as a national park, Grinnell himself did not mention the subject in any of his writing until he had the following to say in his diary in September, 1891: "How would it do to start a movement to buy the St. Mary's country, say 30×30 miles, from the Piegan Indians at a fair valuation and turn it into a national monument or park. The Great Northern R.R. would probably back the scheme and T. C. Power would do all he could for it in the Senate . . . and certainly all the Indians would like it. This is worth thinking of and writing about."

He did write about it later that year in an article entitled "The Crown of the Continent," which, although not published by *Century* until September, 1901, has been generally regarded as the opening gun in the campaign for national parkhood for the region.

[6] It was around this time that the usually imperturbable Grinnell became somewhat irked with Stimson, the latter apparently not yet having acquired the tact and diplomacy that were one day to make him secretary of state. In his diary for September 16, 1891, Grinnell wrote that he didn't care for some remarks that Stimson had made, adding that "on the strength of his few weeks in Colorado, he thinks he 'knows it all.'"

In his memoirs, Stimson concluded the story of his visit to the St. Mary country as follows:

After a month with the party, my vacation ended and I'returned to New York and the bar, Seward and Grinnell remaining for several weeks' further exploration. Billy Jackson escorted me to the railroad with my packs lashed behind our saddles.[7]

With the departure of Stimson, Grinnell was able to undertake what he referred to as his work. This comprised two activities, the first of which was to visit or revisit the areas shown on his 1885–92 "Map of the St. Mary's Lake Region" and complete the mapping as accurately as possible. In the course of a month's time, the explorers climbed, among other peaks, Mount Grinnell and Mount Allen; explored Cataract and Boulder creeks and adjacent areas; and gathered the data that would enable them to draw a reasonably accurate map of the region, showing practically all the names that are to be found on present-day maps.

Grinnell's second objective was to complete the research necessary to complete the manuscript of the book he was preparing for publication the following year; it was to be called *Blackfoot Lodge Tales*.[8] The character and contents of the book were such that the materials for it were procurable only through research in Montana, and the time factor was such as to make the visit of 1891 the last opportunity to complete that research; it would afford the final chance to huddle with Schultz and, through him, to consult members of the tribe who might contribute legends or other useful material.

Actually, odds and ends of what he needed were still being clarified by correspondence between Grinnell and Schultz as late as June 26, 1892. These had to do with the names of the Pikuni gentes and the positioning of their lodges in the great circle of the tribal encampment. In all such matters, Grinnell had to rely on Schultz, who not only authorized the

---

[7]Stimson and Jackson headed for the railroad on September 25, 1891, taking the party's outgoing letters with them.
[8]It was published by Charles Scribner's Sons in 1892.

use of his own material but committed himself to supplying such further information as might be needed.[9]

The trip was one during which many names were conferred. Some topographical features were named for members of the party, such as Seward Ridge for William H. Seward III, Mount Stimson for Henry L. Stimson (this being the peak now known as Mount Logan), and Mount Jackson for Billy Jackson the guide. The naming of Blackfoot Glacier, at that time the largest in the Rockies south of the Canadian border, has been described; the mountain on the northern slope of which the glacier lay was named Blackfoot Mountain. The naming of Gunsight Pass, Mountain, and Lake also has been described. Fusillade was the name laughingly suggested by Grinnell for a mountain to which Stimson and Seward went to hunt goats. The rest of the party heard twenty-seven shots in quick succession, but the young hunters returned with the head and hide of but one small goat.

---

[9] *Blackfoot Lodge Tales*, xv–xvi. For a detailed discussion of Schultz's role in the writing of *Blackfoot Lodge Tales*, see Chapter 25.

CHAPTER 18

Emerson Hough Visits the Future Park

EMERSON HOUGH was really not the usual client so far as James Willard Schultz and Schultz's experience as a mountain guide were concerned. Hough was the only person Schultz ever took through any part of the future park on a winter excursion, and he was the only one to visit the region twice in the same year. Moreover, he was the only client Schultz ever guided west of the Continental Divide, an area with which Schultz had no familiarity.

Hough's visits took place in 1902, one in February, the other in autumn, suggesting a purpose not confined to a mere desire to explore, to hunt game, or to vacation. Hough was a well-known writer on outdoor topics, but he was also the western representative of George Bird Grinnell and *Forest and Stream* magazine. Grinnell's article entitled "The Crown of the Continent" had finally been published by *Century* magazine in September, 1901, and Grinnell felt that the time had come when public interest in national-park status for the region could be given impetus with the publication of articles by such a popular writer as Emerson Hough.

Unaware of these developments, Schultz was taken by surprise when he received a letter from Grinnell asking him to make arrangements for a visit by Hough in the month of February, 1902, stating that the latter would bring with him everything necessary for a party of three men to spend several weeks, if need be, in high mountain country during the winter season. Since no mention had been made of horses, Schultz concluded that the terrain to be explored would be too rugged to make horse travel feasible.

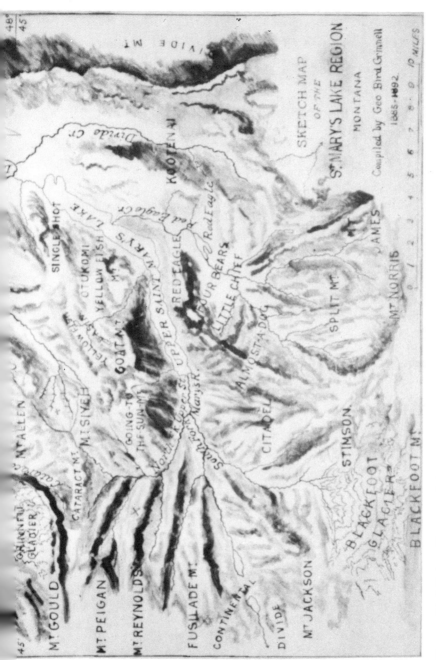

George Bird Grinnell's map of the St. Mary Lakes region, prepared in 1885–92. Courtesy Glacier National Park Headquarters, West Glacier.

Schultz confirmed all arrangements for the trek and reported that the third member of the party would be William Jackson. Schultz, Jackson, and Joe Kipp were at Blackfoot Station when Hough arrived; it was snowing hard, and an icy wind cut like a knife as he stepped from the train. Kipp had a wagon waiting to take Hough's rather considerable baggage to his house for the night. By morning the storm showed some signs of abating, and with Kipp's help they unpacked the equipment Hough had brought with him. Schultz was by now thoroughly experienced in the outfitting of summer parties but was curious to see what equipment Hough had brought with him for a midwinter excursion into the high Rockies. Hough showed them three large, substantial packsacks, each equipped with a tumpline, and explained that everything else would have to be packed into them. Each member of the party, he estimated, would be carrying about fifty pounds.

Spread out on the floor, ready for packing, were a small muslin tent with a stovepipe hole ringed with tin; a sheet-iron stove that folded flat; several lengths of stovepipe; a large coffeepot; two frying pans; tin dishes and cups; knives, forks, and spoons; a canvas ground sheet; an ax; a shovel; three sleeping bags; and a good supply of the usual staple foods. Besides these, each man would have various personal articles that would have to be stowed away in his personal pack and would be equipped with a pair of snowshoes suited to mountain work. Hough carried a rifle upon which they would depend largely for their meat. Schultz and Jackson marveled at the speed and skill with which Hough assembled and packed all their equipment into three packs of equal weight and nice balance for comfortable carrying.

When all was ready, Kipp drove them back to Blackfoot Station. In a few minutes a freight train pulled in and stopped. When the crew, who knew Schultz and Jackson, learned that they were headed for Nyack, many miles west of the Continental Divide and far down the valley of the Middle Fork of the Flathead River, they welcomed the party to come along in the caboose. By the time the train reached Nyack, it had begun to snow in earnest, but the section boss and his wife welcomed them in for the night, providing them with supper and a substantial breakfast. It was bitterly cold when they stepped outside shortly after dawn the next morning. They put on their snowshoes, shouldered their packs, waved good-bye to their hosts, and started upgrade along Nyack Creek. The snow was four or five feet deep but hard packed, and it was not snowing. They were well clothed, and they found it pleasant going.

After a hike of roughly ten miles they found a suitable place to camp near the foot of massive Loneman Mountain. Soon their tent was set up and made comfortable, even though the temperature outside the tent had dropped to thirty degrees below zero. They had a hearty supper consisting of three ruffed grouse shot by Hough, pancakes, syrup, and coffee. A candle was lighted, and, thoroughly relaxed after their climb, they lay back on their bed of boughs to yarn and smoke.

Hough was anxious to secure for mounting an excellent specimen of a full-grown male Rocky Mountain goat, so the next morning they put on their snowshoes and started up the base of Loneman Mountain. They had gone only a short distance when they saw a small band of several females, yearlings, and kids browsing along the foot of a high cliff. Hough admired them through his powerful field glass and was amazed at the agility with which even the smallest of them ran, climbed, and leaped from ledge to ledge. Farther up the valley of Nyack Creek they discovered another band of goats, none of them mature males, so they trudged reluctantly back to camp. As they moved quietly along over the powder snow, they were startled when, with a great whirr, a band of Franklin grouse flew up before them and roosted in the lower limbs of a tree. Fashioning a noose from a piece of cord at the end of a long stick, they had no trouble in taking six of them for that night's supper. Many old-timers considered the Franklin grouse even more stupid than the ruffed grouse and called them "fool hens."

From that time on, the weather deteriorated steadily so that they were confined to their tent nearly all the time. Fortunately, there was plenty of good firewood close at hand

and they had no trouble getting meat. Day after day, long
dark night after long dark night—for their small supply of
candles was exhausted after the first two or three nights—
they lay in their sleeping bags and talked. By now Schultz's
usual reticence had been dissipated by the enforced inti-
macy of their life together in Hough's small tent, now virtually buried in the snow.

During the few brief lulls in the almost constant blizzard,
they managed to venture out along the base of Loneman
Mountain, but even with their snowshoes on it was hard
going and they failed to see a single male mountain goat. On
the eighth day of their sojourn they made another try. This
time they found that the wind had cleared some of the snow
from a ridge a short distance from their camp, and luck was
with them. Within easy rifle range they sighted six fine specimens, any of which would have met Hough's specifications.
He made his selection, aimed carefully, fired, and at long
last had his specimen. They skinned it carefully and back at
camp prepared the skin for shipment as best they could.

By morning there was still no sign that the weather might
be changing. Realizing that the depth of the snow made exploration of that part of the mountains impossible, they
struck the tent, packed their gear, and broke camp. Shoul-
dering their packs and the goatskin, they started down toward the railroad. At Nyack the weather began to clear rapidly, and since no trains were scheduled they decided to
walk along the right-of-way up the Middle Fork of the Flathead River. Soon there was hardly a cloud in the sky and the
mountains were regal in their robes of fresh snow. Time and
again they paused in elation over the spectacle that had been
denied them for so long. Again Hough was astonished at
Schultz's knowledge, even about mountain country he had
never visited. It was a long tramp—seventeen miles or so—
from Nyack to the small settlement of Essex, where they
boarded a train which took them back to Blackfoot Station.
As soon as possible Hough was on the train back to Chicago
and at work on his article or articles for *Forest and Stream*
based on his recent experiences. Several readers later wrote
him that his account of the bands of Rocky Mountain goats

climbing the cliffs of Loneman Mountain convinced them that the habitat of such remarkable animals should indeed, as Hough suggested, be preserved by making it a part of the proposed new national park.

Schultz was not surprised when, during the summer, he got word from Hough that the latter was planning to come west again. This time he wanted to see some of the country on the east side of the mountains, about which both Grinnell and Schultz were so enthusiastic. When Hough arrived in September, he had his wife and Elwood ("Billy") Hofer with him. Hofer, an old-time hunter, had served as the principal guide and outfitter for Yellowstone National Park. He and Hough had become close friends during the many trips Hough made there over the years.

Since Jack Monroe and William Jackson were busy conducting Gifford Pinchot and Henry L. Stimson on a hunting trip, Schultz persuaded an old rancher friend of his, Joe Carney, to help arrange a camping trip for Hough. In leisurely fashion they camped at the Two Medicine Lakes, in the Cut Bank Valley, and at the St. Mary Lakes and finally traveled up the Swiftcurrent Valley to Grinnell Glacier. Afterward they visited Schultz's ranch, were charmed by Nätahki, and enjoyed excellent fishing at various places.

CHAPTER 19

Floating on the Missouri

ONE of the highlights of Schultz's life with Nätahki was their trip down the Upper Missouri in the autumn of 1901. They were still living in the Two Medicine River ranch house which, with the aid of friends, they had built in the latter part of the 1880's. There Nätahki's mother came to live with them for a time, and there they brought up their son, Hart. It had been the scene of much happiness and contentment for Schultz and Nätahki as well as the place where they entertained their many friends and, occasionally, distinguished visitors from Schultz's hunting parties.

There were many opportunities for recreation, including vacations in the nearby St. Mary country and camping trips on the Montana plains with friends or relatives. The idea of a float trip down the Missouri was one that particularly appealed to Schultz because of the impression that parts of the river had made on him when he came to Montana by boat in 1877. In *My Life as an Indian* he mentioned that in addition to the beautiful groves and rolling green slopes of the lower river he had seen "the weird 'bad lands' above them, and the picturesque cliffs and walls of sandstone, carved into all sorts of fantastic shapes and form by wind and storm, which are the features of the upper portion of the navigable part of the river."[1]

Subsequent to his maiden voyage up the Missouri from St. Louis to Fort Benton, Schultz had occasion to make a number of trips through the picturesque sections of the river, usually with Joe Kipp. When they established their last winter

[1] *My Life as an Indian*, 4.

trading post at Carroll in the autumn of 1881, they went
from Fort Benton on the *Red Cloud* and returned on the
Helena the following spring. Schultz had also made a trip on
the *Helena* from Fort Benton to Bismarck, Dakota Territory,
in 1880,[2] all of which meant he had gained a certain familiarity with and appreciation of the scenic features of the
Missouri River landscape as time went on.

Apart from the occasions when Schultz had seen the
Upper Missouri by steamboat, he had also seen many of the
land routes between Fort Benton and the trading posts on
the banks of the river. This was true, of course, of the journey to the post at the mouth of the Judith in 1879 and the
return in 1880. Occasionally there were trips to be made to a
branch of the post at Carroll, and in an emergency during
the winter of 1881–82 Schultz made a special trip up the
frozen river to the mouth of the Judith to replenish the supply of blankets at Carroll.

No longer is it possible for anyone to duplicate the trip the
Schultzes took in 1901, for time and the river are no longer
the same. In the 1930's the federal government, for purposes of flood control and power generation, constructed
Fort Peck Dam and Reservoir, thereby making it impossible
to retrace on a free-flowing river more than half the trip
taken by Schultz and Nätahki only thirty years earlier. The
portion of the river between Fort Benton and Fort Peck
Reservoir is now the last unspoiled section of the Upper
Missouri.

Although few members of the public may be aware of the
fact, the portion of the Upper Missouri that courses through
central Montana is incredibly beautiful. Its best-known section is the white-cliffs region between Fort Benton and the
Judith River where there are seemingly sculptured formations of white limestone and towering buttresses of dark vol-
canic intrusions. As was written in 1833 by Prince Maxi-
milian of Wied:

> Here on both sides of the river, the most strange forms are
> seen, and you may fancy that you see colonnades, small
> round pillars with large globes or a flat slab at the top, little

[2] James Willard Schultz, *Floating on the Missouri*, 93.

towers, pulpits, organs with their pipes, old ruins, fortresses,
castles, churches with pointed towers, etc., etc., almost every
mountain bearing on its summit some similar structure.[3]

The history of the Missouri River may be said to reflect the
early history of Montana. It provided the greater part of the
route of travel for Lewis and Clark on their 1804–1806 expedition to the Pacific coast. Both men left us detailed descrip-
tions of the Upper Missouri, its flora, and its fauna. Many of
the natural features along their route were named by them,
and they were impressed by the beauty of the river.

The explorers were followed by fur traders and trappers,
all of whom arrived via the Missouri and its tributary the
Yellowstone. They in turn were succeeded by a horde of
gold seekers bound for the placer diggings of Virginia City
and Last Chance Gulch. Their means of transportation was
the steamboat until it was made obsolete by the coming of
the railroads. For nearly three-quarters of a century, the
Missouri was the lifeline of Montana.[4]

When Schultz and Nätahki made their 1901 cruise from
Fort Benton to the mouth of the Milk River, they did so in
what he described as "a plain, sharp-bowed, flat-bottomed
skiff, some nineteen feet long and of five-feet beam. Not a
thing of beauty, but staunch, light of draft, and serviceable.
It held our tent, stove, bedding, clothing, guns and ammunition, provisions for a month or so."[5] They named the
boat *Good Shield*, which was the English version of the name
of his Pikuni wife.

The trip began in November and ended more than two
weeks later as the river began filling with cakes of ice. They
traveled at a pace to suit their convenience, covering 40
miles on some days, the total mileage being approximately
275. They camped along the route, availing themselves of
islands wherever possible and subsisting to a substantial extent on the game which he was able to shoot along the river,
mostly deer. On at least two occasions they encountered old

---

[3] See the Introduction to *Floating on the Missouri*, xiii.
[4] *Idem*, xiv.
[5] *Floating on the Missouri*, 3.

friends who invited them to tarry with them, but these kind invitations had to be declined because of the imminence of winter and the need to get to a railroad point before the weather closed in. When they finally reached the mouth of the Milk River, they were within sight and sound of the trains of the Great Northern. The following morning they hired an Indian lad to take them and their things to the railway station and gave the *Good Shield* to him in exchange for his services.

Upon returning home, Schultz prepared a story of their trip down the Missouri in twelve chapters which were published serially in *Forest and Stream*, beginning on February 15, 1902, and ending on May 24, 1902.[6] More than seventy-five years later, it appeared in book form, capably edited by Eugene Lee Silliman and published by the University of Oklahoma Press.

The story that appears in *Floating on the Missouri* is an interesting and romantic tale set forth in the fashion which Schultz thought would have the most appeal to his potential readers. He was never one to let facts stand in the way of a good story, a characteristic illustrated by what actually happened in this case. Schultz and Nätahki did make the trip in question in November, 1901, but not alone. They were serving as guide and cook, respectively, for a party of three men, one of them Sheriff H. E. Benner of Cascade County; Benner's companions were William Silverman and Sam Wilbur. All three of them were from Great Falls. Moreover, two boats were used, and traveling in the Schultz craft was their son, Hart, then 19.

A diary was kept by Sheriff Benner;[7] at least he started to keep a daily diary. Although he missed a few days, he stuck to it long enough to leave a fairly complete record of the trip. Their eighteen-day outing began on November 10 at Fort Benton and ended on the twenty-eighth. The diary contained no entries for the last four days, although these were the busiest, for this is when they did most of their

[6] Introduction to *Floating on the Missouri*, xv.
[7] From the *Rocky Mountain American* of September 9, 1937.

hunting and killed most of the eighteen deer they bagged on the trip.

Part of their progress was made by rowing and part of it by use of a square canvas sail for each boat. The diary contains frequent references to Schultz, as well as to his wife and son, including their camp at the old trading post of Carroll, where Schultz had once worked for Joe Kipp. According to Benner, Schultz told him that he once saw six thousand Indians there, all of them drunk at the time.

Of all the trips taken together by Schultz and Nätahki, whether by rail, to the mountains, or by water, they enjoyed the river trip most. The shifting, boiling flood, the weird cliffs, the beautifully timbered, silent valley—all held a peculiar fascination for them that was possessed by no place in the mountains.[8]

For Nätahki the river trip was the beginning of the end, for it was during this trip that she began to complain of sharp pain in the tips of the fingers of her right hand. Schultz told her that it was nothing but rheumatism and would soon pass away.[9] The pain grew worse, unfortunately. Somehow, they managed to make the last thirty-eight miles to the mouth of the Milk River in a single day. There, at Malta, they were within sight and sound of the trains of the Great Northern Railway. As was mentioned earlier, the following morning Schultz found an Indian lad who, in return for the gift of the *Good Shield*, with which they reluctantly parted, took them and their equipment to the railroad depot.[10]

They took the train to Great Falls and went to the hospital, which she had visited earlier. After a careful examination the doctor confirmed Schultz's worst fears by telling him that Nätahki might live only a year at best. She lived eleven months. The hospital staff and the doctor were diligent in their care and did everything medical science of that day could do for her. Schultz sat by her bedside almost constantly until death put an end to her suffering.[11]

[8] *My Life as an Indian*, 425.
[9] *Idem*, 426.
[10] *Idem*.
[11] *Idem*.

As word of Nätahki's death spread among the Blackfoot people, her relatives and friends, as well as Schultz's many friends, both Indian and white, arrived at the ranch to express their sympathy. Their lodges and tents encircled the ranch house, and the cries of mourning filled the air far into the night. The women of Nätahki's family prepared her body for burial. Dressed in her finest buckskin clothes, which, despite her crippled hand, she had embroidered so beautifully, she was carried to and buried on the hillside where lay her mother, *Patahki*; her beloved uncle, Red Eagle; and other members of her family.

The end of their life together was also the end of the last chapter of Schultz's book *My Life as an Indian*:

... and then one day my faithful, loving, tender-hearted woman passed away, and left me. By day I think of her, at night I dream of her. I wish I had that faith which teaches us that we will meet on the other shore. But all looks very dark to me.

CHAPTER 20

The Pulitzer Poaching Story

IN the annals of the Montana Department of Game and Fish, there has never been another case quite as sensational as that of *State of Montana* v. *Pulitzer*. The prominence of its principals, the period for which it was pending, and the persistence of its prosecution combined to make it the most notorious in Montana history. Moreover, the place where the poaching was primarily perpetrated was on future park property, in the heart of what was soon to become Glacier National Park.

The matter in question, commonly known as the Pulitzer case, attracted wide attention throughout the country because of the identity of the principal defendant, Ralph Pulitzer, a resident of New York City. Ralph was the son of Joseph Pulitzer, wealthy owner and editor of the *New York World*, better known today as the man who established the prestigious prizes in journalism, literature, music, etc. A secondary offender was James Willard Schultz, mountain guide and writer, later to become widely known as the author of more than thirty books dealing with the American Indian.

The various offenses took place in 1903. The first infraction of Montana game laws occurred in the summer of 1903 near Lake St. Mary and was followed within the next thirty days by two others elsewhere in the state. However, the efforts to gather evidence, as well as to apprehend the offenders and bring them to bar, required another eighteen months. Pulitzer was ultimately obliged to face trial and to plead guilty, but Schultz had fled the jurisdiction after the first charges against him were dismissed, and he was never reapprehended.

The story comes to us from two sources, leaving its authenticity beyond question. It first appeared in the pages of the *Second Biennial Report of the State Game and Fish Warden of Montana*, W. F. Scott.[1] It represented a complete report of the affair from the state's view but in what, of course, was a little-read publication. The obverse of the coin came to light more than thirty years later when Schultz chose to relate the details of the story from the standpoint of the defendants.[2] According to Schultz, in the month of June, 1903,[3] Ralph Pulitzer of the *New York World* cabled him from Japan to inquire whether he would take Pulitzer for an outing in the St. Mary Lakes country of northwest Montana. Schultz's beloved wife had just died and he was very depressed, but he cabled Pulitzer to come on and Pulitzer did so. It should be mentioned that for nearly twenty years Schultz had been taking parties for trips to the St. Mary and Swiftcurrent valleys, including such people as George Bird Grinnell, Henry L. Stimson, and Emerson Hough. He had become a licensed guide and was well equipped to provide such individuals with whatever they wished in the way of visits to various parts of the eastern side of the future Glacier National Park.

When Pulitzer arrived at Blackfoot Station with his friend Lieutenant Crimmins and his black valet, Alfred, Schultz was awaiting them with team and wagon, camp outfit, provisions, saddle horses, guides Monroe Arnoux and Dan Purdy, and cooks Nora and Wyola Aspling. They traveled to the foot of Lower Lake St. Mary and after spending a few days there moved to the upper lake and camped on its west side just above the narrows, fishing occasionally but doing no hunting.

One day Pulitzer expressed a desire to shoot a bighorn sheep and asked Schultz to take him out hunting for one. Although it was closed season for bighorns, Schultz agreed to do so. His rationalization for such action was threefold: the party was in great need of meat; the killing of one ram

---

[1] For 1903–1904.
[2] *Great Falls Tribune*, November 15 and 22, 1936.
[3] Actually it would have to have been in May, since Pulitzer arrived in Montana on June 2.

would never be known, he thought; and because of his wife's death he was "reckless and did not care what he did." So early on the morning of June 8, 1903, he and Pulitzer crossed the lake in Schultz's mackinaw boat and headed for Kutenai Lick above Red Eagle Lake. As they peered over its rim, they saw seven old bighorn rams not a hundred yards away. Pulitzer aimed his Winchester at one of them, fired, and kept on shooting in spite of Schultz's protest until he had killed four of the seven. After taking pictures of them, including one snapped by Schultz showing Pulitzer behind all four rams, they got three of the heads and part of the meat back to camp with the aid of Purdy and Arnoux during the next twenty-four hours. Shortly thereafter, Pulitzer sent Purdy with the three heads to Fort Macleod, there to send them by Canadian Pacific express to his New York address.

During the course of the stay at St. Mary Lakes, Schultz told of a houseboat trip he had taken down the Missouri from Fort Benton to the mouth of the Milk River. Pulitzer was so impressed with his description of the scenery and plenitude of game along the river that he asked Schultz to make arrangements for construction of a cabin boat so that the trip could be duplicated. After concluding the St. Mary outing, Schultz and Pulitzer hastened to Fort Benton, accompanied by Monroe Arnoux and Pulitzer's valet, only to find that the boat would not be ready for a few days.

Pulitzer complained of the monotony at Fort Benton, so they repaired to Great Falls, which, Schultz told him, was "a very lively little city." Over Schultz's protests, Pulitzer left the film showing the bighorns at an upstairs print shop and, with Schultz along, proceeded to "have a hilarious time," the evening ending "with a gay foursome at dinner in a restaurant near the Silver Dollar Saloon." When word was received from Arnoux that the boat had been completed, they returned to Fort Benton and took off about July 2. A black cook had been secured from Helena for the trip.

Pulitzer was enchanted with the scenery and took many photographs as they drifted down the river. At the mouth of Armell Creek, they stopped to have dinner with old friends of Schultz, Joe Carney and his wife. Next day, Joe took Ralph into the nearby countryside, where the latter shot a "big, fat buck," the head of which Joe agreed to prepare for mounting and ship to New York. Some of the meat was stored in the boat's icebox.

When they reached the mouth of the Musselshell River, they were again out of meat and went ashore to forage. Pulitzer shot a "fat, blacktail buck," parts of which were put in the icebox, and they continued on to Round Butte, where a man named Darnell lived with his daughters. During the night at this stop, Schultz became "quite sick" and remained in his bunk. Pulitzer, Arnoux, and Darnell arose early the next day and rode off to hunt. About 10 o'clock that morning, Schultz heard someone jump down onto the boat's afterdeck and, peering out from his bunk, recognized Game Warden Green of Glasgow, Montana.

Green asked for Pulitzer, saying he had come to arrest Pulitzer and Schultz for what they had done at St. Mary Lakes and adding that Jack Hall, the game warden at Great Falls, had begun to investigate after seeing prints of the bighorns and Pulitzer as they were drying on the windowsill of the print shop. Green then said: "You've got the heads right here with you. I'll take 'em for evidence, and you two along with 'em." He proceeded to search the boat but found nothing of interest, not even the meat in the icebox, since Schultz had signaled the cook to get rid of it and the latter had thrown it overboard. Frustrated in his search, Green decided it was no use to wait for Pulitzer's return and departed. The trip was concluded a few days later at the mouth of the Milk River; Pulitzer and his valet headed for San Francisco. Schultz, "lonely and grieving," took off for New York "just to kill some time."

When Schultz returned to Fort Benton a month later, he learned that Pulitzer also had returned to Montana, had been arrested for killing the bighorns, and had been put "under heavy bond" to appear at Choteau for trial. When he consulted a lawyer friend, Schultz was told that as a licensed guide he might be tried for conniving in the killing of the game and if found guilty might be sent to prison. Shortly thereafter, Schultz was arrested and taken to Choteau for trial.

When the case was called on the day of the trial, there

were many spectators. Game Warden Hall came forward and whispered with the judge, who announced, "The case is dismissed." Happily, Schultz left the courtroom, but as he was about to leave the building, his friend Wallace Taylor, the sheriff, called him into his office, and warned him to get out of town quickly because the killing of game down the Missouri was being investigated.

Schultz took the advice and the first train for Harlem, Montana, where he hid out with friends until word came that Warden Hall was in Harlem looking for him. He then resumed his flight by boarding the next train to Minot, North Dakota, where he took a room at the Parker Hotel. After only a few days there, he spied Warden Hall in the lobby and hastily left by a side entrance without waiting to get his overcoat, gloves, or overshoes. Although it was a bitterly cold day with six inches of snow on the ground, he hiked up the ice-covered Mouse River toward Canada until, toward evening, he saw a lighted farmhouse, where he asked for shelter. The elderly farmer took him in rather hesitantly but, after hearing his story, let him stay a few days. Then, at Schultz's request, the farmer took him to the first sidetrack west of Minot, where Schultz flagged down and boarded a westbound train.

The next day, an accommodating conductor let him off near Blackfoot Station, where he ran to the home of his good friend William Kipp. There he learned that Pulitzer, who had not appeared on the date set for his trial at Choteau, had forfeited his bond of one thousand five hundred dollars. Now thoroughly frightened, Schultz flagged down another westbound train and stayed aboard to Seattle, from which point he took a steamer to San Francisco. For many years thereafter, he chose to remain in California and Arizona, well out of reach of the Montana law. As he told it:

> While in San Francisco, at Grinnell's request, I began writing [under an assumed name] for *Forest and Stream* the serial that in 1907 became my first book *My Life as an Indian*. . . . Alternately I lived in Los Angeles and . . . in Arizona, 116 miles from a railroad. For a time I was literary editor of the Los Angeles Times.

Well, years passed, years of longing to go to Montana, even for a short visit with my old friends, Indian and white. In 1915 I received a letter from Mr. Louis Hill, president of the Great Northern Railway Company, inviting me to summer in Glacier Park and write what I would about it. At once I wrote to Mr. O. S. Warden, asking him to see the state game warden on my behalf. And soon came Mr. Warden's wire: "ALL IS FORGIVEN STOP COME ON."

I was a happy man when on June 15, I got off the train for the opening day of Glacier Park Hotel. And happily, that summer, I wrote *Blackfeet Tales of Glacier National Park.*

As will be shown, the Schultz version and that of the state game and fish warden dovetail fairly well, with only minor discrepancies between them and a few confusing omissions in each. For the Game and Fish Department, the case was very competently handled by Deputy Warden Jack Hall, who prepared the final report on it. That report opened by saying that Ralph Pulitzer, in company with J. W. Schultz as guide; Alfred, a black valet; and Monroe Arnoux, a half blood, had gone into the St. Mary country near the Canadian line, ostensibly to hunt bear, but that about June 8, 1903, Pulitzer had killed four mountain sheep at a game lick near Upper St. Mary Lake, taking three heads and leaving the carcasses to rot. Thereafter, according to the report, during the last days of June, Pulitzer, Schultz, and their party had come to Fort Benton, from which point they left on July 2 in a boat to float down the Missouri River, intending to land somewhere near the Dakota line. Soon after their departure from Fort Benton, the warden received word that the four dead sheep had been found and that the only party which had visited the locality when the killings could have occurred was that of Ralph Pulitzer.

A deputy was dispatched from Glasgow to intercept the Pulitzer party and search the boat for evidence. He did so and found nothing in the way of incriminating evidence, but, according to the report, the cook, on seeing the deputy, had dumped the venison he was frying and a quarter of venison into the river. When Pulitzer returned to the boat and heard of the deputy's visit, he became frightened; the party landed at Wolf Point, and Pulitzer and his valet took the first train for California. The report was silent as to where Schultz and Arnoux had gone.

When Deputy Warden Hall obtained enough evidence to warrant swearing out a complaint against Pulitzer, word was received from authorities in California that Pulitzer and his valet were on their way back to Monida, Montana, to go through Yellowstone Park. A deputy went to that point and, when Pulitzer returned from his trip through the park, took him into custody. A stop was made at Helena to permit Pulitzer to obtain counsel, and they reached Choteau on the afternoon of August 28. His counsel waived preliminary hearing, and Pulitzer was bound over to the September term of court under a one-thousand-dollar bond.

In the meantime, an affidavit had been secured from Schultz, setting forth that "Pulitzer had brought into camp while they were at St. Mary's three mountain sheep heads and that he, Schultz, had cleaned them and fixed them with arsenic." The case failed to go to trial in September, owing to Pulitzer's nonappearance, for which his attorney had presented a doctor's certificate of illness, and it had to be put over to the December calendar. At this point in the report appeared the following:

> As soon as the case was continued, Schultz left the state under suspicious circumstances and service could not be gotten on him from that time up to the present date. But his whereabouts has been known and it is also known that he has lived in luxury, with plenty of money for "wine, women and song" without doing a tap of work.

In December the case was continued to March, 1904, and several times thereafter until the people of Montana began to think that because of Pulitzer's wealth the case was not being prosecuted in good faith.

While proceedings were pending, Game and Fish Department investigators were checking Pulitzer's activities along the Missouri and had accumulated sufficient evidence to charge him with the killing of an antelope on or about July 6, 1903. He was rearrested, this time in the city of Helena, and taken to the city of Lewistown, where he and his attorney appeared on June 15, 1904, and pleaded not guilty. The case was set for trial on July 15 and continued to July 28, on which date the judge refused to grant a further continuance. Pulitzer did appear on the latter date, and when he perceived that Monroe Arnoux was in court and ready to testify, he realized that further stalling was futile. He pleaded guilty and was fined five hundred dollars.

Incidentally, according to the official report, an attempt was made to "fix" witness Arnoux and he signed an affidavit on July 27, the day before the scheduled trial, to the effect that on July 20 while he was in the city of Lewistown, where he had been staying at the state's expense awaiting the trial, he was

> approached by a certain man who introduced himself and represented that he was a deputy sheriff of Lewis and Clark County and that he asked him to go with him to Helena, which he did; that instead of going to a hotel when they arrived in Helena they went to this man's house and remained there until the 26th; that the man paid all his expenses and gave him money; that he took him to see other parties; that they tried to influence him to change the evidence he had already given in an affidavit.

When the original case was finally called at Choteau on November 28, 1904, Pulitzer pleaded guilty and was fined five hundred dollars. By way of plea bargaining on this occasion, it was agreed that in consideration of Pulitzer's guilty plea in this case, no action would be taken against him for the killing of the two deer along the Missouri on July 4, 1903.

And so ended the case (or cases) of *State of Montana* v. *Pulitzer*, with the warden finally getting his man. Despite the fact that both accounts of the case purported to be factual and reasonably complete, each contained statements or innuendos, the accuracy of which might be open to question. For example, the official report asserted that Schultz, after his disappearance "under suspicious circumstances," was known to have "lived in luxury, with plenty of money for 'wine, women and song,' without doing a tap of work."

Schultz, although fully aware of this calumny, did not choose to dignify it by denial. On the other hand, he may have raised a few eyebrows when he admitted taking a not-inexpensive trip to New York, "just to kill time," this immediately after parting with Pulitzer at Nashua or Wolf Point at a time when both must have been anxious to elude further pursuit by the warden's men.

There were several minor discrepancies between the two accounts. For example, Schultz reported that the three heads had been expressed east from Fort Macleod in Canada, while the warden's account had them checked to New York as personal baggage from Blackfoot Station. Schultz wrote that Pulitzer's one thousand five hundred dollar bond had been forfeited for failure to appear, while the official account mentioned only a thousand dollar bond and reported no forfeiture. It referred to Pulitzer's being charged with the killing of two deer on July 4, 1903, while Schultz reported the killing of only one "big, fat buck." The official report had Pulitzer discontinuing the Missouri trip because he had become frightened and leaving for the West from Wolf Point, while according to Schultz they were confident that the warden could never secure evidence of the killing of the bighorns and they ended the journey at the mouth of the Milk River with rail embarkation taking place at nearby Nashua.

The one major discrepancy between the two accounts, as well as the most puzzling, had to do with the court's unexpected dismissal of the charges against Schultz despite his admitted complicity in the killing of the game. The official report said nothing about a dismissal or concerning a promise to testify, although it did mention that an affidavit had been secured from Schultz. Schultz, on the other hand, told of the dismissal but failed to mention the affidavit or his promise to turn state's evidence. Obviously, it becomes necessary to do some reading between the lines.

The state's primary concern, of course, was to secure the conviction of Pulitzer as the principal offender. To achieve this result, officials were more than willing to offer Schultz immunity from prosecution in exchange for his affidavit and agreement to testify against Pulitzer. Moreover, even though they had the affidavit, they felt it might be wise to ensure his availability at the time of Pulitzer's trial by leaving Schultz's trial on the court's calendar until he had performed as promised.

In their zeal to construct an airtight plan for the conviction of Pulitzer, the authorities overlooked three possibilities for slips between the figurative cup and the lip, to wit: that Pulitzer might fail to appear for his trial on the same date; that this would put the state almost unavoidably in the position of having to agree to dismissal of the charges against Schultz; and that Schultz would promptly vanish from sight before a subpoena for his appearance at the postponed Pulitzer trial could be prepared and served. Unfortunately for the state's plan, all three of these contingencies occurred, and in rapid sequence. But fortunately, on the other hand, Schultz's defection to the West Coast did not destroy the case against Pulitzer, since authorities were able to obtain a similar affidavit and promise to testify from Monroe Arnoux. And fortunately also, the bold attempt to try to buy Arnoux off, undoubtedly made on behalf of Pulitzer, was unsuccessful, thereby eliminating the latter's last hope to escape conviction.

Schultz was successful in escaping punishment under Montana law, but for nearly eleven years thereafter he considered himself a fugitive. He had barely eluded the vigilance of Deputy Warden Jack Hall at Harlem, Montana, and again at Minot, North Dakota. His escape at Minot might be described as hairbreadth, and he endured both physical hardship and emotional trauma before he finally moved beyond the range of subpoena or extradition. As a sensitive man, it was an experience that was to haunt him for years to come, possibly even affecting his health and well-being.

Seemingly, Schultz never made the discovery that the Montana game and fish authorities' only interest in him had been as a means of securing a conviction of young Pulitzer, the real culprit. In any event, Schultz was delighted to receive an invitation from Louis W. Hill to spend, together with his Blackfoot friends, the summer of 1915 in Glacier

National Park at the expense of the Great Northern Railway, an invitation that gave new meaning to the dedication with which he prefaced the book he wrote that summer in the park:

TO

LOUIS WARREN HILL, ESQ.,

True Friend to my Blackfeet People,
and the One who has Done More than
Any Other Individual, or any Organization to Make the Wonders of Glacier National Park Accessible to the
American People, this Book is Dedicated by

THE AUTHOR

CHAPTER 21

The Womanless Years

WHEN James Willard Schultz sought refuge in California in the winter of 1903–1904, he was forty-four years of age; and although he would not then have believed it, he was just beginning the second half of a long and eventful life. For Schultz, it was a time when he felt that his productive years were behind him, when he decided that his future would consist principally of memories, and when he penned a now celebrated paragraph, the second in *My Life as an Indian*:

> I am in the sere and yellow leaf, dried and shrivelled, about to fall and become one with my millions of predecessors. Here I sit by the fireplace in winter, and out on the veranda when days are warm, unable to do anything except to live over in memory the stirring years I passed upon the frontier. My thoughts are always of those days; days before the accursed railroads and the hordes of settlers they brought swept us all, Indians and frontiersmen and buffalo, from the face of the earth, so to speak.

From the foregoing it is obvious that Schultz's morale was at low ebb, but it was the midpoint in his life chronologically, too. The year had brought disaster in the death of his beloved Nätahki, only to be followed by misadventure with the Montana law, which caused him to flee to a state where he had neither friend, acquaintance, nor prospects. Happily, however, whatever the year may have been as either a midpoint or low point, it was destined to be a turning point, and a major one at that, in his life. Little did he dream that here he would attain national recognition as a writer and success in a field which, for him, had been only an interesting side-line up to that time.

It was to northern California, specifically to San Francisco, that Schultz headed after his hasty departure from Montana in late 1903. The fact that San Francisco was then the literary capital of the West may well have had something to do with his choice of destination. In any event, when convinced that Montana authorities were making that state too hot for his comfort, he took a Great Northern train to Seattle, then a coastwise steamer to San Francisco. As he was about to disembark, Schultz spotted three policemen who seemed to be waiting for the ship to dock. Fearful that they might be there to arrest him, he managed, although with heart beating fast, to slip by them unnoticed. Carrying his scant luggage, he walked a short distance from the pier to a small, inexpensive hotel, where he became a guest for the next few days.

While en route by train and ship, Schultz had given considerable thought to what he might be able to do for a living in his new surroundings. He well knew that his experience as an Indian trader and Montana rancher would be unlikely to serve as qualifications for many jobs in the more sophisticated areas where he would have to seek employment. Undoubtedly it was during this westward journey that he conceived the idea of writing the story of his life among the Indians and of proposing to George Bird Grinnell its publication in serial form by *Forest and Stream*. For Schultz it represented an ambitious and thrilling concept.

Although we do not know the length of this first of his several sojourns in Northern California, we do know that it was long enough for him to do three things. One was to get Grinnell's approval for the proposed autobiography, and the second was to get it under way. The third was to look for employment, including any type of job that might be available in the areas adjacent to San Francisco.

One of the job possibilities outside San Francisco was an opening with an oil company which was looking for a publicity agent at its Chowchilla plant. Although totally inexperienced in this type of work, Schultz decided to apply in

person for the job at Chowchilla, a town situated between
Merced and Fresno in the San Joaquin Valley. Whether his
writing experience was a factor or not, Schultz was accepted
and went to work. As the story goes, one day during lunch
hour his immediate superior observed that he was writing in
a notebook and inquired what he was writing about. Schultz
told him he hoped to become a professional writer and
handed him the notebook. The man read aloud:

> Wide brown plains, distant, slender, flat-topped buttes;
> still more distant giant mountains, blue-sided, sharp-peaked,
> snow-capped; odor of sage and smoke of campfire; thunder
> of ten thousand buffalo hoofs over the hard dry ground;
> long-drawn, melancholy howl of wolves breaking the silence
> of the night, how I loved you all! [1]

This, of course, was the opening paragraph of Schultz's classic *My Life as an Indian*. His superior was much impressed
and told him that anyone who could write that well should
not have to be working around the oil fields. Despite this
complimentary statement, Schultz continued with his Chowchilla job until he had accumulated enough money to return
to San Francisco, where he intended to devote full time to
his writing project.

Schultz did return to San Francisco and began to concentrate on writing his *Forest and Stream* material. After a few
months there, however, the serial was still far from finished,
his funds were running low, and he was starting to feel
strangely unwell. In thinking about alternatives, he recalled
a letter received before leaving Montana from James Alexander, superintendent of the Pima Indian School in southern Arizona. He decided to get in touch with Alexander for
two reasons. He surmised that the dry air and open spaces
of the Arizona desert might be just what he needed from a
health standpoint. Also, he felt that it might be possible to
find some quiet and inexpensive spot on or near the Pima
Indian Reservation where he would be able to complete his

[1] In her article "Adventuresome, Amazing Apikuni," published in the
Autumn, 1960, issue of *Montana: The Magazine of Western History*, Jessica
Donaldson Schultz-Graham recounted this incident on p. 7.

Schultz excavating a refuse heap in Arizona about 1906. Courtesy Renne Library Collection.

work on the serial. Alexander replied at once, suggesting that Schultz would be welcome to come and stay with him.

This was a generous offer because the two men had never met and Schultz's reputation as an author had yet to be established. Schultz gladly accepted, and the two men took to each other at once. Conditions for continuing with the writing proved to be ideal. The two would have an early breakfast together, after which Alexander would leave for his day's work on the reservation. When he returned at the end of the day, Schultz would have the evening meal ready. During the warm months, they would sit outside and enjoy the cool of the early evening.

Schultz was pleased to find that Alexander was knowledgeable about other tribes of the region, the Papagos as well as the Pimas. Often Schultz would ride out through the surrounding countryside, where he found the Indians to be friendly and willing to converse despite the difficulties posed by the language barrier. It interested him to compare the Pimas' way of life with that of the Pikunis. During these occasional visits, Schultz saw evidences that the Pimas were beginning to abandon many of their old ways, a conclusion with which Superintendent Alexander sadly agreed.

One evening Alexander told Schultz of the Casa Grande ruins only a few miles away and explained some of the features that made them unique among the ruins of Arizona's ancient Indian villages. For example, the main building of the ruins, which was responsible for their name, meaning "great or grand house," was more than forty feet high, sixty feet long, and forty feet wide. It had been constructed of the local adobe called caliche, which contained a high percentage of lime and dried to a cementlike hardness.

Schultz expressed such great interest in the ruins that Alexander arranged for him to meet Jesse Walter Fewkes, who was planning to excavate and, to some extent, rebuild part of the ruins. When they arrived, they found that Dr. Fewkes and his small staff had their camp well established. When Alexander had finished his business with Fewkes, the latter led them through the ruins, telling of his plans for excavation and rebuilding. As Alexander and Schultz were about to leave, Fewkes turned to Schultz and said: "You seem so interested in what we plan to do here, why don't you join us and give us a hand?"

Schultz accepted the offer and found working with Fewkes a memorable experience. As the work progressed, many artifacts were found, including seashells and others etched with animal and geometric designs. In his field notes of January, 1907, Fewkes reported that Schultz had unearthed a most interesting small coiled snake nicely carved from stone. A photograph of this find is in Fewkes' Casa Grande Report in the *Twenty-eighth Annual Report of the Bureau of American Ethnology* (1905–1907).

While his stay of nearly two years in the southern Arizona desert enabled him to complete "In the Lodges of the Blackfeet," which *Forest and Stream* ran in twenty-five installments during 1906, it also came to an unexpected conclusion with a mysterious ailment that required treatment at a Phoenix hospital. While thus confined, Schultz chanced to read several issues of the *Los Angeles Times* and was impressed by the paper's sympathetic policy in reference to the Indians of Southern California. As a result he decided to betake himself to Los Angeles forthwith.

Upon his arrival there in the early part of 1907, Schultz applied for a position on the news staff of the *Times*, undoubtedly using his *Forest and Stream* accomplishments as a reference, and was given the position of literary editor. Little can be learned of his early years on this assignment because part of the paper's personnel records were destroyed in the bombing of the *Times* building on October 1, 1910, by the McNamara brothers, climaxing a lengthy labor dispute. Nor does the *Times* index disclose anything that might have been written by Schultz during his years there, because use of the byline was not customary at that time. Book reviews for that period were simply designated as "By a Times Reviewer."

Schultz had embarked upon his new job with a profound feeling that he was now entering a critical stage of his career, as well as into a wholly different type of occupation. He had had no experience as a literary editor but found the task of preparing book reviews a congenial one, even though it was his first work of this kind. Despite the fact that it left him little time to pursue his own writing, it had the advantage of being a job amid pleasant surroundings and with a steady income.

CHAPTER 22

Life with Celia

W HEN Schultz went to Los Angeles in late 1906 or early 1907, it was as a stranger without so much as a single friend or acquaintance.[1] His new surroundings brought home to him the fact that for several years he had been a widower on the move, and he began to realize that his return to a state of single blessedness was really, for him, a state of lonesomeness. Depressed by the lack of familiar associates as well as by the complexities of an unaccustomed life style, he was overwhelmed by a need for friendly companionship. Never had he been so lonely in his life. Nor did there seem to be any practicable way of dealing with the problem, particularly in the land of many strangers that was Los Angeles.

As usual, his diffidence kept him from making new friends quickly, although in his job at the *Los Angeles Times* the members of the editorial staff were pleasant and tried to be helpful. Of course, there could never be an adequate replacement for his beloved Nätahki, and at first he did not even consider the possibility. Moreover, during his adult life he had known few white women, and as he approached fifty he had little idea of how to go about meeting potential mates. Certainly it was no longer possible, as he had done in the case of Nätahki, simply to point his finger at an attractive female and say, in effect, as one might in choosing a French pastry, "I'll take that one."

---

[1] Except as otherwise indicated, the contents of this chapter are based on the personal recollections of Harry C. James and his many years of friendship with the Schultzes.

As Schultz's urge for feminine companionship grew, so also did his knowledge of some of the more unorthodox ways of seeking a mate. In desperation he decided to advertise for one, and shortly after going to Los Angeles he put an ad in a heart-and-hand magazine, presumably seeking responses from women with an interest in writing and marriage. He received answers and invited one of the women to come west and meet him. She was a young woman from Michigan to whom he took an immediate dislike, and she returned home. Soon the second woman arrived in response to the advertisement. Her name was Celia Belle Hawkins and she, too, had come from Michigan, where she had been employed as a writer for a small paper. Presumably, with her response to the ad she had provided a photograph and the usual vital statistics; if so, these were not preserved or disclosed to other than Apikuni, and there is no record of her age. At his request she came to Los Angeles, met with his approval, and they were married at once.[2]

When news of the marriage got around at the *Times*, members of the staff dropped by Schultz's desk to congratulate him. Among them was Harry Carr, who had been with the *Times* since 1900 and was one of its top writers; he invited the newlyweds to have dinner with him that evening. This was the beginning of another of Apikuni's lifelong friendships. His desperate loneliness was coming to an end.

A few weeks after her arrival in Los Angeles, Celia, manuscript in hand, began to haunt the editorial offices of the *Times*. One day, to her husband's great embarrassment, she marched into the managing editor's office and demanded a job. According to Harry Carr, there was a mighty roar and Celia came dashing out, followed by the irate editor, who yelled after her, "Keep out of here, I tell you and don't you ever dare come back in!" He then gave Schultz a piece of his mind. "You keep that damn woman of yours at home where she belongs! Do you hear me?" Schultz heard him, all right!

---

[2]The date of their marriage is not known, although it was during the first few months of 1907.

Celia.
Courtesy
Renne Library
Collection.

By that time Schultz was beginning to think that one of Celia's reasons for marrying him was the hope of furthering her own career as a writer; but after reading some of the things she had written, he realized that she did not have what it took to write for the *Times*. If he had ever entertained any idea of having her as a collaborator, it was quickly shattered. In fact, as the days passed, the only interest shared by the two of them seemed to be a liking for good food. When Harry Carr was asked one day how on earth Schultz came to marry Celia, his quick response was, "She's a hell of a good cook."

The reason or reasons for Celia's being willing to marry a total stranger can only be the subject of conjecture. After all, Schultz was approaching forty-eight years of age and was therefore at least twenty years her senior.[3] The probabilities are that she was without encouraging marriage prospects in Michigan and perhaps was dazzled by the prospect of a marriage, though loveless, to a writer who had made his mark in the literary world,[4] and had a steady job as an editor on a metropolitan newspaper.

Be that as it may, the newlyweds rented an apartment in Los Angeles at 324 East Avenue 60 on the edge of the Arroyo Seco. Adjoining the apartment was a pleasant natural garden under gigantic sycamore trees where Apikuni often took his typewriter and spent the mornings at work. Here, now and then, he and Celia would entertain friends and he would occasionally pass an afternoon with old western cronies. Los Angeles was not then the metropolitan center it is today, but it seemed a great city to a man from the plains of Montana and a woman from a small town in Michigan. Since both were newcomers, neither had friends other than Harry Carr, who had gone out of his way to be gracious to them.

The reviews of *My Life as an Indian* were good all over the country, and soon in Los Angeles Schultz began to be something of a celebrity. Frequently he was requested to give talks, and on occasion he and Celia were invited out together. He shied away from all such invitations, but Celia loved them and urged him to accept; enjoying a bit of reflected glory as the wife of an author was better than no glory at all. In time, Celia made several friends in Los Angeles and led a social life separate from that of her husband.

In 1909, Apikuni relocated his son, Hart, after being out of touch with him for several years. Hart had decided to attend a good art school and with his father's approval enrolled at the Art Students' League in Los Angeles. He also came to live with his father and stepmother. But Hart and Celia did not hit it off well, and she proceeded to make life

[3] Celia's date of birth and age at time of her marriage are not known, but it is believed from the fact of her death in 1961 that in 1907 she was probably between twenty-five and thirty.

[4] Since *My Life as an Indian* was published in January, 1907, it is almost a certainty that she was aware of that event before she agreed to marry him.

miserable for him. He learned that away from home she had once referred to him as "that half-breed." Hart, on the other hand, was unhappy over the fact that his father had remarried so soon after the death of his mother.

In spite of his love for his father, Hart stayed away from home as much as possible, and that made his father unhappy. When the three of them were at home together, the conversation between father and son would nearly always turn to happenings among their Pikuni friends, and Celia would sulk. When they unconsciously lapsed into Blackfoot or made a point by sign talk, Celia would explode. Her intense jealousy of the young man put such a strain on the relationship that Hart soon decided to get his art training somewhere besides Los Angeles.

Except for a few short stories, Schultz did not find it possible to resume his writing career for several years after his marriage to Celia. It was 1912 before his second book was published. *With the Indians in the Rockies* was "affectionately dedicated to my wife, Celia Hawkins Schultz whose good comradeship and sympathy have been my greatest help in writing the tale." This elaborate dedication was, as we shall see, directly contrary to her total lack of interest in his books, particularly with the subject of Indians.

The development of income from Schultz's books enabled him to give up his job at the *Times*. Moreover, he became sufficiently prosperous to build himself a log cabin, or shooting lodge, at the eight thousand five hundred-foot level in the remote White Mountains of Arizona. Schultz had looked forward to the time when he could own a mountain retreat where there was an abundance of wildlife, including even grizzlies, and fabulous hunting. His dream cabin was to be completed as the year 1913 drew to a close.

The site selected by Schultz was a small open meadow beside the clear headwaters of the Little Colorado River. It was surrounded by a veritable garden of wild flowers, and there were countless butterflies everywhere; Schultz aptly named it *Apuni Oyis*, or Butterfly Lodge. The nearest community was the hamlet of Greer, a small village of the Latter-Day Saints. To reach it, he had to take a Santa Fe train to Hol-

Schultz and Celia at Butterfly Lodge. Courtesy Renne Library Collection.

Schultz's Arizona lodge. Photograph by Frank O. Stephens, 1984.

brook, then hire a taxi, usually a touring car, for the last one hundred six miles to Springerville, high in the White Mountains, then negotiate what was then a steep one-way dirt road for a dozen more miles to Greer. Traveling the route between Springerville and Greer was always an adventure, since it was not unusual to get stuck in the mud.

It was the first week in January, 1914, when the Schultzes were at last able to occupy their mountain cabin. There was snow on the ground, but a good fire in the fireplace soon made the house comfortable, and the hospitality of their Mormon neighbors added to their pleasure. Springerville, with a population of several hundred and situated seven thousand feet above sea level, was their base of operations for the necessities of life. Their neighbors provided invaluable service by bringing them mail and supplies, as well as taking them into town for an occasional shopping spree.

In the meantime, during the decade of his self-imposed exile from Montana, Schultz had never ceased to yearn for the plains and mountains he had known so well and to see the people there who had been closer to him than all others. All through the years he had maintained a correspondence with a few Montanans, including his onetime associate and close friend Joe Kipp, who had remained in Browning. So it was that Schultz began to lay plans for a return to his former stamping ground.

As early as 1913, in the course of his correspondence with Kipp, Schultz had suggested that they meet in San Francisco in the summer of 1915 to see the Panama-Pacific Exposition there, then travel together to Montana. Unfortunately, late in 1913, Schultz received word from Eli Guardipee that Kipp had died. Schultz was devastated. According to Harry James, Celia said he could neither talk nor eat. Day after day he sat under a large sycamore tree near the apartment, his head bowed, his face tear-stained. It was two weeks or more before he could bring himself to resume his writing.

Late in the summer of 1914, Schultz and Celia left their Arizona retreat and took the train to Montana. Guardipee's letters had prepared him to expect many changes, so he made the long-anticipated journey with a heavy heart. However, when they reached Browning, he was glad to renew old friendships, and it was reassuring to find that the unpleasant experiences that had taken place in connection with his services as a guide for Ralph Pulitzer had in no way clouded his reputation in Montana—at least not among his friends.

At Browning the Schultzes rented a small house and had no sooner started carrying their baggage inside when some of his old friends, mostly Indians, since Browning was the capital of the Blackfoot Reservation, crowded around to welcome him. Most of their talk was in Blackfoot, of course. He introduced them to Celia, and they responded pleasantly in the halting English spoken by a few of them. But this part of the country was not home to her, and she made little effort to conceal her annoyance when, everywhere they went, Schultz was the one greeted with affection by both Indians and whites. For Celia it was an unhappy situation and led her to remain in Browning when he went off, often for several days at a time, to visit among the Pikunis and other Blackfoot tribes, a decision they both tacitly accepted. Celia made a few friends among the white women of Browning and even became a member of their small bridge club.

Schultz's old friend Eli Guardipee and his family were still living on the ranch where Schultz and Nätahki had spent so many happy years. Eli urged Schultz and Celia to visit them, but Schultz found it impossible to take Celia with him. He went alone and spent a few poignant days among familiar scenes and with old friends. After a memorable final feast, he trudged slowly back to Browning; he was relieved to find Celia sound asleep. It would have been difficult for him to explain to her how profoundly moved he had been by the events of that evening.

This visit to Montana was Schultz's first since Glacier became a national park and since his business became that of writing books. Consequently, he now viewed his former haunts in the eastern valleys of the park as prime material for his pen. He perceived the idea of telling the story of the Blackfoot presence to be one of great interest, provided he could find a way to gather the necessary materials from Indian friends who might be knowledgeable concerning them. He felt this could best be accomplished by inviting those old-timers most familiar with the legends and history of the region to join him during the summer of 1915 in a camping trip through the eastern valleys.[5] Much of the planning for this project had to be done during 1914.

When Schultz and Celia returned to the park in the summer of 1915 for the camping projects in question, she had a frightening experience about which he later wrote and as a result of which his Blackfoot friends named her *Kut-ai-ko-pak-i*, or No-Coward Woman.[6] It seems that Celia and a friend from Boston were sitting together one day near the edge of a high bank overhanging the Cut Bank River while

[5] For the story of this camping reunion, see Chapter 23.
[6] See *Blackfeet Tales of Glacier National Park*, 82–83.

Schultz and his Blackfoot friends were meeting elsewhere in the valley. Presently they heard the slow, heavy, twig-snapping tread of an animal back in the brush and to their horror saw a big grizzly coming toward them. They crept hastily to the very edge of the high bank, grasped one of the limbs of a dwarf juniper growing there, and let themselves down over the bank. Then the limb broke with a loud snap, and down they tumbled into the river with a noisy splash. Neither was seriously injured, and after fording the waist-deep stream they arrived at camp dripping but safe. After all, what were bruises and a wetting compared to being mauled by a grizzly!

It was before 1920 that a friendship between Schultz and Harry James became firmly established. As long as Celia and her husband were in Los Angeles, rarely a week went by without a get-together by the Jameses and the Schultzes. Often the latter had lunch or dinner with James and his wife, Grace. Rarely, however, did Schultz and Celia come together. He would always arrive first, and often it would be half an hour, or even a full hour, before Celia appeared, usually just as the meal was about to be served. Neither ever explained why they did not come together, but as time went on all who knew them well were aware that the pattern of their lives differed decidedly from the one most people follow.

One of the sources of difficulty between Celia and her husband was that they were always in financial trouble. They both enjoyed good food but appeared to live rather simply otherwise. Celia's only extravagance was a liking for expensive clothes. She took particular pleasure, it was said, in astonishing the natives of Browning, both white and Indian, by wearing clothes better suited to New York's Fifth Avenue.

Whatever they may have had in common was outweighed, it seemed, by their differing likes and dislikes. Although Celia in her own right was a very pleasant and even amusing person, she had little interest in her husband's great concern for the American Indian and was totally disinterested in his writing. In fact, their incompatibility was such that friends found it difficult to understand why they had ever married.

According to Harry James, his first visit to Butterfly Lodge was in 1920 when he was invited, along with Stewart Edward White and others, to be Schultz's guests for a week of hunting and fishing. Subsequently, Schultz insisted that James bring up to camp for a few days some of the members of a boys organization he had founded some years earlier in Southern California; James took advantage of the offer on several occasions. Every night, with due ceremony, the boys built their council fire inside the lodge of James Willard Schultz, whose books they much admired.

Beginning with the end of World War I, Schultz's popularity as a writer began to increase, and by the mid-1920's his star was at its zenith. At the same time, this period was among the most productive of his long career as a writer. In addition to such books as *Rising Wolf, Friends of My Life as an Indian,* and *William Jackson, Indian Scout,* he wrote a number of magazine articles on behalf of Indian causes he was supporting. For example, he wrote "The Case of the Hopi," which appeared in *Sunset Magazine* in 1921, and "America's Red Armenians," published in *Sunset* in 1922, as strong articles telling the plight of the Hopi and Pikuni people, respectively.

In February, 1921, Schultz was commissioned by Marshall Neilan Productions to prepare a scenario for a motion picture to be called *White Chief*. He was also, according to plans at that time, to write publicity material for the picture and to go to New York for its release to assist in the publicity planned for its first showing, including talks before various organizations concerning the Blackfeet and the picture. In connection with the publicity work to be done in New York, Schultz had planned to consult George Bird Grinnell for the purpose of securing Grinnell's support for the Indian Welfare League, which he had been sponsoring, as well as Grinnell's assistance in raising money for the Blackfoot Relief Fund. Consequently, he was bitterly disappointed when he received word from the New York office of Marshall Neilan Productions that release of the film had been postponed indefinitely and the trip was off. The scenario was never published.

Schultz in Los Angeles, about 1922. Courtesy Renne Library Collection.

In 1922 the Schultzes made a belated visit to Glacier National Park, arriving on August 5. By mid-October they had returned to California and had moved into the Harwan Apartments at Crown Hill and Witmer streets in Los Angeles. Here they were domiciled until the following summer, although Celia paid a visit to her father in Illinois during March, 1923. They left for the park again on July 9, 1923, and spent an uneventful summer there. On October 18 from Los Angeles, Schultz sent Houghton Mifflin, his publishers, a wire saying he had just signed a contract with William Hart to write, in conjunction with Vance Thompson, a scenario for *The Sun God's Woman*. There is nothing to indicate that such a scenario was ever written.

The Schultzes continued to spend much time in Glacier National Park during the 1920's. By 1923, Schultz had practically become an unpaid member of the hotel company's personnel, with all expenses for himself and his wife assumed by the company for any time they were in the park. For a while it also furnished their transportation from California to the park and return; and beginning in 1925 the Great Northern provided substantial financial aid to Schultz to make possible the gathering of material for his books.[7]

With the Great Northern subsidy taking care of most of their summer expenses, Schultz was able in the spring of 1924 to buy an automobile, that is, to make a down payment with a promise to pay the balance of eight hundred dollars out of royalties due November 1. Thus it was that they drove that year to Glacier Park for the first time. They reached Montana early in June, 1924, intending to have Francis Monroe, son of old Hugh, meet them at Browning and accompany Schultz to the Edmonton area, where he hoped to get some material for a second book on Hugh. In the meantime, Celia would head for Highland Park, Illinois, for a visit to her former home.

On Celia's return at summer's end, she met Schultz on September 10 at Great Falls, from which point they drove back to California. They arrived in Los Angeles in mid-October, the car showing mileage of 10,380 since April. After checking in with the Jameses, they decided to drive on

---

[7] This benevolence, according to Great Northern correspondence on file at the Minnesota Historical Society, amounted to $2,408.48 for the year 1925 and to $3,310.65 in 1926. It ended in 1929 when Great Northern officials became disenchanted by word of his intemperance.

to Baja California, but returned a few days later when suitable quarters for the purpose of his writing could not be found. It was at this time that they rented for occupancy during the winter of 1924–25 a brown bungalow at Arch Beach, two miles below Laguna Beach,[8] their ownership of a car having given them the mobility that would enable them to live outside metropolitan Los Angeles.

The summer of 1925 was spent by Schultz in Glacier Park, this being the year of his third reunion with old Blackfoot friends for the purpose of gathering material for a book, this one to be entitled *Signposts of Adventure*. It also required some contact with the Kutenai tribe in Alberta, and while there he suffered a touch of pneumonia, which necessitated hospitalization at Macleod. The Schultzes had returned to Southern California by October 24.

In February, 1926, Ferris Greenslet, the Houghton Mifflin editor assigned to Schultz's account, happened to be in Los Angeles and made it a point to call on Schultz. They had lunch and a pleasant visit at the University Club. By June 12 the Schultzes were again on their way north to Glacier Park, where they spent most of the summer. Cecil Baring,[9] of the English banking family, joined Schultz on August 7 for a three-week outing in the park. By September 26 the Schultzes were back in Southern California and promptly wired Houghton Mifflin for an advance, saying they were "flat broke."

As will be mentioned later,[10] this impecunious state of affairs was more or less characteristic of their financial condition throughout the more than twenty years during which Celia and her husband carried on their marriage. They were, for the most part, apartment dwellers, and when Harry James first knew them in 1919 they were still living at 324 East Avenue 60 along the Arroyo Seco. They had been

[8]Letter from Schultz to Ralph Budd, Great Northern president, dated January 14, 1925, advising that their mail address was c/o Knight & Leach, Laguna Beach.
[9]For the story of the Baring family, see Chapter 14.
[10]See Chapter 26.

at this address since at least 1913 and continued there until they moved to the Harwan Apartments at Crown Hill and Witmer streets in the fall of 1922. They moved to Laguna Beach on returning to California in the autumn of 1924, residing there while in California through the spring of 1928.

Despite all of their wanderings and the fact that they never owned any property there, it was to Los Angeles or its environs that the Schultzes always returned from Montana and Arizona. Because of the city's advantages and conveniences, more than half their time was spent there. Not only the literary contacts and the enjoyable facilities of the University Club, but the benefits of a warm climate for Schultz's rheumatic pains were important factors to be considered.

James Willard's and Celia's last trip together was to Glacier Park in 1927. Schultz had particularly looked forward to the summer in Montana, not only because of special dance ceremonies to be staged by the Pikunis at Browning, but also because of the Okan ceremony, or Sun Dance, that would be staged in the Belly River Valley by the Blood tribe of the Blackfoot Confederacy; the latter was to be a ten-day event. It was Schultz's intention to attend both ceremonies, but Celia remained at the Glacier Park Lodge while he was in Browning and at the Many Glacier Hotel while he was at Belly River.

With him when he returned was a woman who had attended the ceremonies. Her name was Jessica Donaldson, and she was a professor at Montana State College. Schultz had suggested to her that if she accompanied him to the Many Glacier Hotel it would be easier for her to arrange transportation back to Bozeman; also, while there, she could meet and visit with Celia. When they reached the Many Glacier, Miss Donaldson met Celia and spent an afternoon with her. This was the only meeting of Schultz's second and third wives, and when asked about it many years later Jessica wrote:

> Celia said definitely she had never been in love with Schultz and that she hated Indians! She belabored Hart and Naoma, said they were just no good. Was very ugly about them. I

spent an entire afternoon with Celia in their bedroom, listening to her tales of persecution by Apikuni.[11]

It was during that same afternoon, according to Miss Donaldson, that Celia confided that she was going to start divorce proceedings that winter.

Despite this threat, Celia and Schultz returned to California together that autumn and rented quarters at Laguna Beach, where they resided until May or June, 1928. At that time they parted, she to go to her father's home in Illinois, he to spend at least a part of the summer in or near Waterton Lake National Park, with headquarters at the Cahoon Hotel in nearby Cardston, Alberta. There is nothing to indicate that Schultz and Celia ever cohabited again or even that she filed a California divorce action. If she did so, she failed to follow through with it, preferring to remain with her father and presumably relying upon him for financial support.

In view of this situation, Schultz filed his own suit for divorce in Montana and was granted a decree on September 5, 1930. However the decree did not resolve their dispute over how the royalties on his books should be divided, a dispute which was not brought to a conclusion until the latter part of 1932, and only after Schultz had secured legal representation in Chicago. That agreement provided:

(1) That Celia would relinquish her interest in all contracts between Schultz and Houghton Mifflin, as well as all copyrights, in return for one-half of all royalties from Schultz books published before September 5, 1930, date of the divorce, but accruing thereafter.

(2) That the same arrangement would apply to the royalties from any of such books if Schultz should authorize their publication by agents other than Houghton Mifflin.

(3) That Schultz should not have the right, without her written consent, to abrogate or modify any existing agreement with Houghton Mifflin relative to books published before September 5, 1930.

[11] Letter from Apaki to Harry C. James dated May 22, 1974.

Thus ended more than twenty years of marital discord between Schultz and his mail-order bride. Celia spent her last years in a retirement home in Maywood, Illinois, passing away in 1961.[12] Under the 1932 agreement, she continued to receive part of the royalties on pre-1930 Schultz publications until the end of her life.[13]

[12] Letter from Apaki to Harry C. James dated May 22, 1974.

[13] *Idem.* Manifestly the contents of this chapter do not begin to embrace all of Schultz's activities during the twenty years when Los Angeles served as his home base. For the story of the campaigns he waged against Indian mistreatment, see Chapter 29. For the part of his writing activities during that period, see Chapters 25 and 26.

CHAPTER 23

Summer Reunions in Glacier Park

WHEN James Willard Schultz returned to Montana in 1914 after an absence of more than ten years, he became thereafter a regular summer visitor to the Blackfoot Reservation and to what had become Glacier National Park.[1] Not only did he return each year, but in each of three summers he was host on camping trips in the park for his Pikuni friends and their families. The unique feature of these camping trips was that each was planned to, and did, culminate in the publication of a book about the legends, lore, and people associated with the part or parts of the park which served as campsites.

Schultz's favorite locale for reunions was Two Medicine Valley, although in one season they camped at several spots on the east side of the park. His reasons for including Two Medicine on every trip were several. To begin with, it had long been a meeting place for a number of tribes, the Bloods and Kutenais as well as the Pikunis, and had derived its name from that fact. It was highly scenic, with a string of three beautiful lakes, and was especially suitable for camping purposes. From a purely practical point of view, it was the nearest of the park's valleys to the homes of most of his Blackfoot guests on the reservation, as well as to the railroad station and Glacier Park Hotel. Especially important to Schultz was its richness in the Blackfoot lore that he would need for the books he planned to write about the park.

The summers when these special get-togethers were held were those of 1915, 1922, and 1925. Sometime well in ad-

---

[1] Glacier National Park was established May 11, 1910.

vance of the summer of 1915, Schultz had conceived the idea of writing a book about the part the Blackfeet had played in what was now the Glacier Park region, to be called *Blackfeet Tales of Glacier National Park*,[2] and of taking a group of his old Blackfoot friends on an extended camping trip through the park as a means of gathering additional material for the book and to provide a background for its presentation. He realized, however, that the financing of such a project was beyond his personal means. In considering ways to finance what he had in mind, he felt that the publicity value of such a project would have a strong appeal to his publicity-minded friend Louis W. Hill, president of the Great Northern Railway and owner and operator of the park's hotels and chalets. Schultz readily gained Hill's approval, and Hill agreed that Great Northern would pick up the tab.

The summer of 1915 was an important one for Glacier Park. On July 4, Many Glacier Hotel was completed and opened for business in the heart of the park. It was also the summer when a large group of white visitors, to wit, the Howard Eaton party, paid its initial visit to the park, although there was no connection between it and the Schultz safari. The latter got under way on July 12 in Two Medicine Valley and eventually concluded in Swiftcurrent Valley on September 10.

With no worry about cost, Schultz was able to invite many of his old-time Blackfoot friends and their families for a free two-month outing. Apart from Schultz himself, the party numbered thirty-three persons, consisting of eight men and their eleven women and fourteen children. They made up, as Schultz said, "a considerable camp of people." The men were Yellow Wolf, Tail-Feathers-Coming-Over-the-Hill, Big Spring, Two Guns, Black Bull, Stabs-by-Mistake, Eagle Child, and Eli Guardipee, whose Blackfoot name was Takes Gun Ahead.[3] Yellow Wolf and Tail-Feathers were uncles of Schultz's first wife, Nätahki.[4]

[2] The title Schultz had in mind was *Last Camps with My People*. As things turned out, it was not to be the last of his camps with his people.

[3] In *Signposts of Adventure*, 7, Guardipee is referred to as Takes-Gun-First.

[4] According to Schultz, at least. However, the 1907–1908 reservation records do show Yellow Wolf as her uncle.

All of the men were special friends of Schultz, and each had been to war—some of them many times—and had counted coup on the enemy. Tail-Feathers had many battle scars, and Schultz recalled being with him when he got the last one in a fight with the Crees. With all of these men, particularly Guardipee and Tail-Feathers, Schultz had traveled and hunted in the old days; hence they had much to talk about.

One of the principal subjects for Schultz's chapter on Two Medicine Valley was Hugh Monroe, the white Blackfoot, since it was his Indian name, Rising Wolf, that had been given to the most dramatic peak in the valley. However, Schultz also told his friends that the Indian name of Rising Bull Mountain had been replaced by the whites with Mount Rockwell and that Running Eagle Falls had been renamed Trick Falls, to which they responded with understandable indignation. The mention of the falls, however, gave Schultz an opportunity to have Tail-Feathers relate the story of the Blackfoot warrior maiden Running Eagle, or *Pitamakan*, who distinguished herself in combat until she was killed in a raid against the Flatheads; he featured the story in *Blackfeet Tales*.

Schultz and the Pikunis moved to Cut Bank Valley on July 18, to Little River on the Blackfoot Reservation on August 2, and to the foot of Upper St. Mary Lake on August 5. Around the evening campfires Schultz would invite his guests to recall legends pertaining to the locale, to recount adventures that they or their friends might have had there, and to reminisce generally concerning the lakes and mountains with which they were familiar.

Schultz himself told of Hugh Monroe's experiences in the St. Mary country, as well as some of his own. He told how he had named Red Eagle Mountain and Red Eagle Lake, as well as Singleshot, Kutenai, Almost-a-Dog, Yellow Fish, Goat, Four Bears, Going-to-the-Sun and Divide mountains, the last-named being the outermost mountain on the Arctic-Atlantic watershed. He told also how he and Jack Monroe had named Grinnell Glacier and Grinnell Mountain in the Swiftcurrent Valley; how Grinnell himself named Little

Chief Mountain above Upper St. Mary Lake; and how Grinnell, William Jackson, and he had named Blackfoot Glacier, Gunsight Pass, and Mount Jackson. Finally, he told how his own name, Apikuni, had been given by Lieutenant Beacom to the high mountain between Swiftcurrent River and Kennedy Creek.

Shortly before September 1 the party moved into Swiftcurrent Valley, camping beside the lake (then McDermott) and recalling the legends of the area. Here they lingered until September 10, when they broke camp and the Blackfoot members of the party returned to the reservation. Schultz and his wife returned to the Always-Summer-Land[5] to complete the writing of what was finally given the title *Blackfeet Tales of Glacier National Park*. It was published the following year.

Friends of My Life as an Indian was written as a result of a similar reunion Schultz held for his Indian friends in the summer of 1922. *Blackfeet Tales* had provided attractive and unusual publicity for the park and for the Great Northern Railway as owner and operator of the park's hotels and chalets, a fact of which President Louis W. Hill was quite cognizant. It was Hill who in the summer of 1920 had suggested to Schultz the writing of a historical-biographical book about the personalities with whom the latter had come into contact during his early Montana years. Hill even suggested a title for the book, *Friends of My Life as an Indian*, to capitalize on the great popularity of *My Life as an Indian*.

The suggestion could not have come from a more auspicious source. Moreover, Schultz liked the idea as well as the title. He sought and obtained tentative approval from Houghton Mifflin and suggested that early publication be planned. He did not foresee that writing the book would be one of his most difficult tasks. Whereas not more than one year would elapse between the dates of conception and publication of most of his books, the period of gestation for *Friends of My Life* was a full three years.

Schultz's difficulties sprang from many sources. In the

---

[5] To their home in Southern California.

first place, he began to realize that with respect to biographical subjects he lacked sufficient material about enough people to make up such a book and that, accordingly, it would be necessary to refresh his information and memory from available sources, principally his Pikuni friends in Montana. This, of course, would require making the necessary arrangements, as well as allowing sufficient lead time to do so, that is, to set up a time and place convenient to his friends. Furthermore, as previously indicated, he began to realize that dealing with historical and biographical subjects, unlike the fiction he was accustomed to writing, was more difficult than he had anticipated. He wrote to Houghton Mifflin and asked for more time to submit his manuscript. "This historical stuff is the hardest I ever tackled. I wish I had never attempted to write the story," he said.

Apart from the foregoing, everything else seemed to conspire to interfere with the project. A serious dental infection required the removal of Schultz's upper teeth, causing much discomfort and a serious loss of working time. Financial problems grew out of the rejection of a serial by *Youth's Companion* and an unfortunate delay in the payment for another by *National Stockman and Farmer*. An individual who had been counted on to supply certain key information declined to talk after Schultz went to Oregon to interview him. A printers' strike in 1921 and a railway shopmen's strike in 1922 contributed to delays in his plans. So desperate did Schultz become that in spite of the profound reverence with which he held the religious observances of the Indians he began to plan to commercialize the Pikuni Medicine Lodge ceremony for the next summer. Visitors would be welcomed, and he would publicize the event so as to attract them. He was certain each one of them would not object to paying two dollars to view the ceremonies. He quickly abandoned this unfortunate idea.

It was early October, 1921, before he could get to Montana to lay plans for a reunion of his Pikuni friends in Glacier Park during the summer of 1922, this time to include his son, Lone Wolf, and the latter's wife, Naoma. The date finally set for the 1922 encampment was August 5; the place, Two Medicine Valley. In fact it was held entirely in that valley, finally winding up on September 19. The number of participants was probably about the same as that in 1915, comprising ten Blackfoot men and their families: Boy Chief, Francis Monroe, Curly Bear, White Grass, Raven Chief, Many-Tail-Feathers, White Dog, Short Face, Wonderful Child, and Crow Feathers, the last-named a young man. Few of them had attended the 1915 encampment.

Whereas the earlier reunion and *Blackfeet Tales* had been concerned principally with the park's eastern valleys and stories in connection with each, this session was to be primarily people-oriented; as the proposed book title suggested, it was to tell about Schultz's friends in his Pikuni days. The book did include brief biographies of Joseph Kipp, Charles Rivois, and Francis Monroe, with two chapters devoted to Monroe's father, Hugh, without at least a mention of whom no Schultz book would have been complete. That seemed, however, to exhaust the list of Schultz's biographical subjects, and the rest of the book covered such stories and legends as "I am White Dog, Assiniboine," the Sacred Buffalo Stone and the Buffalo Stone ceremony (three chapters), and a final chapter entitled "The Story of the Sacred East-Plant."

Friends of My Life as an Indian is a fascinating book, well written in the Schultz style despite his disappointment in being unable to secure some of the material he had hoped to obtain. Yet even a casual comparison of the book's contents with the subject matter suggested by Hill makes it evident that there is not a great deal of resemblance between them. Historical stuff, as Schultz had complained, was not the kind of writing that he cared to tackle.

Signposts of Adventure, the last volume of Schultz's trilogy on the Blackfeet and Glacier National Park, was published in 1926. Although it grew out of the park reunion of 1925, its inception can be traced to that of 1915, when Schultz and his Indian friends met for the first encampment. It was then that his comrades had learned with much bitterness that many of the Indian names for Glacier Park landmarks had been replaced with "foolish names of no meaning what-

ever." According to Tail-Feathers-Coming-Over-the-Hill, the
Blackfeet names for the region were, "in a way, the history
of our people to far-back times." He added that "the whites'
names should at once be wiped out and our names restored
to the maps of the region, that our children who come after
us may ever be reminded of the bravery, the dignity, the in-
every-way fine character of their once powerful ancestors."

Those present in 1915 had agreed with these sentiments,
and they agreed also that Schultz was the man who could
and should undertake the restoration. He told them that he
would accept the assignment but that other commitments
would prevent immediate action. As year after year went by,
his friends continued to urge that the work be done, but it
was not until 1925, with the cooperation of Ralph Budd,
Hill's successor at Great Northern, that it was possible to
plan for appropriate action. For the third time in a decade,
accordingly, Schultz sounded the call to his Blackfoot friends
for a get-together in Glacier Park.

> On June 1, 1925, I again camped with the older men of
> the Pikuni and their families upon the shores of Two Medi-
> cine Lodges Lake. But how many were missing of those who
> had been there with us ten years before! Gone to the Sand
> Hills—dread abode of the dead of the Blackfeet tribes—
> were the shadows of Tail-Feathers-Coming-Over-the-Hill,
> Medicine Owl, Boy Chief, and a host of less noted friends.[6]

Prominent among those present were Curly Bear and Eli
Guardipee, or Takes-Gun-First,[7] and they and Schultz, coun-
seling with the men of the group around the evening fire in
Curly Bear's sacred Beaver Medicine Lodge, agreed on a
plan of action:

> (1) All white-man names on the eastern side of the park
> should be eliminated except for those of individuals who had
> been closely identified with the Indians as their true friends.
> (2) Indian names should then be given to all east-side fea-
> tures that the tribes had not theretofore named.

---

[6] *Signposts of Adventure*, 6.
[7] In *Blackfeet Tales of Glacier National Park*, Schultz referred to Guardipee
as Takes-Gun-Ahead (see pp. 9, 108, 110).

(3) The Kutenais and other west-side tribes should be asked to restore to that area the names they had given to its various features.

(4) Curly Bear and Guardipee should serve as Schultz's "close and constant assistants in the prosecution of the work."

The pages of *Signposts of Adventure* did not disclose how long the encampment continued at Two Medicine Lake but merely stated that "camp was broken and we went our various ways."

In due course Schultz and his two assistants traveled north to Fort Macleod, Alberta, to meet with members of the Canadian branch of the Kutenai tribe. One of them was a half-Kutenai and half-Pikuni man of great intelligence, named by his Pikuni mother *Kakitos*, or Star, who served as their interpreter. The Kutenais not only agreed with the project but in the course of daily sessions for a week succeeded in providing names for all west-side features from the international boundary to the southern border of the park. The names the Kutenais came up with were, as Schultz said, "for the most part, simply the names of men of the tribe who were successful hunters, or 'magicians,'" Brief explanations were given with reference to fewer than a dozen of the names.

For the topographical features of the east side of the park, one hundred sixty-one in all, the committee was able to provide pre–white man Pikuni names in perhaps thirty or forty instances. For the rest of the east-side features, names of noted warriors or other tribal members were proposed as replacements for the current names. Of course, quite a few of the latter had been supplied in earlier times by Schultz, and these were retained.

The task of thinking up more than a hundred names to replace those assigned by the white man to east-side features was not an easy one. Some of the committee chose their own names, such as Curly Bear Ice for Hudson Glacier[8] and

---

[8] Although this recommended change was never implemented, the Geological Survey map of 1938 showed the name *Curly Bear Mountain* where Kutenai Mountain had been.

Takes-Gun-First Mountain for Chapman Peak. Long Hair Mountain was suggested for Mount Custer. A bit of nepotism crept into the process. Interestingly, Appekunny, as it was spelled by Schultz in the 1880's, was left unchanged on the *Signposts of Adventure* map although it appears as Appikunny in the text. The committee thought the name of Logan Glacier should be replaced with Lone Wolf Ice, to honor Schultz's son,[9] and that Lake Francis should be renamed Fine Shield Woman Lake in memory of Lone Wolf's mother, who was Schultz's first wife.[10]

Quite a few additional Blackfoot or Indian names have appeared on the official maps that have been issued since the publication of *Signposts of Adventure* in 1926. Among them are Curly Bear, Natahki, and Sinopah, as well as Mount Kipp, Kipp Creek, and Raven Quiver Falls. Sinopah, Hugh Monroe's woman, had been recommended as a replacement for Mount Rockwell. In the 1938 revision of the official map this change was implemented, with Mount Rockwell being relegated to a less-conspicuous position on the Continental Divide to the west of Sinopah. Whether directly or indirectly, each of these changes was the result of Schultz's crusade.

What was the white-man reaction to *Signposts of Adventure* and its objectives? On the whole, it was not unfavorable. In the first place, it brought the unhappiness of the Indian to the attention of thousands of Schultz's loyal readers, most of them not previously aware of it. Undoubtedly, most white men would have agreed heartily with the changes mentioned in the preceding paragraph; and many, if not all, would have been sympathetic to restoration of most of the names used by the Indians in pre–white man times. On the other hand, many whites would have felt that Schultz was making a mountain out of a molehill issue and would have

[9] The Lone Wolf recommendation was not adopted, and Logan Glacier is still Logan Glacier.
[10] Although this recommendation has never been adopted, the name of *Natahki Lake* (in Apikuni Basin) has appeared on the official map for 1938 and subsequently.

been unable to understand how or why the Indian could claim the right, or even wish, to rename park features he had never taken the trouble to name when they were his. A large percentage of the three hundred fourteen names involved were intended for features which had never borne Indian names and had no connection with the Indians for whom it was proposed that they be renamed.

Almost every white man would have regarded the Schultz proposal as an exercise in futility in view of the difficulty in getting even one name changed for good reason. Except for whatever indirect effect Schultz's recommendations may have had with reference to Curly Bear, Nätahki, Sinopah, and Kipp, the only one which has actually borne fruit is the change in 1980 from Trick Falls to Running Eagle Falls.

What would have been the probable reaction to *Signposts of Adventure* on the part of Pikunis who became fully aware of it? Undoubtedly it would have been one of unqualified approval, appealing to their ethnic pride and feeling of grievance at white-man treatment in general. They would have felt, as did Tail-Feathers-Coming-Over-the-Hill, that Schultz's book would, if nothing else, provide a permanent record for the benefit of their children and grandchildren. As Curly Bear said when their task was finished:

> . . . the whites put their knowledge upon paper before they die and that knowledge lives forever. But now our children are learning the whites' ways; they will read this our work, and their hearts will be glad. *Kyi*! Let us smoke and rest.[11]

As for Schultz himself, long the champion of Indian causes, *Signposts of Adventure* completed the trilogy of books which he had planned to write in or about Glacier National Park. With its publication he was enabled to get another grievance over the white man's mistreatment of his beloved Pikunis off his chest and into the form of a permanent document. But why did he tilt at windmills, as it were, in proposing the renaming of a large majority of the park's topo-

---

[11] *Signposts of Adventure*, 18–19.

graphical features? Answers at this late date will serve no purpose, but one of them has to be that had mention of all features which had never borne Indian names been eliminated, this would also have eliminated the greater part of the material he needed for a full-sized book, leaving him with only a pamphlet or long magazine article.

CHAPTER 24

Life with Apaki

JESSICA DONALDSON met James Willard Schultz in June, 1927.[1] While she was a house guest at the ranch of the Ernest Millers, they invited Schultz to be an overnight guest. They knew that Miss Donaldson, a professor at Montana State College in Bozeman, was interested in the American Indian and accordingly would find much in common with Schultz.[2]

Schultz was glad to accept the invitation, even though it did not include Celia, who in the early summer of that year had again driven with him to Montana. The Millers frequently had interesting visitors at their small guest ranch, but when he arrived Schultz was surprised to learn that the guest they wanted him to meet was Miss Donaldson.[3] He recalled receiving a letter from her a year or so earlier asking him to be one of the sponsors of a masque she and her students were planning to stage at the college. It was to be based, she had written, upon the traditions of the Crow, or Absaroka, Indians. One of her students had written the script for the masque and she had made several visits to the Crows' reservation to secure their approval and coopera-

[1] Schultz's friends in the Blood tribe, a Canadian branch of the Blackfoot Nation, named Miss Donaldson *Apaki*, or White Weasel Woman. She liked it. Schultz preferred to translate it as Ermine Woman.
[2] Grace Miller, in an article in *The Piegan Storyteller*, Vol. V, No. 1, January, 1980, 5, tells the story of how Apikuni met Jessie Donaldson.
[3] Tom Gilmore, in an article entitled "St. Helenan Tells of Life with Indians," appearing in the *Napa* (California) *Register* of July 22, 1975, and reprinted in *The Piegan Storyteller*, Vol. I, No. 2, April, 1976, 13, tells the story of her adoption and naming by the Bloods.

tion. Schultz agreed to permit his name to be used as one of the sponsors. He did not see a performance of *The Masque of Absaroka*, but from what he read of it in the newspapers, it was a success. Now, as he talked with her about it, he was impressed by the depth of her knowledge regarding the Crows, and even more so by her enthusiastic interest in all things Indian.

That evening, Apikuni and Miss Donaldson had a long talk together. He was pleased to learn that her interest in Indians had been aroused by reading his books and that it was his *Bird Woman* which had interested her in the Lewis and Clark Expedition. He discussed with her several places in Glacier National Park which he thought would be suitable for staging a pageant based on the experiences of the expedition. She was delighted when he offered to meet with the park superintendent and one of the Great Northern's top officials for the purpose of interesting them in her idea. He assured her that he was confident the Pikunis would be cooperative.

The next morning at breakfast, Apikuni mentioned that the Bloods were planning to stage their Medicine Lodge ceremony, Okan, often referred to as the Sun Dance, in July. The Indians would cross the border into Glacier National Park and make camp on a wide slope between the Belly Buttes and the Belly River. It would be a wonderful sight because about two thousand Indians would be encamped in a giant circle of beautifully painted lodges. As Apikuni described the scene he could see how excited Miss Donaldson had become. He suggested that she try to meet them in Cardston and he would be glad to take her over to meet some of his friends among the Bloods and to witness some of the ceremonies. She was thrilled at the prospect.

On her return to Bozeman, she immediately told her two close friends, Dorothy Chamberlin and Martha Maxey, who had worked with her on *The Masque of Absaroka*, of her meeting with Apikuni and of her plans to attend the Belly River ceremonies. She urged them to come with her, and was deeply disappointed when they found it impossible to do so.

When she arrived at Cardston, she learned that Mrs.

Schultz would not attend the ceremonies but that Schultz would nevertheless take her (Jessica) there. When he arrived, they soon had her baggage and books stowed away in the car and drove her to Belly River, up a rough, winding ravine, and then past one butte after another until they finally sighted the tops of the lodge poles in the Indian camp. A few moments later the whole camp came into view: a great circle of painted lodges, with no two alike. Schultz stopped the car as his passenger gave a gasp of amazement, then pointed out some of the details of the camp. Inside the main circle were the lodges of the two societies which played important parts in the Okan ceremonies of the Bloods, the Horn Society of the men and the Matokiks of the women.

As they approached the camp and stopped, several Indians ran out to greet Schultz, all welcoming him as Apikuni. As he led her through the camp, Indians were constantly hailing him in friendly fashion. When they finally stopped in front of a very large and richly decorated lodge, an imposing Indian stepped out and greeted Schultz with great affection. Schultz then introduced her to *Imitaikwan*, Little Dog, the head chief of the Blood tribe.[4] The chief told Apikuni that he was to share his lodge while visiting with his people. He then introduced his daughter to Schultz and Jessica.

To Jessica's surprise, the chief's daughter spoke English and used her English name, Violet Creighton.[5] She invited Jessica to share the tent she had directly back of her father's lodge. Only then did Jessica realize that she would be the only white woman in that camp of two thousand Blood Indians. In fact, it turned out that she and Apikuni were the only non-Indian visitors during the entire ten days of the ceremonies.

[4]This is the story as Schultz told it. Actually, Little Dog was Percy Creighton, whose father had been an army deserter named Abe Creighton. He was only a minor chief or counselor, not the head chief of the tribe as stated by Schultz. He was well educated and would act as an interpreter; consequently, white people, on entering a Blood camp, would make a beeline for his tipi. Many considered him more white than Indian.
[5]There was really no reason for surprise that Violet spoke English. All her family did.

Apikuni spent most of the night visiting his many friends throughout the camp. Drums and singing were to be heard everywhere, and the members of the Horn Society sang their preliminary songs all night long. Near morning it began to rain, and Violet Creighton's tent began to leak. She suggested that they had better move over to her father's lodge, and they quietly did so. Violet showed Jessica where they could put their bedding in the space between the couches and the fire without disturbing anyone. There they spent what was left of the night very comfortably.

At dawn, *Imitaikwan*'s women woke Jessica and Violet and helped them move their bedrolls far enough away from the fire so that breakfast could be prepared. As new wood was put on the fire and the flames danced up, the whole lodge was soon astir. Schultz was amazed to see Jessie inside the big lodge. *Imitaikwan* began scolding his daughter in a joking way for bringing Jessica inside the lodge among so many men.

Apikuni had brought a large quantity of food to help provide for *Imitaikwan* and his family during his visit with them. As soon as everything was ready, Jessica was invited by *Imitaikwan*'s Sits-Beside-Him-Wife to sit with all of them around the fire and enjoy breakfast.[6] As they ate, Apikuni explained to Jessica that the Matokiks, the women's sacred society, would complete the ceremonial construction of their lodge that morning. Jessica was very anxious to observe this, so Apikuni led her to a spot where she could sit undisturbed and make whatever notes she wished.

When the Matokiks lodge had been completed and the women began furnishing it with the usual couches, backrests, and other necessary articles, Apikuni came by and Jessica showed him her notebook. As he was looking at it, the Matokiks women suddenly appeared in full costume and walked solemnly into their lodge. Apikuni pointed out to Jessica that the members of each of the four bands of the Matokiks—Snake, Young Buffalo, Old Buffalo, and Bird—

---

[6] This statement from Schultz leaves the implication that *Imitaikwan* had more than one wife. He had only one.

wore costumes and hairdresses appropriate to their band and that their ceremonies inside their lodge would occupy the next four days.

When the Matokiks ceremonies had been completed, the men of the Horn Society, wearing their magnificent beaded buckskin costumes and eagle-feather warbonnets, staged the first of their ceremonies. Holding high either long crooked staffs or lances, they danced in groups of four abreast. With drums beating fast and furiously, they danced in rhythm inside the entire circle of the camp. From then on, a variety of ceremonial activities were carried on constantly. Medicine men were dancing around their lodges, holding their sacred pipes out in front of them as they did so.

The climax of the Okan came with the erection of the impressive Medicine Lodge. Everything pertaining to it was performed with the greatest of solemnity by the Bloods of that time, as were the ceremonies that were enacted within it. In *The Sun God's Children*, written jointly by Schultz and Jessica and published by Houghton Mifflin in 1930, there is an account of these observances, which it seems likely that Apikuni had been allowed to witness during his early days with the Pikunis. Apikuni himself always considered Clark Wissler's *The Sun Dance of the Blackfoot Indians* to be the most authoritative account of the ceremony. It was published in 1918 as Part 3 in Volume XVI of the *Anthropological Papers of the Museum of Natural History*.

As the time to leave drew near, Apikuni suggested to Jessica that she should drive with him to the Many Glacier Hotel, where she could arrange for transportation which would be simpler than the route she had to take to get to Cardston. She accepted his invitation and met Schultz's wife, Celia, at the Many Glacier Hotel.

Miss Donaldson returned home to Bozeman to make preparations for her year's leave of absence from teaching duties and for her attendance during that period at the University of California. Schultz and his wife drove back to Southern California, where they remained in rented quarters at Laguna Beach until May or June, 1928. By what was

not coincidence, Schultz and Jessica spent the summer of
1928 near Calgary, Canada. She was engaged in research
for the book entitled *The Sun God's Children*, on which they
would soon collaborate. He spent most of the summer with
the Northern Blackfeet, arriving by October at Bozeman,
whither she had gone to resume her teaching duties in
September.

The Sun God's Children was written during the winter of
1928–29 when Schultz and Jessica were living in Bozeman.
It was at the end of that school year, under circumstances to
be related later,[7] that Jessica severed her ten-year relationship with the college and cast her lot with Schultz. Soon
thereafter they left Bozeman and spent several weeks visiting his Indian friends in the vicinity of Browning, followed
by a sojourn with the Northern Blackfeet near Calgary and
a short stay in British Columbia with Kutenai friends.

By this time the summer of 1929 had ended, and with no
home base to return to, the couple decided to accept the invitation of Schultz's son, Lone Wolf, to spend some time with
him and his wife, Naoma, at Butterfly Lodge, their mountain retreat in Arizona. After a few weeks there they returned to Bozeman, where they rented a cabin for the
winter—the first winter of the Great Depression. Since Jessica was now unemployed and since his royalties had been
tied up by his divorce suit, Schultz was forced to borrow
money to get them through the winter.

With assistance from her brother, Jessica returned to
Berkeley in January, 1930, to continue her studies toward a
master's degree in anthropology. Schultz, of course, lived
with or near her in the university city. By the autumn of
1930, funds were no more plentiful than before, and they
were glad to be able to revisit Lone Wolf and Naoma at
Butterfly Lodge, where they remained until the chill of the
Arizona mountain winter forced the four of them to move
to a house in Tucson. In January, 1931, Jessica returned to
Berkeley to complete her postgraduate work and to receive
her master's degree in the month of May. Anticipating that

[7]See Chapter 34.

event somewhat, the couple drove to Winnemucca, Nevada, and were married on April 27, 1931. They felt that most of their troubles were behind them and that they could now look forward to a more pleasant way of life.

Unfortunately for Apikuni and Jessica, things were destined to become worse before they would get better. For more than three years after their marriage, Jessica was unable to find work of any kind. As for Schultz, he had the misfortune to suffer a severe back injury that took him through a series of hospitals and treatments with a succession of doctors. The ensuing painful disability and its complications made him a virtual cripple for the rest of 1931 and much of 1932, and they were fortunate to be able to return to Butterfly Lodge and Tucson for the autumn and winter of 1931.

Frustrated by the persistence of Apikuni's disability, the couple decided that it might be best to return to Berkeley for purposes of convalescence, since they had been advised that surgery was not indicated. They arrived there in the early part of 1932, and during the next few months, under competent medical supervision, his condition became much improved. However, Jessica was still unemployed, and since their personal resources as well as the economy in general were still at low ebb, they returned to Butterfly Lodge for the autumn of 1932 and to Tucson for the winter of 1932–33.

With conditions still failing to improve, the Schultzes decided to move back to Bozeman, where they could economize by living in their fishing cabin on the Madison River, which they called Cherry Grove. Meanwhile, of course, his income from book sales had been nominal, not only because it was frozen by the still-unresolved settlement of royalty payments, but also because his disability had brought his output of work to a standstill.

It is probable that the Schultzes spent the fall of 1933 at Butterfly Lodge and the winter of 1933–34 at Tucson, since Jessica continued to be unemployed during that period, despite intensive efforts to find work. But it was at Cherry Grove that they were living, apparently, when Jessica re-

Schultz about 1928. Courtesy Renne Library Collection.

*Schultz
in his sixties.
Courtesy Renne Library
Collection.*

ceived the welcome news that a job was available to her at
Choteau in September, 1934. She hastened there and was
hired as a community worker by the Federal Emergency Relief Administration. After barely three months, she was
transferred to a similar post at Browning, only a few miles to
the north.

For Apikuni and Apaki the year 1934 held significance. It
brought them to the end of the long tunnel of adversity and
frustration through which they had been struggling since
1929. It brought them to the end of their itinerant existence, with its impermanence of residence and inability to
plan for the future.

For Apikuni, 1934 represented his seventy-fifth milestone
in life and the beginning of the end of his productive years.
Although he would carry on for another 13 years, his increasing health problems and diminishing powers of con-
centration were such as to reduce to a total of three his output of books for this period. There was none after 1940. He
did devote some time during the latter part of the 1930's to
the compilation of a series of articles which he referred to
as his reminiscences. These were recollections of his early
Montana years, first published in the *Great Falls Tribune* and
submitted by him to Houghton Mifflin Company in unedited form in 1940. With considerable editing they were
published in 1962 as *Blackfeet and Buffalo.*

The Schultzes moved to Browning in December, 1934,
when Jessica was transferred there. The necessity for co-
existence in a difficult economy required the newlyweds to
live wherever she might be able to find employment suited
to her talents—or, in fact, any kind of remunerative work.
This was the reason their years after 1934 were spent entirely in the Northwest, first in Montana and finally in Wyoming, a situation beyond Apikuni's control, although it had
benefits as well as drawbacks.

Her employment in Browning returned them to a familiar area, although the number of Apikuni's cronies had been
decreasing each year. The Schultz home in Browning became a magnet for their many friends, both red and white.
The proximity of Glacier National Park was especially enjoy-

able for Apikuni, not only because of the nostalgia it evoked but also because it re-created opportunities for visits to St. Mary Lakes and other familiar areas and particularly because St. Mary had become the site of the summer studio of Schultz's artist son, Lone Wolf. The latter was five years older than Apaki, but Hart's wife, Naoma, was several years younger. Fortunately for all concerned, Apaki was on excellent terms with both.

During the Browning period, despite being in his late seventies, Apikuni would usually spend parts of each summer in the nearby national park, sometimes accompanying out-of-state guests or other friends. Harry James made trips to the area from time to time, usually in the role of counselor to a group of Boy Scouts. It was on one of these visits that Apikuni and James, the latter with the approval of the Blackfeet, attended a Beaver Bundle ceremony, which was being held that summer at an isolated group of tipis on Lower St. Mary Lake. The daylong ceremony impressed James.

It was a sad day for the Schultzes when they were unexpectedly transferred to Fort Washakie, Wyoming, in 1940. Readjustment at eighty-one is difficult for anyone, but for Apikuni the circumstances of their uprooting were doubly difficult. As for Apaki, she could only look forward to starting a new life with new people she did not know in a new environment with a new staff and a variety of new situations involving two dissimilar tribes. As she pondered the new challenge, she felt rather low. Eventually, of course, they arrived at Fort Washakie and for living quarters were given the use of a large stone house on a hill above the river.

Life for Apikuni in the wilds of Wyoming proved to be anything but exciting. However, he satisfied his lifelong love of music by listening to concerts and opera on the radio and records. So long as his eyes permitted, he read newspapers, magazines, and books: mystery stories, histories, accounts of archaeological findings. And he managed to keep up his correspondence in some fashion to the end.

There were occasional visitors. Hart and Naoma came north from Arizona to visit, and the men had good laughs

Apikuni chatting with Bear Cap in Glacier National Park. Courtesy Renne Library Collection.

Apikuni and Apaki with the Haynes family. Courtesy Renne Library Collection.

together as they recounted, in the Blackfoot language, events of the past. Hart painted some fine canvasses during these visits, which would sometimes last a whole winter. Some of the Blackfeet came to visit, too: Wades-in-the-Water and his wife, Julia; Mr. and Mrs. Running Rabbit; Mr. and Mrs. Eagle Ribs; William Spanish and his wife, Nora.

One summer Harry James brought a group of boys from California for the purpose of retracing the western part of the route followed by Lewis and Clark. In the party were Eaton Randolph, David Jackson, and Finn Burnett, lineal descendants of Captain William Clark, young George Shannon, and Sacagawea, respectively. Finn Burnett was a Shoshone boy who had come to the group from Fort Washakie. Apikuni drove out with the group to the old cemetery where Sacagawea was said to have been buried. Slowly he walked with them to the grave. Then they asked the aged Episcopal minister, the Reverend John Roberts, who had officiated at Sacagawea's funeral to tell them about it, and he did. Schultz seemed happy to be spending the day with the group and was deeply touched by the respect and affection shown him by the boys. Tears came readily to his eyes at any little demonstration of their regard for him.

A visitor of personal interest was J. Donald Adams, a writer for the *New York Times*. By special invitation from the Schultzes, he spent several days with them. Later he had kind words to say about his visit and his hosts:

> I shall always be thankful that I met and stayed with James Willard Schultz, when he was living on the Shoshone Indian Reservation at Fort Washakie, Wyoming. That was in 1941, and Schultz, then a very old but still vigorous man, made me a living link with the old West.
>
> It seemed almost incredible when I sat with him—a few months, mind you, before our entry into World War II—that this hawk nosed man whose blue eyes were still undimmed . . . had, as an adopted member of the tribe, gone on war parties with those dread marauders, the Blackfeet, one of whose girls he was to marry. . . .
>
> My days with Schultz, who was then married to Jessie Donaldson of the Indian Service, are an unforgettable memory. I happened along, luckily for me, in time for the annual Sun Dance of the Shoshone and Arapaho who share the same reservation. There I saw an old white sheepherder fast and dance with his Indian friends. . . . I saw the old Shoshone Medicine Man—more spiritual looking than most bishops I have seen—conduct the sunrise ceremony, and was moved to deep emotion. Another day I woke to hear the drums

pounding at dawn and hurried down with Lone Wolf,
Schultz's half-Indian son (and a gifted painter) to the ceremonial lodge, to stand and watch all day. But old man Schultz
wouldn't stir. "There's only one real sun dance left," he said,
"the dance of the Bloods in Alberta." And that, too, I was to
see some years later.[8]

---

[8]Quoted by Jessie Donaldson Schultz in "Amazing, Adventuresome
Apikuni," 17.

CHAPTER 25

The Story Behind the Stories

J AMES WILLARD SCHULTZ began writing for publication in the early 1880's, sending articles from time to time to *Forest and Stream*, a popular weekly journal to which he was a subscriber. He was barely twenty-one when the first of these appeared in the issue of October 14, 1880. It was entitled "Hunting in Montana" and gave the author's name as AP-WA-CUN-NA. The second appeared on April 21, 1881, under the title "The White Buffalo Cow" and over the name of AP-WE-CUN-NY. The third article, entitled "An Elk Hunt by Moonlight," was published June 19, 1881, and gave the author's name as AP-PE-CUN-NY.[1]

Each of the articles had to do with some phase of hunting. As time went on, however, and Schultz learned more about the people with whom he had come to be closely associated, he undertook the writing of a series of articles setting forth his observations concerning their customs, tribal divisions, and family life. The pieces were published in nine installments as "Life Among the Blackfeet," commencing with the issue of November 26, 1883. It was in connection with these

[1] The variance in spelling of the pseudonyms used in each of Schultz's first three ventures into article writing suggest that he was not quite sure how his Indian name should be spelled. This uncertainty had been remedied by the time George Bird Grinnell first visited the Northwest, as his *Forest and Stream* articles, the earliest appearing in 1885, show. Schultz himself seems to have resolved the difficulty not later than 1883, since the second of his "Life Among the Blackfeet" series (which appeared on December 6, 1883) used the spelling *Appekunny*. Although one of his later hunting parties (the men of Troy) referred to him in 1888 as Appecani, this was probably a phonetic spelling based on the way it sounded to the hunters when others addressed Schultz by his Indian name.

articles that he first used the name of J. W. Schultz as their
author.

By the latter part of 1884, Schultz had made two trips to
the St. Mary country, thereby discovering another topic
fully as interesting as hunting and Indians. As a result, he
wrote "To Chief Mountain," which appeared in the December 10, 1885, issue of *Forest and Stream*.[2] A year later, the
story of his 1886 trek with the Barings to the St. Mary region, entitled "White Goats and Bull Trout," was published.[3]
The story of his first trip to the area with George Bird Grinnell in 1885 already had been fully covered in a lengthy series
of articles by Grinnell entitled "To the Walled-In Lakes."[4]

Apart from the 1883 series on the Blackfeet, Schultz wrote
only articles and stories during the 1880's and 1890's, giving
no thought to entering the book-writing field. In fact, it is
rather startling to learn that he rejected an opportunity to
write a book about his favorite Blackfeet when the offer was
made by Grinnell. When Schultz declined to undertake the
assignment, Grinnell himself did so and the book was published in 1892 under the title *Blackfoot Lodge Tales*.[5]

Grinnell had written other books about western Indians,
notably one entitled *Pawnee Hero Stories and Folk Tales*.[6] It
dealt with Indians from the standpoint of the Indian, and it
aroused so much public interest that he was inspired to
sponsor a similar book about the Blackfeet. He was aware,
of course, that much of the material for such a volume was
already available in the form of articles and stories written
by Schultz; hence Grinnell felt that Schultz was the logical
man to undertake such an assignment. With this in mind, he
wrote Schultz suggesting that he do so and

urging him, as I had often done before, to put his observations in shape for publication, and offered to edit his work
and see it through the press. Mr. Schultz was unwilling to
undertake this task, and begged me to use all the material

[2] P. 362.
[3] *Forest and Stream*, Vol. XXVII, 443.
[4] *Forest and Stream*, Vol. XXV, 382, through Vol. XXVI, 122.
[5] Charles Scribner's Sons, 1892.
[6] Charles Scribner's Sons, 1889.

which I had gathered and whatever he could supply, in the preparation of a book about the Blackfeet.[7]

In view of the foregoing, Grinnell prepared the text of *Blackfoot Lodge Tales*. He wrote in the Introduction:

It is proper that something should be said as to how this book came to be written. About ten years ago, Mr. J. W. Schultz of Montana, who was then living in the Blackfoot camp, contributed to the columns of the *Forest and Stream*, under the title "Life among the Blackfeet," a series of sketches of that people. These papers seemed to me of unusual interest, and worthy of record in a form more permanent than the columns of a newspaper; but no opportunity was then presented for filling in the outlines given in them.

A portion of the material contained in these pages was originally made public by Mr. Schultz, and he was thus the discoverer of the literature of the Blackfeet. My own investigations have made me familiar with all the stories here recorded, from original sources, but some of them he first published in the columns of the *Forest and Stream*. For this work he is entitled to great credit, for it is most unusual to find anyone living the rough life beyond the frontier, and mingling in daily intercourse with Indians, who has the intelligence to study their traditions, history and customs and the industry to reduce his observations to writing.[8]

Grinnell thus made it clear that Schultz's sketches had been the inspiration as well as the principal source of his material. That being so, specific identification or attribution in the text itself became unnecessary; however, his chapter on "Medicine Pipes and Healing" is almost pure Schultz, including a quotation of the latter's description of a special "medicine dance" he had witnessed.

Since Grinnell's book is one which made a substantial contribution to anthropological knowledge, it was republished many years after its original issue, as well as after the death of both Grinnell and Schultz. Those worthies would have been gratified to know that the University of Nebraska Press

[7] Introduction to *Blackfoot Lodge Tales*, xv.
[8] *Idem.*

in Lincoln republished the book in paperback form in May, 1962, and found it necessary to make a second printing in December, 1965.[9]

After declining the opportunity to become the author of *Blackfoot Lodge Tales*, Schultz continued to confine his literary output to occasional articles and stories for the next ten years. Most of them were published by *Forest and Stream*, but a few of them began to appear around the turn of the century in the *Great Falls Tribune*, *Outing* magazine, and on one occasion at least in a London publication, *Wide World* magazine. Apparently the idea of a book or serial did not occur to him in the 1880's or 1890's.

Schultz's first work to be published in installment form in a periodical and as a book during his lifetime was his western romance *My Life as an Indian*, which was issued in January, 1907,[10] after appearing in twenty-five installments in the columns of *Forest and Stream* in 1906 under the pen name of W. B. Anderson as "In the Lodges of the Blackfeet." This is the book which has been described as "the story that proves that truth is not only stranger than fiction, but that it can be more interesting."[11]

For Schultz, the writing of *My Life as an Indian* not only was a fascinating and rewarding experience but initiated a new phase in his life as an author. Through its success, he came to find the writing of books a profitable field, as well as a medium to which he could devote full time because of the steady income which it made possible. Books thereafter, either with or without serialization through magazine publication, became his specialty.

Despite the fact that *My Life as an Indian* was his first book, it is still regarded as his finest work. This may be due to its being a tender and unusual true-life love story for mature readers. For the author, its writing was more than a colorful

[9]This was a Bison Book edition prepared from the original edition published in 1892 by Charles Scribner's Sons.

[10]Originally copyrighted January 31, 1907, extended thereafter to January 31, 1963, and by statute applicable to second-term copyrights to December 31, 1969.

[11]Matthew J. Conway of Boonville. See *The Piegan Storyteller*, Vol. I, No. 1, 8.

account of his life among the Indians; it was a panegyric and farewell to Nätahki, his Pikuni wife, whom he idolized.

In some respects the title may be said to overstate its content. Although Schultz did live for a time "in the lodges of the Blackfeet," he did not do so for long or as a blanket Indian; nor was he ever formally adopted or inducted into the tribe. For most of the period covered in depth by the book, he was employed in the operation of a series of trading posts patronized by a number of tribes. During those years he resided principally at the posts and thereafter at his ranch on the Blackfoot Reservation.

The perceptive reader will recognize Schultz's exercise of an author's prerogative to include or exclude material from a semiautobiographical work of this kind. Although the story purports to cover a period of twenty-six years (1877–1903), to all intents and purposes it ends in 1884 with the disappearance of the buffalo from the plains. The final nineteen years are covered briefly in the book's last fifteen pages. With his fine sense of the dramatic, Schultz undoubtedly realized that it would detract from the unique appeal of his story were he to include any reference to whatever non-Indian activities he happened to engage in during his Indian-oriented years, such as the articles written for eastern or European magazines and his service as a guide in the Rocky Mountains. The same intuition was undoubtedly responsible for the omission from *My Life* of any mention of the birth of a boy child to himself and Nätahki during his trading post years in the early 1880's. In other words, *My Life as an Indian* is not an autobiography in the usual sense of the word. It should be read as a novel, not with a critical eye toward dates, history, or biographical accuracy. When thus approached, it represents an entertaining and extremely readable story revolving around the unusual life the author led for a time among the Blackfeet Indians of Montana in the days of the buffalo.

Schultz's first book after *My Life* was *With the Indians in the Rockies*, published by Houghton Mifflin in September, 1912, followed by *Sinopah, the Indian Boy* in 1913. These two books launched him on his career as a full-time book writer and

freed him from the necessity of having to hold down a desk
or other job while writing in his spare time. Not only was
With the Indians the first of Schultz's books written for boys
and about boys, it follows a pattern based on his own life,
that is, of a lad in St. Louis with a yearning to see the West
who makes the long journey up the Missouri to Fort Benton,
where he becomes acquainted with a Blackfoot boy somewhat older and more experienced and they have many adventures together. Serialized like many of his later books, it
appeared in the pages of *Youth's Companion* under the title
"Indian Winter."

The year 1914 saw the publication of two more books by
Houghton Mifflin Company, these being *The Quest of the
Fish-Dog Skin* and *On the Warpath*. Significantly, Schultz retained the copyright to his books from here on out. But
after the success of the first two books and the exhausting of
the first edition of *My Life*, it became apparent to Houghton
Mifflin that its new author was a winner. Schultz, in turn,
hoped the company would take over further publication of
the book.

In April, 1914, Schultz received the copyright on *My Life*
from George Bird Grinnell's *Forest and Stream*, and Doubleday, Page & Company offered to sell him, for one hundred
dollars, the plates used in printing the first edition. Houghton Mifflin was evidently as interested in issuing a second
edition of the book as was Schultz himself for he was offered
a royalty of 30 per cent if he succeeded in obtaining both the
copyright and the plates. Not having a hundred dollars,
Schultz tried to persuade Doubleday to accept for its magazine *Country Life in America* an article he had just finished
entitled "Virginia Beef Country." However, *Country Life* rejected his manuscript, saying it was too local, so Houghton
Mifflin accepted a plan Schultz had proposed in such an
eventuality: that Houghton Mifflin put up the one hundred
dollars and lower the royalty from 30 per cent to 20 per
cent. As the book was to sell for a dollar fifty, this would
mean a return of thirty cents for Schultz on each sale, but as
things turned out the reduction cost him thousands of dollars. It was also Schultz's suggestion that when Houghton

Mifflin took over publication of the book the title be changed
to *Nätahki and I*, with *My Life as an Indian* as a subtitle. The
publisher said no.

With one exception, all of the books issued before Schultz's
death were published by Houghton Mifflin Company or
under its authorization. That one exception, of course, was
the Doubleday first edition of *My Life* in 1907. Among authorized editions were those published in Europe, as well as
Boy Scout editions of *Lone Bull's Mistake* (1921) and *The
Quest of the Fish-Dog Skin* (1923), both issued by Grosset &
Dunlap at the special price of one dollar each. The only
Schultz books issued by Houghton Mifflin after his death in
1947 were editions of *With the Indians in the Rockies*, *The Quest
of the Fish-Dog Skin*, and *The Trail of the Spanish Horse*. They
were republished about 1960[12] and issued by the company's
juvenile division, apparently from new plates and with illus-
trations by a different artist but otherwise identical to the
original editions. Although no longer in print, they are said
to have been available into the 1970's.

That Schultz's stories have been considered a combination
of good writing and interesting material is attested by their
inclusion in various anthologies over the years. Among
these were two stories used by Ginn & Company in 1936: "A
Warrior and His War Horse" ("The Gray Colt") from *The Attack and Other Stories* and "The Sacred Rock Vision" from *Too
Many Bears and Other Stories*. Published shortly thereafter
was "Skunk Cap's Medicine," which Ross, Peterson & Company put in *Best Short Stories for Boys and Girls, 1938*.

Holt, Rinehart & Winston, in its 1966 college textbook
Culture in Process, was granted permission to include an excerpt from *My Life as an Indian*. In the following year, Har-
court, Brace and World was authorized to do the same in *De-
sign for Good Reading, Level 1*, directed to the junior-high
market. Especially interesting is the fact that the Fawcett edition of *My Life as an Indian* was transcribed into Braille in
1968 by the Monterey Peninsula Volunteer Braille Tran-
scribers of Pacific Grove, California.

[12]Schultz-Graham, "Adventuresome, Amazing Apikuni," 8.

Several Schultz books have been published in Europe. Interestingly, the foreign edition most frequently found is that of *In the Great Apache Forest*, probably because George Crosby, the youthful hero of the book, was a Boy Scout; thus the book had a potential readership in countries where the Scouting movement was popular. In Sweden it was published as *I Den Stors Apacheskogen* (Stockholm, Hugo Gebers Foring, 1939); in Norway it was *Indianarskogen an fortelling fra Arizona* (Bergen, J. W. Eides Boktrykeri A/S, 1956); and in England it was published by Hodder & Stoughton of London. *Fasornas Flod* is a Swedish edition of *The Quest of the Fish-Dog Skin*, published by Falun, B. Wahlstrom Bokforlag in 1973. A British edition of *Rising Wolf, the White Blackfoot* has been published by Nelson of London. Some of Schultz's short stories also were published in England, including an article in the September, 1899, issue of the London periodical *Wide World Magazine* entitled "On the War-Path with Redskins."

Of Schultz's forty-six book-length works, forty-two were published during his life, consisting of twenty-seven serialized books, ten that were books only, and five that were serials only. The four books published after his death were *Floating on the Missouri*, a 1902 serial published in 1979, and three anthologies comprised of earlier-published articles and stories: *Blackfeet and Buffalo* (1962), *Why Gone Those Times?* (1974), and *Many Strange Characters* (1982), all were from the University of Oklahoma Press. *Blackfeet and Buffalo* was edited by Keith C. Seele, the other three by Eugene Lee Silliman.

It is hard to realize that Schultz was nearly fifty years old before his first book was published and before he had an opportunity to appreciate the possibilities of combining magazine publication in installment form with book publication. When he wrote "Floating on the Missouri,"[13] for example, it was not with its subsequent book publication in mind. Indeed, whether he wrote "In the Lodges of the Blackfeet"

[13] Published in *Forest and Stream* in twelve installments beginning February 15 and ending May 24, 1902.

with anything in mind other than its publication in *Forest and Stream* is conjectural.

The secret of serialization, as Schultz soon discovered, was the element of adventure or romance or both with a plot that would hold the reader's interest from installment to installment. Ten of his books failed to qualify for serialization, although for reasons which are not always obvious. In the case of his books dealing with Glacier National Park, such as *Signposts of Adventure* and *Blackfeet Tales of Glacier National Park*, no plot or connected story was involved. Similarly, *Friends of My Life as an Indian* was comprised of biographical sketches and legends, while *The Sun God's Children* had to do with historical and religious phases of Indian life.

A surprising reason for sales resistance on the part of magazine publishers—as well as one that Schultz seemed to have difficulty in appreciating—was the fact that his stories about Indian heroines had little appeal for the boys who read his tales of adventure. Hence such stories as *Bird Woman* and *Running Eagle* (the Pikuni warrior maiden) aroused little interest in magazine publishers with an eye to circulation figures. *In the Great Apache Forest* was a book which Schultz had written expressly for serialization by *American Boy*. To his astonishment, the magazine unhesitatingly rejected it because one of the principal characters was a girl.[14]

The reasons for other rejections are somewhat obscure. As for *In Enemy Country*, the asking price of one thousand dollars seemed to be a stumbling block, and even though Schultz offered to accept as little as six hundred dollars, no taker could be found. There is no information as to why *Sinopah*, published in 1913, went unserialized. It is believed that *White Beaver* was serialized under the title "Star Woman," although the magazine in which it would have appeared about 1930 remains unknown.

Of Schultz's serialized books, all but six had appeared in

[14] Houghton Mifflin gave Schultz the same message, to wit, that its sales had suffered when the hero of the story was the heroine. The company turned down his story entitled "Lance Woman" in 1933 and suggested that he "defeminize" the story.

either *Youth's Companion* or *American Boy*[15] before coming
out in book form. These six included the early serials in *Forest and Stream*, one of them the previously mentioned "Floating on the Missouri" in 1902, and the other, of course, "In the Lodges of the Blackfeet" (*My Life as an Indian*) in 1906. Of the remaining four, three appeared in *National Stockman and Farmer* and included *The Dreadful River Cave* in 1918–19, *The Danger Trail* in 1922, and *Sahtaki and I* in 1923. The fourth was *Sun Woman*, which was serialized in condensed form by *Frontier* magazine in 1926. Still another serial that appeared in none of the foregoing magazines was one that came out in *Boy's Life* for July, August and September, 1935, under the title "The Sacred Otter Bowcase." Though it was never published as a book, it did appear in condensed form in *Blackfeet and Buffalo*. Many Schultz short stories appeared in *Youth's Companion*, *American Boy* and *Forest and Stream*, thirty-two of which are listed in the Appendix.

The last Schultz book to be published by Houghton Mifflin during his lifetime was *Short Bow's Big Medicine* in the year 1940. It grew out of a story entitled "Warring Medicines," which had been published in serial form in 1934 by *American Boy*. Houghton Mifflin had declined that same year to publish it,[16] presumably because of its insufficient length. In 1938, when he again broached the subject of its publication as a book, Houghton Mifflin editors told him plainly that it was not long enough for book purposes, for which they felt 55,000 words was the minimum, whereupon Schultz indicated his willingness to expand it to at least that length. He commenced work on the lengthening project forthwith but was hampered by a variety of ailments with which he was afflicted during his final years at Browning. Ultimately, he got the word count up to 54,875 and resubmitted the manuscript. He had planned to ask one thousand dollars for it, but by the time it was completed and in the hands of

---

[15] After amalgamation of the two magazines about 1927, the further serials appeared in *American Boy*.

[16] Letter from Houghton Mifflin to Schultz at his Bozeman address dated April 21, 1934.

the publisher, he was in such financial straits that he agreed to accept an offer of five hundred dollars.

Schultz left one important book unfinished, although it had supposedly been under way during all of his declining years at Fort Washakie. This was *Bear Chief's War Shirt*. After her husband's death, Jessica authorized its completion by Wilbur W. Betts of Seattle, Washington, a retired Boeing Aircraft Corporation executive. Her choice was motivated by two things: Betts had been a close friend of Schultz and was much interested in Indianology, and Betts was a descendant of the Seneca tribe. Despite the circumstance that the manuscript left by Schultz consisted of only sixty-two pages and that Betts's efforts to reach certain persons who might have information about how the shirt was retrieved from the Assiniboines were unproductive, he was able to complete the book[17] and it was published in 1983 by Mountain Press of Missoula, Montana.

There is no complete bibliography of Schultz works. However, a chronological compilation of his books has been prepared by Arthur H. Clark, Jr. It shows not only the names of the thirty-seven books published during the author's lifetime but also the dates of first issue and the original prices. A copy in revised form has been included in the Appendix, along with a table showing his serials. Also, for ready reference, there is in the Appendix a table of the forty-one Schultz books mentioned heretofore, shown in correlation with his thirty-three serials. Of his thirty-seven books, ten were not serialized for one reason or another, as shown in the same table. The five serials that never became books were "The Sacred Buffalo Hunt," "The Warring Tribes," "The Wolfers," "The Peace Trail," and "The Sacred Otter Bowcase."

What are the possibilities that other Schultz books may yet be published? The plans for *Bear Chief's War Shirt* have been mentioned, and the James Willard Schultz Society has similar plans with respect to "The Wolfers." As a matter of fact,

---

[17] For the story of *Bear Chief's War Shirt*, see *The Piegan Storyteller*, Vol. I, No. 3, July, 1976, 11, and Vol. II, No. 2, April, 1977, 1–2.

the society hopes to publish all of the serials that have never become books, this having been one of its various objectives, as resources permit.

There is at least a possibility that additional Schultz stories and articles may yet be discovered. Included among the potential sources for such finds are the back issues of the *Great Falls Tribune* for the years 1895 through 1942. Other possibilities are the magazines to which Schultz is known to have contributed from 1900 to 1941; these include *Boy's Life*, *Open Road for Boys*, *True Western Adventure*, *Outing*, *St. Nicholas*, and similar periodicals of the 1900–1940 era during which Schultz was producing stories that might have interested their readers.[18]

[18] I have reviewed the issues of *Forest and Stream* for the period 1879–94. It is possible that later issues of that publication might reveal articles or stories not listed herein.

CHAPTER 26

Thirty Years with Houghton Mifflin

I T was in the year 1912 that James Willard Schultz and Houghton Mifflin Company of Boston began their long and mutually beneficial relationship. From that date forward, Houghton Mifflin was his sole publisher; in fact the exclusive arrangement did not terminate until several years after his death in 1947. In all, the Boston firm published thirty-seven Schultz books, a remarkable fact when one considers that he was fifty-three when the first volume was published. Of course, there were many reprints and editions of the thirty-seven, including special editions issued with Houghton Mifflin authorization in the United States and abroad, some of them years after his death.

No figures are available as to the number of Schultz books printed and sold to date by Houghton Mifflin or under its banner. It has been estimated that *My Life as an Indian* alone may have accounted for half a million, although this figure does not include hundreds of thousands sold after 1956 by other publishers.[1] The probabilities are that close to two million Schultz books have been published, including those in Europe, with an aggregate value of a possible three million

[1] According to records in the possession of Schultz's widow, three editions were brought out by various publishers after the copyright on *My Life as an Indian* was relinquished by Houghton Mifflin in 1955. One was an abridged paperback (90,000 words) brought out by Fawcett Publications in March, 1956, which went through many printings and by 1968 had sold 145,000 copies. The second was a juvenile edition (abridged to 45,000 words) edited by Robert E. Gard of the University of Wisconsin and published in 1957 by Duell, Sloan and Pearce. The third, a photographic reprint of the original by Corner House Publishers of Williamstown, Massachusetts, appeared in 1973.

dollars, since most of them sold for a dollar-fifty and none for more than three dollars.

Something of the story of the unique relationship between Schultz and Houghton Mifflin Company is told in more than seven hundred letters exchanged between them over a period of thirty years.[2] An interesting feature of this relationship is that it was entered into and conducted entirely by correspondence. In the thirty-five years of its duration, Schultz's only personal contact with anyone connected with the company was a casual luncheon meeting of a social character with a junior executive who happened to be in Los Angeles on other business one day in February, 1926. This was Ferris Greenslet, who handled the Schultz account for his company during the years 1914–26. Taking up the correspondence chore as of January, 1927, was Ira Rich Kent,[3] who joined the Houghton Mifflin staff at that time after many years in the editorial department of *Youth's Companion*. In his capacity there he had become familiar with Schultz's work, since the magazine had been publishing short stories by Schultz since 1910. Despite his nearly twenty years of handling the correspondence with Schultz, the opportunity to meet him personally never came about.

Schultz had become a member of the company's stable of writers in the usual way, that is, by submitting a manuscript that met the firm's criteria with respect to salability. In a few years, of course, he came to be counted as one of the regulars, from each of whom a book of popular interest could be expected each year. Ironically, however, when in 1940 he submitted for Houghton Mifflin's consideration the material for what would have been the thirty-eighth Schultz book, it was not given the usual automatic acceptance and, as we shall see, did not reach the point of publication.

In the early part of his relationship with the company, Schultz was given to understand that the market for juvenile books would not absorb more than one book a year and that

[2] Preserved on microfilm in the Houghton Library at Harvard University.

[3] Kent continued to serve as the Houghton Mifflin editor for Schultz until his death on January 5, 1943, after a brief illness.

its appearance on the market should be timed to coincide with the opening of school in the fall. As the popularity of Schultz books grew, however, Houghton Mifflin was forced to revise its thinking in this regard, and for a period of more than fifteen years it planned regularly for the publication of one Schultz book in the spring and another in the fall. In some years, when he was at the peak of his popularity, as many as three of his books were published each year.

The contracts with Houghton Mifflin for each book provided for the payment of royalties twice a year, on May 1 and November 1. However, Schultz was rarely able to manage his budget and living expenses to conform to these contractual provisions. He found it difficult to live within his means, and his correspondence file is replete with letters and telegrams imploring Ferris Greenslet or his successor to send advances to keep the wolf away from the door. When Greenslet happened to be in England or on vacation, Schultz's pleas were largely disregarded. However, many of his requests indicated that his plight was desperate, saying, "We don't have enough money for food and clothing" (Fort Washakie, Wyoming, June 24, 1944), or "Arrived today from Glacier Park. Flat broke. Please wire $400" (Los Angeles, September 26, 1926), or "We haven't a cent left for living expenses" (Los Angeles, April 23, 1922), or "In all our lives we were never so hard up as now" (Greer, Arizona, September 22, 1915), to cite a few examples.

Although the Schultzes enjoyed what was considered a rather substantial income, it seemed never to be enough to meet their expenses. Of course, their way of life included the maintenance of two and sometimes three part-time residences, plus their rather considerable travel expense to and from California, Arizona, and Montana. He was generous with his friends, frequently having Houghton Mifflin send people copies, and often complete sets, of his books, charging them to his account. There were innumerable expenses connected with his prolonged campaign on behalf of the Blackfeet and Hopi Indians in 1920–22. Moreover, his medical, dental and hospital bills must have been enormous.

In response to his many requests for advances, the staff at

Houghton Mifflin did its best to hold Schultz to contract provisions governing the time for royalty payments. This need for funds seemed to accelerate after the Schultzes moved back to Browning in 1934, despite the fact that they now had the salary of Mrs. Schultz with which to pay expenses. Being well known in Browning, he was able to devise a rather ingenious system for obtaining what amounted to advances against his royalties by means of assignments. For example, he would go to the First National Bank of Browning and in exchange for a loan give the bank an assignment against his royalties due on a specified date. Houghton Mifflin did not particularly like this procedure but nevertheless cooperated as long as the assignee was a bank.

The correspondence between Schultz and Houghton Mifflin was filled with references to the possibility of undertaking a lecture tour. He expressed an interest in going east to talk before clubs, college groups, Boy Scouts, Woodcraft Leagues, and others. The talks would have to do with his life as an Indian and in Glacier Park, and presumably the Great Northern Railway would furnish suitable slides or motion pictures. Schultz always expected to do this on a salary, with all expenses paid for himself and his wife, so while there was much discussion from 1915 to 1926 about doing such talks, nothing ever materialized.

It had been Schultz's dream to write the Great American Novel, a romance of the fur-trade days. As far back as 1914, in his letters to Ferris Greenslet, he had made known his desire to write such a book and had even set forth an outline of what he had in mind. He also had chosen a title for his novel, to wit, *Sun Woman*, and kept saying that he would write a few chapters as soon as he had finished a more urgent adventure story. Greenslet never gave him any encouragement, since it might imperil the established success of his reputation as a writer of adventure stories for boys. Finally, after nursing the project for more than a decade, Schultz did write the novel of his dreams. *Sun Woman* was one of three Schultz books published in 1926, and it sold for two dollars (instead of a dollar-fifty) in token of its being a book for mature readers. It had been published in condensed form by *Frontier* magazine.

Schultz had collaborated only once in a literary way, that having been on *The Sun God's Children*, published in 1930 after he wrote it with his wife-to-be, Jessie Donaldson. However, he frequently mentioned the possibility that he might collaborate with other authors in the preparation of a book. In the summer of 1915, when Mary Roberts Rinehart was in Glacier Park with the well-known Howard Eaton party, Schultz was able to spend considerable time with her and supposedly helped her with the writing of an article on the dire need and suffering of the Blackfeet.

According to Schultz, two of the best-known novelists of the period had indicated a desire to collaborate with him on a novel of the early fur trade: Henry Herbert Knibbs, author of *Overland Red*, and Harold Bell Wright, author of *The Winning of Barbara Worth* and other popular novels of the 1900–1925 era. In May, 1926, Schultz advised Houghton Mifflin that the well-known author Agnes C. Laut[4] was planning to spend the summer in Glacier Park and that together they would write a scenario of fur-trade days, she the white part, he the Indian side. None of these interesting ideas materialized.

As a rule, Schultz received royalties of 10 per cent of the retail price of the first five thousand books sold and 15 per cent thereafter. However, there was a special arrangement wth respect to *My Life as an Indian*, for which his share was 20 per cent. For his magazine stories published by *Youth's Companion* he had received seven hundred dollars in 1915 and one thousand dollars for a serial, the latter, of course, subsequently being sold to Houghton Mifflin for publication in book form.

Near the end of his productive years, Schultz conceived the idea of writing a series of sketches dealing with his early years in Montana. As he wrote them from time to time, they were published by the *Great Falls Tribune*, and it occurred to him about 1939 that he might assemble a group of these articles, possibly with the addition of some of his earlier magazine stories, and arrange for their publication in book form

[4] Author of *Enchanted Trails of Glacier Park*, published in 1926 by Robert M. McBride & Company of New York.

under the title *Reminiscences*. At least that was the working title under which the unedited material was submitted to Houghton Mifflin in February, 1940, to consider for publication.

When certain preliminaries had been cleared up, Houghton Mifflin began to give careful consideration to the material Schultz had submitted. The editors realized that the newspaper clippings would require extensive editing, which they were not prepared to provide. Moreover, questions were raised among the staff as to the content of parts of the material. One staff member recommended against acquiring the material because of what he called plagiarism. In a short note to Ira Kent, he had this to say:

> I went over the Schultz material and found that at least two of the stories in the manuscript have been stolen from FRIENDS OF MY LIFE AS AN INDIAN. "Charles Rivet's Tale of Hardship" is a rewrite of "Charles Rivois's Tale of Hardship" (Chapter VII), and "The Passing of Back-in-Sight" is a rewrite of "How Apsi and I Found, and Lost, Old Back-in-Sight, in the Long-Ago" (Chapter XIII).
>
> The stories are rewritten and improved, but they are definitely the same stories, with whole paragraphs lifted intact from the book version.[5]

Despite the various problems posed by the material, Houghton Mifflin finally offered a 10 per cent royalty plus five hundred dollars to be paid on signing of the contract. The offer was promptly accepted by Schultz, who by this time was living in Wyoming. The contract was mailed early in January, 1941, but the five hundred dollar check went to the First National Bank of Browning to satisfy an assignment from Schultz.

[5] The staff critic might have added that a substantial part of the Schultz material, later published in *Blackfeet and Buffalo* as "Some Adventures of Old Fort Conrad," was a rewrite of Chapter XII of *Friends of My Life as an Indian*, entitled "Many Tail Feathers Tells Us of a Terrible Enemy and How he Fulfilled his Sun Vow to Kill Him."

"The Passing of Back-in-Sight" appeared in *Youth's Companion*, on January 5, 1911, and "Rivois' Tale" appeared in the *Companion* on February 29, 1912.

It is interesting to note that neither "The Passing of Back-in-Sight" nor "Rivois' Tale" appeared in *Blackfeet and Buffalo* but that the story of Many-Tail-Feathers, extensively rewritten, did.

At the time it signed the contract with Schultz for *Reminiscences*, it was undoubtedly Houghton Mifflin's intention to edit and publish the material. But the editors were dilatory about it, and nothing had been done by the time war broke out in December, 1941. That was an event, of course, which caused the revision of many priorities, and so it was that in January, 1943, when Schultz was in the hospital at Lander, Wyoming, Houghton Mifflin wrote him that it was still trying to get the material "in shape for publication." But the editors continued to temporize and the project was still on high center at the time of his death in 1947. As a matter of fact, Mrs. Schultz was to learn that in 1953, thirteen years after the material was submitted, the company still had no plans for editing or publication. Accordingly, she undertook to edit and market the material herself; after submitting the result to a number of publishers without success, she enlisted the assistance of a friend, Keith C. Seele. Finally, in 1962, the material was published by the University of Oklahoma Press as *Blackfeet and Buffalo*.

In 1955, Houghton Mifflin, upon request, consented to a termination of the agreement (June 16, 1914) for the publication of *My Life as an Indian*. The purpose was to enable Jessica to negotiate with other publishers who might be interested. Houghton Mifflin, however, declined to consent to a termination of the agreements covering four other early Schultz books: *With the Indians in the Rockies*, *Sinopah, the Indian Boy*, *The Quest of the Fish-Dog Skin*, and *The Trail of the Spanish Horse*. The company refused to terminate the agreements because it had decided to publish new editions of three of them (all but *Sinopah*) and in fact did publish such new editions in 1960.

From the pages of the Schultz–Houghton Mifflin correspondence, it is sometimes possible to glean information about his books that is not otherwise available. For instance, Schultz's original title for *Blackfeet Tales of Glacier National Park* was *Last Camps with My People*. *Son of the Navaho* had been serialized in *Youth's Companion* as "Wampin." Schultz's title for *In the Great Apache Forest* was *The Boy Scout of the Mountains*. The working title for *Sun Woman* had been *The Sun God's Woman*. *White Beaver* had once been called *Star*

Woman and may have been serialized under that name. In the months before its publication, *Red Crow's Brother* was usually referred to at Houghton Mifflin as "the Hugh Monroe story" and was given its final title because that was the name under which it had been published in *American Boy*. It was Ira Rich Kent who supplied the imaginative name *Signposts of Adventure*, which undoubtedly sold many more books than would have been the case had Schultz's title, *Glacier National Park as the Indians Knew It*, been used.

From time to time throughout the relationship between Schultz and Houghton Mifflin, the latter would prepare for publicity purposes a circular entitled "APIKUNI, The Story-teller." It usually contained a short and colorful blurb about Schultz in the role of APIKUNI and included a list of his books under the headings "Mr. Schultz's Books for Boys and Girls" and "For Older Readers." Schultz frequently reordered quantities of these small circulars for his personal use and to leave at various places in Glacier National Park.

CHAPTER 27

Acclaim as a Writer

OR more than two centuries the American frontier has supplied an attractive milieu for writers dealing with adventure and romance. Peopled with thousands of Indian tribesmen both willing and able to defend their home territory against the relentless incursions of the white man, it was a setting without equal. Among the hundreds of writers who chose to deal with this magnificent phase of history, two giants have stood out: James Fenimore Cooper in the 1800's and James Willard Schultz in the 1900's.

The two men shared a number of interesting similarities. Both were born into well-to-do families and grew up in upstate New York. Both had the same first name and both used their middle names for literary purposes. As authors, both were widely read in this country as well as in Europe. Each in his day was almost a household name, and the former popularity of each has been undergoing something of an unexpected renaissance.[1] Beyond this point, however, the likenesses do not extend.

Schultz knew his Indians intimately; he lived with the Piegan tribe, married one of its women, and learned to speak the language fluently. He made it his business to become the chronicler of the Blackfeet, to acquaint himself with their history and legends, to know personally as many of them as possible, and to identify himself with their causes. Most of his characters were drawn from among his real-life friends and acquaintances, although he sometimes concealed their identity. As Schultz presented his Indians, he showed that they possessed the same human qualities as

white people. His stories told frequently of tribal life, showing that his Pikuni people loved, hated, feared, warred, and
even worshiped in the same way as whites. His friends among
the Pikunis were true and dear.

Schultz's books were primarily stories of adventure rather
than romances, simply but skillfully written, with the youthful reader in mind. Most of them appeared in serial form in
Youth's Companion or *American Boy*. A large proportion of
them were based upon personal knowledge of actual incidents involving himself or Indians that he had either known
or known of. Many of the writings had to do with adventures or legends of the Blackfeet or other western tribes.

Because he wrote for a mostly juvenile readership, it is
difficult to predict Schultz's ultimate place in literature. The
fact that in the 1980's more than thirty-five years after his
death, he had an enthusiastic following throughout the
country in a group known as the James Willard Schultz
Society is significant, as is the society's publication at regular
intervals of *The Piegan Storyteller*, devoted exclusively to extolling the virtues of its hero and his works. The evaluations
of him by his contemporaries speak eloquently of his ability
as a writer in his particular field. Although he has never
achieved the breadth of recognition accorded Cooper
throughout the world, he has not been without tributes
from distinguished and knowledgeable people. Among
many such was J. Donald Adams, who wrote in his *New York
Times* column, which he called "Speaking of Books":

> *My Life as an Indian* is the real McCoy. It gives, in vivid de-
> tail and at first hand, the life of the Plains Indian in the days
> before the buffalo had vanished. And no people, in my es-
> timation, ever lived a better life, or one of deeper and fuller
> satisfactions. We, who destroyed it—as was inevitable—have
> not substituted a better; most certainly not for the descen-
> dants of those who lived it.[2]

---

[1] With reference to Cooper, see *The Leatherstocking Saga*, published in
1954 by Pantheon Books of New York and edited by Allan Nevins.
[2] Schultz-Graham, "Adventuresome, Amazing Apikuni," 2, 17.

Professor Verne Dusenberry of the English Department at Montana State University has written a perceptive appreciation of Schultz:

Good writing of any kind required knowledge of the subject and understanding of the peoples involved. Schultz had both of these qualities. But not only does he stand practically alone in the literary interpretation of the Indian, but he has made a distinct contribution to the science of anthropology. True, he did not consciously attempt to analyze the lives of his Indian companions. He let his good friends—men who were professional anthropologists like George Bird Grinnell—do that. But anthropology owes a debt to Schultz. His close observations of Indian life in many instances are excellent ethnographic accounts. Reading Schultz for this detail gives us a picture of Blackfeet life that is unobtainable elsewhere.

Many of us envy him the opportunity he had of knowing and of living with the Blackfeet in the last days of their glory. Few of us, I fear, would have shared our knowledge or recorded our information as Schultz did. His was a great opportunity and one that he utilized well—both for himself and for American literature.[3]

In his book entitled *Outlines of American Literature*,[4] William J. Long had this to say:

The most remarkable work that has ever been done in the western field with the Indians as a character appears in the little books of James Willard Schultz who is ignored by literary critics because he writes only adventure stories for boys. Would that those who write for men and women had the secret of his method! The heroes of all his tales are a white boy, the son of a fur trader, and his "almost brother," Pitamakan, a young Blackfoot Indian. The adventures and escapes of these two are a marvelous reflection of the habits and beliefs of savage riders of the plains in the days of the buffalo. Schultz's way of telling—simple, straightforward, with constant action and dramatic dialogue—is near perfection and

[3] Verne Dusenberry, "An Appreciation of James Willard Schultz," *Montana: The Magazine of Western History*, Autumn, 1960, 22, 23.
[4] Published by Ginn & Company in 1925.

was evidently learned by listening to Indian tale-tellers while
he was a member of the tribe. Of all our writers, early and
late, he is the only one who comes near to knowing the soul
of an Indian.[5]

Writing in the *Dallas News*, the able western writer Stanley
Vestal observed on July 13, 1930:

> Among writers on the American Indian, Willard Schultz is
> distinguished by a rare combination of virtues. In the first
> place, he knew the Indian in the old buffalo days, and knew
> him well, sharing his life. Throughout a long lifetime he has
> retained the confidence of these friends of his youth. In ad-
> dition to these advantages, Mr. Schultz is something of a
> scholar, and his work is in accord with the most authentic
> records of the Plains tribes, both on the historical and eth-
> nological sides. And to crown their merits, he can write.

One writer offered this comment in reference to the popularity of Schultz stories among youthful readers:

> They like the simple, direct style of the narratives, beside
> which the polished and labored efforts of Cooper seem to
> them the work of some elephantine *literateur* who doesn't
> know how to keep his feet on the path of a story. Schultz gets
> in a great deal more accurate detailed description of the In-
> dians and their customs than Cooper, but he does it so well,
> and mixes it so cleverly with his true-to-life narrative, that
> boys never object to it.[6]

In a February 16, 1961, letter to Jessica Schultz, Stuart W.
Conner, Billings, Montana, attorney and chairman of the
Billings Archaeological Society, wrote:

> It is unfortunate that a man such as Mr. Schultz can never
> know in his lifetime the pleasure he has created for genera-
> tions of readers. Mr. Schultz stands alone in his field, but if
> there had been thousands reporting identical experiences, I
> am confident none could have conveyed the feeling and hu-
> manity he did. . . . Mr. Schultz's books are not only a valuable

---

[5]See Part 1, p. 208. Quoted in Schultz-Graham, "Adventuresome,
Amazing Apikuni," 8.

[6]Hubert V. Coryell, "James Willard Schultz," *St. Nicholas*, July, 1934,
433.

insight into the personality and life of the Indian, but contain anthropological information of great value.

Keith C. Seele, the University of Chicago professor who served as editor of *Blackfeet and Buffalo*, was a Schultz aficionado from childhood, having read thirty-three of Schultz's thirty-seven books. He considered *My Life as an Indian*, an American classic destined to live forever in the literature of this country and carried it with him on his travels, reading and rereading it. He stated in his introduction to *Blackfeet and Buffalo*:

> While [I have] long been convinced that . . . *My Life as an Indian*, is an American classic of the old West, [I see] now more than ever that Apikuni—to refer to Schultz by his Blackfoot name—will forever be remembered as the greatest interpreter of a noble Indian people to all who are capable of appreciating them. Apikuni, however, in contrast to many of the distinguished writers who in their turn have added to our knowledge and understanding of Indian life and history, has permitted the Blackfeet—more strictly the Pikunis (Piegans), southernmost branch of the great Blackfoot Confederacy—to interpret themselves in their own words. Without being a journalist, he has been a reporter, and a very faithful one, on the daily life and conversations as well as the deeper side of the Indian as revealed by his prayers, his religious ceremonies, and his unswerving conviction of the indwelling presence of the Above Ones in all his acts.
>
> Apikuni's reporting is unique for the reason that, though a white man, he was also truly an Indian. . . . He learned the difficult Blackfoot language at the age of eighteen and spoke it constantly with his family and Indian friends for more than fifty years. Thus he not only spoke Blackfoot, he *thought* it as well.
>
> . . . Apikuni listened to the Indian storytellers, and he became one of the best of them. But, unlike them, he could transfer their stories of the lodge fires to paper for thousands to enjoy forever. His literary style is unique; it is Blackfoot talk in English words and sentences. He is an artist of narrative and a master of suspense. One follows his stories with breathless interest and deplores the thinning pages at the end of the book. If only there were more and more

and more! If only his books were not so few—only thirty-seven. . . .

George Bird Grinnell, the eminent anthropologist, naturalist, editor, and author, wrote in his introduction to *My Life as an Indian*:

> In this account of his long residence with the Blackfeet, Mr. Schultz has given us a remarkable story. It is an animated and vivid picture of Indian life. The scene is on the plains in the old days, in the picturesque period when the tribe lived in a primitive way, subsisting on the buffalo and at war with hostile neighbors. It is a true history and not romance, yet abounds in romantic incident. In its absolute truthfulness lies its value.
>
> The book has extraordinary interest as a human document. It is a study of human nature in red. The author has penetrated the veil of racial indifference and misunderstanding and has got close to the heart of the people about whom he writes. Such an intimate revelation of the domestic life of the Indians has never before been written. The sympathetic insight everywhere evident is everywhere convincing. We feel that the men and the women portrayed are men and women of actual living existence. And while in the lodges on the Marias the elemental passions have fuller and franker sway, we recognize in the Blackfoot as here revealed a creature of common humanity like our own. His are the same loves and hates, hopes and fears. The motives which move him are those which move us. The Indian is the white man without the veneer of civilization.

Some, though not all, of these favorable comments were from contemporaries of Schultz, yet note should be taken of a more recent feather in his literary cap. In a 1982 survey conducted in the pages of *Montana: The Magazine of Western History* to determine reader opinion concerning "the best books about Montana," the works of 398 authors received votes, with the result, according to Harry W. Fritz, professor of history at the University of Montana, who conducted the survey, that

> James Willard Schultz who, with A. B. Guthrie, Jr., placed nine winners, ranked highest with *My Life as an Indian*.

CHAPTER 28

Problems of an Author

As a writer, James Willard Schultz made no pretense of being anything other than a faithful portrayer of Indian life and a storyteller of western adventure designed primarily to entertain the youthful reader. Whether his charm lay in his special style or in the choice and handling of his subject matter or both, Schultz enjoyed between World Wars I and II a readership popularity that amounted almost to a cult—a popularity that has had something of a resurgence during the 1970's and 1980's. The loyalty of his followers has continued unabated in spite of faults they seem to overlook entirely.

The principal complaint of his more perceptive readers and those having a familiarity with Montana history seems to have been that Schultz, in dealing with dates and sometimes with characters of Montana history, was often guilty of inaccuracies. Particularly did this criticism have reference to events concerning which he had first-hand information or a ready means of verifying its accuracy.

One of the more notable of Schultz's gaffes on dates, and perhaps the perfect example of his strange inability to achieve accuracy in this respect, had to do with the date of birth of his only child, Hart Merriam. Here was a date of which Schultz, above all others, had intimate personal knowledge and which there was no point or purpose in even mentioning, particularly in a publication of general circulation, unless it was to be strictly factual. Regardless of that, however, he managed to misstate not only the month but also the year of his son's birth, reporting that this "blessed event" of February, 1882, occurred in March, 1884.[1]

Schultz also demonstrated that he could be equally erratic with respect to dates of death. Since he had helped bury his good friend Hugh Monroe and later had served as biographer of parts of Monroe's life, it would seem that Schultz was the one person who had every reason to remember and to report correctly the year, at least, of Hugh's demise. Yet in two of his articles or books he stated that it occurred in 1896, this despite the fact that it had been widely publicized by the Montana press that Monroe died in December, 1892.

While each such error with regard to family or close friend was an inexcusable faux pas on the part of Schultz, they were not such as to attract readily the notice of a casual reader. But Schultz was seemingly oblivious to dates, even to those he had previously reported, being strangely consistent in his inconsistency. Frequently when he had occasion to recount the same events in two or more of his books, they would reflect material variations in his dates. Another series of comparisons will serve to illustrate the point. In telling the story of guiding Grinnell and others through parts of the future Glacier National Park during the 1880's and early 1890's, which he did in two of his books, Schultz gave dates that were often inconsistent. In *Blackfeet Tales of Glacier National Park*, Schultz wrote that he first visited St. Mary Lakes in 1882; in *Blackfeet and Buffalo*, he said it was in October, 1883. Similarly, in *Blackfeet Tales*, Schultz reported that the first visit of George Bird Grinnell to the St. Mary country was in the autumn of 1883, while in *Blackfeet and Buffalo*, he stated correctly that it occurred in 1885. In *Blackfeet Tales*, Schultz said it was in 1885 that he first took Grinnell up the Swiftcurrent Valley, but it was in 1886 according to *Blackfeet and Buffalo*. In *Blackfeet Tales* he told how the Kutenai Indians had led him to a spot that he named Kutenai Lick in

[1]This was in an article published in the *Great Falls Tribune* on January 10, 1937, when Schultz was living at Browning and republished in *Blackfeet and Buffalo*, 82. Hart was born on February 18, 1882, more than two years earlier.

1883, but the incident happened in 1887 according to *Blackfeet and Buffalo*; he demonstrated his versatility by reporting in *Signposts of Adventure* that it occurred in 1885. The discerning reader who happens to detect a discrepancy in dates given by Schultz in two or more of his books for the same incident or event would naturally assume that one or the other of the dates must be correct. Not necessarily so. The bewildering fact is that sometimes neither of such cited dates for a historic event is correct. For example, although Schultz dated the exploration of the glacier that bears Grinnell's name at 1885 in *Blackfeet Tales* and in 1886 in *Blackfeet and Buffalo*, the actual date was 1887, a fact correctly reported by himself in still another book, *Signposts of Adventure*. And although the year of Grinnell's exploration of Blackfoot Glacier was 1891, Schultz placed it at 1888 in *Blackfeet and Buffalo*, apparently having forgotten that he had reported the year to be 1886 in *Blackfeet Tales*.

Schultz's inability to deal successfully with the date problem on a personal history level explains, of course, why he had similar difficulty in coping with it in respect to Montana history generally. This mental blind spot represented a quirk or trait of which he may not have been aware. Certainly he had no intention of misleading his readers but was simply incapable of factual precision so far as dates were concerned.

Another fault, according to readers, has been Schultz's tiresome repetition of certain episodes and stories, such as the christening of St. Mary Lake and the career of Hugh Monroe, each appearing in at least five of his books. As interesting as these incidents or episodes may be when first read in *My Life as an Indian*, they lose something of their charm when encountered again and again, and then sometimes again, in his other books. Moreover, it can become progressively more confusing as the discovery is made that the various versions do not agree with one another in respect to essential names and dates, especially when the variance among the latter is by as much as two decades. A glaring example of both repetition and inconsistency is to be

found in Schultz's different accounts of the St. Mary Lake
christening with regard to the date of the incident and the
identity of the priest who assertedly participated, as is shown
below:

NAME OF BOOK	PAGE	NAME OF PRIEST	DATE OF EVENT
Blackfeet Tales of Glacier National Park	146–47	DeSmet	"in the 1830s"
My Life as an Indian	185	DeSmet	"in the early eighteen fifties"
Signposts of Adventure	122	Lacombe	"in the eighteen fifties"
Blackfeet and Buffalo	70	Lacombe	1846
William James, Indian Scout	32	Lacombe	no date given
Friends of My Life as an Indian	65	"a Black Robe"	no date given

It is fairly obvious from the foregoing that Schultz not
only did not know who was present or when but that he had
neither records nor reliable memory on the subject. Unfortunately, the facts are that none of the four mentioned dates
could possibly have been correct and that neither DeSmet,
Lacombe, nor any other priest was present at the ceremony.

Nearly every Montana history buff knows that Father De-
Smet was never in the St. Mary region, or even in the Northwest, in either the 1830's or the 1850's. Likewise, it is not difficult to verify the fact that Father Lacombe did not visit
Montana before 1869; moreover, as of 1846, he had not
seen the Northwest, nor had he completed his studies for
the priesthood. Incidentally, although Monroe was unquestionably a key figure at the ceremony, Schultz apparently
took no note of the fact that Monroe had frequently stated
for publication that those with him at the christening were

his Kutenai friends, thereby in effect denying the presence of a priest; nor had Schultz noted the fact that books written by or about DeSmet and Lacombe contained no mention of the incident.

Although the foregoing are but a few of Schultz's many errors in the way of positive misstatements or inconsistencies, he was also capable of conveying misinformation through the omission of a fact or set of facts. For example, although Hugh Monroe had fathered nine or ten children, Schultz stated repeatedly that Monroe's family consisted of three boys and three girls, and he gave their names. He apparently never did discover that the Monroe offspring also included Felix, Oliver, and William, Alberta residents who had grown up during Hugh's second and rather lengthy employment in Canada by the Hudson's Bay Company but who did not cross the line into Montana.

While the litany of Schultz errors seems to have escaped the attention of his readers in general, as well as that of the literary critics and others who extolled his work in the preceding chapter, the mistakes have at least been mentioned by the knowledgeable editors of his posthumously published works. Commenting in the foreword to one of these anthologies, one editor stated:

> It should be understood that Schultz was a storyteller, not a historian. He did not carefully study, as a scholar would, historical records, journals and reports in order to reach objective, documented conclusions. Rather as a sympathetic listener, he recorded the stories and oral traditions of an Indian culture before its demise.[2]

The same commentator made the same point a little more emphatically at another time:

> Schultz's style of writing has not endeared him to scholarly historians. When accurate information about names, dates and places is of prime importance, James Willard Schultz's writing cannot be relied upon. What is certain is his veracity in recording the attitudes, customs, religious beliefs, occupa-

---

[2] Eugene Lee Silliman in *Why Gone Those Times?*, x.

tional practices and reminiscences of the Indian and white friends he knew intimately. This he did with consummate skill.[3]

In full agreement with the foregoing was Keith C. Seele, one of Schultz's greatest admirers, as well as the editor of *Blackfeet and Buffalo*, who commented:

> Apikuni . . . *was a storyteller, but he never set himself up to be a historian or scientist.* It is of the utmost importance that the historian and searcher after facts neatly verified not look to him for definitive historical truth. This was not his forte nor his aim.[4]

That Schultz was not a historian's historian must be conceded. He was primarily a storyteller, a writer of Indian legends, lore, and life, a field in which he had no peer. His principal purpose was to entertain rather than to inform. His tales of life among the Indians had a realistic charm based on his intimate knowledge of their customs, beliefs, and day-to-day activities; yet the fact that his stories were sometimes given an inaccurate historical background was not always understood or appreciated by some of his readers.

On the other hand, Schultz was also a writer of biographical and autobiographical articles and books. These ranged from *My Life as an Indian*, a romanticized version of a part of his life among the Pikunis, to articles purporting to represent unvarnished reports of his activities as a frontier Indian trader and mountain guide. These were not history per se, but they did have a factual basis in names, dates, places, much of the value of which depended upon their accuracy.

In his autobiographical material, it was unquestionably his intention to be as accurate as possible with dates and names; hence the various inaccuracies listed above, particularly those having to do with dates of birth or death or other important events of family or close friends, are puzzling and appear to show that he committed such errors in spite of himself. They go even further in helping to explain his vul-

---

[3] Eugene Lee Silliman in *Many Strange Characters*, xiii.
[4] *Blackfeet and Buffalo*, ix.

nerability to error in ordinary biographical material, into which inconsistent and erroneous dates and names could have crept more easily when he did not have personal knowledge of the facts.

Although readers of Schultz books and articles have been briefly and rather generally alerted as to his weakness in dealing with historical material, until now no in-depth review of the subject has been available. Readers who have reached this point must be wondering about the effect of Schultz's errors on the quality of his work and the sale of his books.

It could be said that in Schultz's case evaluations are probably made by three types of critics, including those who have read and appraised his material primarily from a literary standpoint, those who have judged him as a recorder of native culture, and those who have considered his work from the standpoint of history. By those in the first two categories he has, as we have seen been given high marks, without comments on the shortcomings in his treatment of material. Those who have sought to rely upon his work as history have found his errors in dates and other important features of Montana history distressing.

Fortunately for Schultz, the overwhelming majority of his readers fell into none of the foregoing categories. They were teenagers who read what they enjoyed and were oblivious to historical accuracy. Whether Schultz's son was born in 1882 or 1884 or whether Hugh Monroe died in 1896 or 1892 were matters of no concern to these youngsters. They were interested in adventure, and it is safe to say that the Schultz errors, numerous and flagrant as they were, nevertheless were of a type that went unnoticed by all but a very few of his readers; and therefore their effect upon his reputation, upon his enthusiastic young following, and, finally, upon the sale of his books and articles has been minimal.

CHAPTER 29

Champion of Indian Causes

SCHULTZ began to live intimately the life of an Indian almost from the day he arrived in the West. He ate their food, slept in their lodges, and began to learn the difficult Blackfoot language; he eventually was able not only to speak it well but to think as the Indians did. He began to see the world through the eyes of the Blackfeet. Though his skin was obviously white, his soul had become that of a red man. He became familiar with the record of broken government promises to and mistreatment of the tribes of the Northwest and, later, those of the Southwest. He was as much disturbed, if not more so, about these indignities and inequities as if he had been an Indian himself. In fact, throughout his life he regarded himself as a member of the Blackfoot tribe and felt honored to be so.

When situations arose in which his Indian friends needed a champion, Schultz became their self-appointed spokesman—and an effective one. With his pen as well as in person, he did everything possible to eliminate injustices, beginning with the so-called starvation winter on the Blackfoot Reservation in the 1880's and continuing for more than half a century as other Indian problems came from time to time to his attention.

It was in the spring of 1883 that indications of trouble first appeared. In April, the New Grass Moon, several lodges of Pikunis came down to camp near Fort Conrad, where Schultz was then located. He and Nätahki were delighted because among them were many of their friends, but the news they brought was sobering. Depending for food—as they had to do now that the buffalo were gone—upon the antelope and deer in the country around Badger Creek, they had killed off nearly all of the game there. The agent, Major John Young, known to them as *Ahsi Tupi*, or Young Person, did not have sufficient rations for them. Adding to their plight, their horses had contracted a skin disease (scabby mange) which was spreading rapidly, causing the hair to slough off in great patches. Many of them died.

As the summer progressed, there was no improvement in conditions among the Pikunis. Schultz became concerned and tried to ascertain whether Major Young and the agency at Badger Creek were making any plans to aid the Pikunis if, as was beginning to seem likely, their plight became desperate with the approach of winter. Young, however, had issued orders prohibiting any whites, other than his employees, from entering the reservation, so it was necessary to set up a secret meeting with friends among the agency employees at which Schultz learned that there were no plans to meet the emergency. Important Pikuni chiefs who came to talk with Schultz warned him of the shortage of food. Although he listened attentively, he still did not comprehend the full extent of the tragedy that was then only just beginning.

As Schultz became increasingly concerned, he began to ponder ways and means of doing something to help. He bethought himself of the friendly correspondence he had been having with George Bird Grinnell, editor of *Forest and Stream* magazine. He wrote Grinnell asking for help, and Grinnell wired him to visit the reservations and write him a full report on conditions. Schultz, then only twenty-four, rode over to the reservation to see for himself how the Pikunis were faring. Everywhere he went he found many of the elderly and those weak from illness already at the point of death. Several had died. The shortage of food was alarming, and the big-game animals were all gone; even such small animals as rabbits, grouse, and porcupines were hard to find. He knew that the Pikunis could not be persuaded to

eat either horse or dog, for both of these animals were considered sacred; nor would they eat fish, since these were
considered the property of the dreaded Water People.

Schultz met with thirty or forty of the leading men of the
tribe in Chief Red Paint's lodge. They pleaded with Schultz
and Father Peter Paul Prando, who also attended the meeting, to do everything possible to secure food for them before the arrival of winter; otherwise, they emphasized, the
Pikunis were doomed. The priest promised to do everything
he could. Schultz again called on his friends among the
agency employees and learned through them that no plans
were being made to cope with the situation. They told Schultz
how Major Young had for years been sending reports to his
superiors in Washington about his great success in making
self-supporting farmers of the Indians under his authority.
Now, of course, he dared not ask for help for them and thus
prove himself a liar.

Schultz returned to Fort Conrad and worked late into the
night preparing for Grinnell a report of all he had learned.
It was a month before he received a reply telling him that
Grinnell had gone to Washington to consult influential men
in the government, including President Arthur himself,
who had promised to do everything in his power to see that
ample supplies of food would be dispatched to the tribe.

In the meantime, Schultz learned that Father Prando had
also written authorities in Washington, but without results.
Prando then made contact with Colonel (later General)
Edward A. Moule, who, with some of his staff, had reported
the situation among the Pikunis to the War Department. As
a result of this action, Inspector C. H. Howard was sent to
the reservation in November. He found that the Indians
were starving for meat, the rations due them having been
cut to one and a half pounds of meat and two and a quarter
pounds of flour per person per week, and that this was usually exhausted by the middle of the week.

Back at Fort Conrad, everyone was doing everything that
could be done to aid old friends and relatives among the
Pikunis. Day after day Schultz would find Nätahki in tears
over the death of someone she loved. Earth Woman and

Crow Woman still had about one hundred fine buffalo robes, which they had Kipp sell in Fort Benton for nine hundred dollars. With this they bought food for the destitute. Kipp was constantly giving food to those he knew to be in desperate need.

It was well into December before the action of Grinnell and Father Prando brought results. That month, Fort Shaw soldiers arrived at the agency with several wagons loaded with food and driving a herd of cattle that had been donated by Charles Conrad. The food in the wagons consisted largely of flour, beans, and bacon. Unfortunately, the bacon was alive with worms and made such a stench that the agency doctor ruled it unfit to eat.

In April, 1884, according to Schultz, there were dramatic developments at the agency. An Inspector Gardner arrived on the mail stage, went directly to the agency office, and informed a startled John Young that he was fired and that he and his family were to get out at once to make room for his replacement, who would arrive shortly.

The new agent was Reuben A. Allen. Schultz lost no time in meeting him and found him to be kind and well disposed toward the Indians. Unfortunately, with Allen's replacement of Young conditions among the Pikunis did not improve automatically. The food the army had supplied in December was soon exhausted, and in early May, Allen reported that little flour remained and that the supply of meat was gone. In desperation he examined the supply of condemned bacon, sorted out 2,112 pounds and issued it, with grave misgivings, to the starving Pikunis. Later that spring when Allen issued 5,000 pounds of potatoes to the Indians for planting, most of them were eaten and those that were planted soon had to be dug up for food. In June many Indians were reduced to eating the inner bark of cottonwood trees. In August conditions improved somewhat when the Pikunis were able to gather berries and kill small game. However, it was not until January, 1885, that Congress approved the special appropriation that finally brought an end to the frightful period of starvation among the Pikunis.

In retrospect, Schultz was in error in concluding that

Young had made no move to secure adequate help for the
Indians for whom he was responsible. Several letters to the
Commissioner of Indian Affairs provide evidence of Young's
efforts to secure adequate food for his charges during this
period of desperate need. On May 8, 1883, he telegraphed
the Commissioner: "There will not be provisions enough to
prevent suffering. Can anything be done?" In late September, Young received a reply informing him that the appropriation for supplies for his agency had been spent and
there was nothing to be done. On receipt of this, Young
tendered his resignation; nevertheless, he remained on the
job through that terrible winter.

The famine toll among the Pikunis was heavy. Chief
Almost-a-Dog had cut a notch in a willow stick for each Indian who died. On that stick, according to Schultz, were five
hundred fifty-five notches. It has been estimated that one-
sixth to one-quarter of the Pikunis died during the winter of
1883–84.

The highly respected Indian Rights Association of Philadelphia made a painstaking investigation of the disaster, the
results of which it issued in an open letter to newspapers. In
this it placed the major blame on Congressman Ellis, chairman of the House Subcommittee on Indian Appropriations,
for the subcommittee's failure to approve the necessary special appropriations so urgently requested by officials of the
Bureau of Indian Affairs and advocated by the Indian Rights
Association as well as by other organizations and individuals
interested in the welfare of the Indians.

An unmarked monument to the Winter of Death remains.
When Harry James visited the site of the agency on Badger
Creek with Hart Schultz, the latter pointed out a ridge
where many of the hunger victims were buried, so many, he
said, that the Pikunis still refer to the place as Ghost Ridge.

History has an unfortunate way of repeating itself, and
when Schultz visited the Pikunis in 1921 he was disturbed
by the conditions he found. He became gravely concerned,
fearing that the tribe might be in for another starvation period unless prompt action were taken by the Bureau of Indian Affairs. After consultation with interested friends, he

prepared a comprehensive report over his own name. In it he pointed out that although the land of the Blackfoot Reservation was not suitable for farming it was excellent for grazing and the Pikunis had done well in raising cattle, especially when prices were high during World War I. However, drought in the summer of 1919 made it impossible to harvest hay for winter feeding, and the winter that followed was one of the worst in Montana history. Consequently, when General Hugh L. Scott, a member of the Board of Indian Commissioners, visited the reservation in the fall of 1920 he found that the future of the Blackfeet had not looked so hopeless since the winter of 1883–84.

Schultz rose to the occasion at once, writing a powerful pamphlet entitled "The Starving Blackfeet Indians" and seeking contributions to the Blackfoot Relief Fund at Browning to assist Indians without food or money. He wrote for *Sunset Magazine* an article entitled "America's Red Armenians,"[1] depicting the plight of the Blackfeet, plus articles for leading newspapers throughout the nation.

Soon after his articles appeared and despite protests from the Bureau of Indian Affairs, donations began coming in, some of them sizable, to the Blackfoot Relief Fund. The fund was being administered by Dr. Wilson, a respected citizen of Browning, where an account was opened in Stockmen's State Bank. Harry James worked with Schultz in taking care of the donations as they were received in Los Angeles, where they were acknowledged and forwarded to Browning.

As a result of contributions to the Blackfoot Relief Fund, a large number of Indians were enabled to survive. Money from the fund helped to keep many of them from losing their homes as well. Several of the Montana Blackfeet had been allotted three hundred twenty acres in a small area of irrigated reservation land, to which they were given title. During the 1920–22 stringency, many of these Indians were kept from starving by being allowed to buy food on credit from reservation traders. Certain of these traders com-

[1] *Sunset Magazine*, Vol. 49, November, 1922, 17–19, 70–74.

Schultz with General Hugh Scott about 1931. Courtesy Renne Library Collection.

pelled the Indians, ignorant of the gravity of what they were doing, to sign liens against their land as security for their accounts. When the Indian was unable to settle his account, the trader would foreclose and acquire the Indian's land and home for a trivial sum. In checking the records of Glacier County Court in May, 1922, Schultz found that there had been more than a hundred such foreclosures. Fortunately, Dr. Wilson was able to prevent several by advancing money from the relief fund to enable the Indian to pay his bill and thereby save his land and home.

It is ironic that when the spring of 1922 was well advanced and the crisis was over the Bureau of Indian Affairs appropriated several thousand dollars to help the Indians who had been starving for the past winter. However, because the money was no longer needed for that purpose, the agent, according to Schultz, used it to build a good road from Browning to Heart Butte, where he had some real-estate holdings.

The Hopi Indians of Arizona also were having problems about 1920, as Schultz discovered in the course of visits to Hopi villages as well as from reports he received from Harry James. Schultz felt the time had come for action in reference to the Hopis in particular and the American Indian in general. White missionaries to the Hopis had tried to discourage participation in ancient tribal ceremonies of religious character. However, the Hopi leaders were being pressured in other ways to put a stop to their religious ceremonials. Much of this pressure was from Commissioner of Indian Affairs Charles H. Burke, an appointee of the notorious Secretary of the Interior Albert Fall.

As a first step in his concept of creating better conditions for the Indians, Schultz in 1920 invited Stewart Edward White, Harry James, and Emerson Hough to have lunch with him at the University Club in Los Angeles. Hough was then in the area in connection with plans being made for the filming of a novel he had written, *The Covered Wagon*. At this luncheon, Schultz asked James, who had been in the Hopi country the previous summer, to relate some of the unfortunate conditions he encountered there. When he had finished, Schultz spoke of similar experiences in Hopi villages when he visited them. In the course of their discussion, one of the group suggested that some sort of organization be formed as the first step toward alleviating the immediate problems of the Hopis and the Pikunis, after which it could see what might be done to correct abuses by the Bureau of Indian Affairs. Schultz agreed and said he would take the lead if the group would be supportive. The others agreed.

One evening early in the winter of 1920–21, Schultz invited a few people to dinner under the sycamores adjacent to his Los Angeles apartment. Among those who responded to the invitation were Ida May Adams, an attorney who had been active for some time on behalf of the Indians of southern California; Marah Ellis Ryan, author of two novels about the Hopis, *Flute of the Gods* and *Indian Love Letters*, who was knowledgeable about many southwestern tribes; Edward S. Curtis, then concluding his monumental twenty-volume masterpiece *The North American Indian*; and Frederick Webb Hodge, editor of the invaluable two-volume Bureau of American Ethnology *Handbook of American Indians North of Mexico*, who was at the time engaged in editing Curtis' work. It was a beautiful evening and Schultz had prepared a delicious dinner. He was an excellent host, and although several in the group were meeting for the first time they were soon chatting like old friends. Presently, however, the small talk gave way to serious discussion of a subject in which all had interest: the maladministration of Indian affairs.

Ida May Adams surprised everyone with the depth of her knowledge of the multitude of problems faced by the United States and with her determination that indeed an organization should be set up to do something about solving them. She insisted that the first thing to be worked for was full voting citizenship for the Indians. After considerable discussion, all present agreed with her. Before the meeting was over, the group had decided to form not one but two organizations.

The more important was to be called the Indian Welfare

League, and its purpose was to decide policy and draft plans for a campaign to gain voting citizenship for the Indian and thorough reform in Bureau of Indian Affairs personnel and policies. These objectives were to be carried out as diplomatically as possible so as not to antagonize the bureau into exercising its power to ban league members from Indian reservations. Both Curtis and Hodge still had work to do on *The North American Indian*, while Schultz had planned important work among the Blackfoot tribes; for the bureau to close the reservations to them would be catastrophic.

The second organization would be given a rather pompous name, the National Association to Help the Indian, although it consisted of only two people: Mr. and Mrs. S. A. R. Brown of Santa Barbara, a highly-respected, dignified, soft-spoken, gentle-mannered, and rather wealthy couple. The purpose of this "organization" was to write letters and issue statements criticizing the tragic conditions among the Indians of the United States as a result of negligence and corruption in the Interior Department's Bureau of Indian Affairs.

Both organizations were decidedly informal. If the weather was pleasant, they met under the sycamores near Schultz's apartment; if it was foul, they met at the Southwest Museum. According to the letterhead of the Indian Welfare League, Dr. John Comstock was chairman of the executive council, although Schultz usually functioned in that capacity. Routine expenses were met by the council members. No minutes were kept because there was no secretary. Attending frequently was Frederick Webb Hodge, whose connections with the Smithsonian Institution and whose encyclopedic knowledge of the Indian were invaluable to the group.

Early in 1921 the Indian Welfare League was in full swing. Its most informal executive council consisted of Schultz; Edward S. Curtis; Marah Ellis Ryan; Jo Neeley; Dr. John Adams Comstock (director of the Southwest Museum); Ida May Adams; William S. Hart; Walter W. Woehlke, editor of *Sunset Magazine*; Stewart Edward White; Anita Baldwin; Harry James; and William Jennings Bryan, Jr. One of the first actions approved by the group was the publication in

Sunset Magazine of an article by Schultz entitled "The Case of the Hopi"[2] and subtitled "Is the Indian Bureau Forcing a New Culture and Religion Upon Them Against Their Will?" The article was based not only upon the personal observations of Harry James and Schultz but also upon the vast fund of knowledge of such an authority as Frederick Webb Hodge.

The Hopis' religion was embedded deeply in their daily lives. It permeated the all-important system which was responsible for the extensive calendar of religious ceremonials as well as the government of every village. To wipe out the Hopi religion in order to facilitate the work of the missionaries would, Schultz and the members of the Indian Welfare League executive committee were certain, gradually destroy one of the most significant cultures of the North American Indians.

Despite a heavy writing schedule and dedicated attention to the Blackfoot relief project, Schultz did not by any means neglect the affairs of the Indian Welfare League generally. As its founder, he never missed a meeting. Ida May Adams, good attorney as she was, decided in 1922 that the league was engaged in work too important to continue in its extremely informal manner; consequently, she presented the league with a constitution and bylaws. An executive council consisting of Dr. Comstock, Ida May Adams, Anita Baldwin, William Jennings Bryan, Jr., Edward S. Curtis, and Marah Ellis Ryan was elected. Headquarters was the Southwest Museum, but most of the meetings continued to be held under the sycamores alongside Schultz's apartment.

In retrospect it seems astonishing that such a small organization could accomplish as much as it did. Besides assisting Schultz in his plan to help the Montana Blackfeet, the league worked diligently to bring back freedom of worship for Indians everywhere. When the campaign to forbid the Hopis to continue their religious ceremonials reached a crisis in 1922, the Indian Welfare League gave its full support to the Hopis. Schultz met with their leaders in Arizona at his

[2] *Sunset Magazine*, Vol. 47, October, 1921, 20–22.

own expense and strongly encouraged them to go on with their ceremonials.

At a meeting of the league's executive council in March, 1924, Ida May Adams said she felt the time was right for her to go to Washington and consult with the senators and representatives who had approved her plan to secure passage of legislation to guarantee voting rights for all Indians in the United States. Schultz and other members of the league, who had been in communication with their own representatives in Congress, agreed heartily.

In May, 1924, Miss Adams boarded a train for Washington, where she met with her supporters and Senator Dill of Utah invited her to make use of his office. Dill and Representative Howard of Nebraska were her chief advisers. After several days spent in consultation with various members of Congress, they agreed with her that the wise thing to do was to draft a bill embodying the legislation she wanted and have it introduced in Congress as promptly as possible. When Dill and Howard conferred on what should be done about drafting the bill, Miss Adams laughed and handed them copies of a bill she had already written. The two men looked at the short slip of paper, and as soon as he had read it Dill said, "Short as it is, it ought to do it. I'll be happy to support it in the Senate." Howard agreed to introduce it in the House of Representatives. On June 2, 1924, H.R. 6355, having been approved, became the law of the land:

> Be it enacted by the Senate and House of Representatives of the United States of America in Congress assembled, That all non-citizen Indians born within the territorial limits of the United States be, and they are hereby, declared to be citizens of the United States: Provided, That the granting of such citizenship shall not in any manner impair or otherwise affect the right of any Indian to tribal or other property.

When Ida May Adams returned to California, her fellow members in the Indian Welfare League honored her at a large dinner attended by many important members of the legal profession and other civic organizations. Schultz was on his way to Montana at the time but wired his congratulations, which Edward S. Curtis read at the dinner:

How splendid it is that you, such a small modest person, have been able to do such a truly great thing for the benefit of such multitudes of people by writing such a few words! I think that only an Ida May Adams could do such a thing. With a full heart I congratulate you.

It had been the league's unwavering support of Miss Adams that made her accomplishment possible, and it was Schultz who provided the spark that fired the zeal of its members.

Schultz never failed to be diligent whenever Indian problems were concerned, even small ones. Among other projects to which he dedicated himself during the 1920's was that of restoring or attempting to restore Indian names to the mountains, lakes, and other natural features of Glacier National Park. The replacement of Blackfoot titles with white-man names long had been a sore spot with the Indians. The story of what Schultz undertook to do about it is told more fully elsewhere in this volume.

Even when Schultz had reached his eighth decade his interest in his beloved Blackfeet did not diminish. While at Browning in 1940, where his wife was doing social work among the Pikunis for the Indian Service, he became aware that there was no library. The Schultzes launched a campaign to remedy this deficiency. With the aid of such friends as Joseph Henry Jackson of the *San Francisco Chronicle*, Walter Woehlke, of *Sunset Magazine*, and others, hundreds of books were contributed to the agency library.

CHAPTER 30

Apikuni and His Addictions

ALTHOUGH *addiction* and *habit* are somewhat similar terms, the former suggests a craving or compulsion rather than custom or use; it usually connotes an involvement with a deleterious substance as well as a lesser amenability to control. So far as James Willard Schultz was concerned, such distinctions would have been academic since he had no interest in exerting control over his chronic addictions, regardless of the label to be pinned on them. Among his friends his fondness for alcoholic beverages was no secret, although it was never the subject of their criticism. He imbibed, in later years at least, on a regular basis and by today's standards probably would have been considered an alcoholic. In any review of his career the subject of his drinking recurs with sufficient frequency as to call for some consideration of its nature and extent and its effects on his life and work.

That he may have had a drinking problem was a subject he never discussed, even with his intimates; hence any evaluation of its extent can be derived only from a review of comments by people who knew him well enough to be familiar with his day-to-day conduct and activities. Such an approach is necessary to any rational assessment of his lifestyle because of the exaggeration which seems to have developed over the years with reference to his drinking.

Schultz's contacts with the world of alcohol began in his teens when his strong-willed attitude led him to visit bars in New York City and occasionally those in his hometown. Of course, when at the age of eighteen he became associated with Joe Kipp in the latter's trade with the Montana Indians, a substantial part of his duties consisted of dispensing liquor to the customers, usually by the cupful. In effect he was acting as a bartender, and whiskey was always available to him.

For the early-day Indian trader an indispensable part of his stock in trade was in liquid form, to wit, whiskey. Unprincipled traders not only watered down their whiskey but adulterated it with tobacco juice, cayenne pepper, and other evil things. Kipp and Schultz sold what they called weak whiskey, the pure thing diluted with water. Nevertheless, Schultz made no apology for the whiskey trade, saying in *My Life as an Indian*: "It was wrong, all wrong, and none realized it better than we when we were dispensing the stuff. It caused untold suffering, many deaths, great demoralization among these people of the plains." As to his own drinking, his friends were sometimes astonished by the fact that despite his modest size he could consume more than the average man without seeming to show any unfortunate effects. He was an extremely diffident and reticent man, and a few drinks seemed to break down whatever barriers there were and enable him to speak fluently and with greater ease.

During many a winter in Los Angeles according to his friend, Harry James, Schultz would watch hopefully for royalty checks. When one arrived, he would cash it at once, then pay a brief visit to James and hand him all but fifty dollars or so of the money to be taken care of for a few days. Three or four days later, neat and shipshape as ever and showing no signs of having been on a binge, he would return to retrieve the funds entrusted to his friend, all of this without knowledge of his wife, Celia. He never made any explanation, knowing that none was needed. However, James was told by the manager of the University Club, to which they both belonged, that at such times Schultz would go on a grand spree with two or three old-time cronies, sometimes at the Uplifters Ranch in Santa Monica Canyon, and finally land at the University Club to sober up.[1] Since these get-togethers took place during Prohibition, rumor

[1] Letter from Harry James to Apaki, April 17, 1975.

had it that certain members of both of these excellent organizations enjoyed connections with friendly bootleggers.

According to James, Schultz's passion for good whiskey
made enactment of the Volstead Act in 1919 hard for him to
bear. Often he spoke sadly of the barrel of fine whiskey he
and Jack Monroe had hidden near their cabin at the lower
end of Upper St. Mary Lake; so well had they hidden it, in
fact, that they were never able to find it. The thought that it
was still there and well aged became especially distressing
during Prohibition, although his anguish was somewhat as-
suaged by the good relations between his University Club
friends and the best of local bootleggers.

The University Club group included Harry Carr, a top
writer for the *Los Angeles Times*, and others who shared a
common interest in everything pertaining to the West and
an appreciation of good sippin' whiskey. Another of Schultz's
special friends was Stewart Edward White, a well-known
writer on western topics. The two men had hunted together
in Arizona and Schultz had visited White in Santa Barbara.
In later years, when contact between them had been lost,
Stewart wrote Harry James:

> And thanks for letting me know about old Schultz. He must
> have an enormous number of years to his credit. Certainly
> you can't kill off those tough old timers. I saw him in 1936 in
> Montana. Also, just between ourselves, it is a wonderful testi-
> monial to the preservative qualities of alcohol, it seems to me.
> But he is a unique bird in himself and could not be held up
> as an example.

One of Schultz's admirers was J. Donald Adams of the *New
York Times*. In the latter's column "Speaking of Books," which
appeared regularly in the book review section of the *Times*,
he frequently gave high praise to the Schultz books. In 1941
he spent several days in Wyoming with Schultz and his wife,
subsequently writing in a column on March 31, 1957: "Now
Apikuni lies under the cliffs with the Blackfoot chiefs he
loved. God rest him. He was a powerful drinker, a wonderful storyteller, and a loyal friend."

It was Schultz's use of alcoholic beverages that terminated
fifteen years of friendly relations with the Great Northern

Railway. The company's substantial support and financial aid had made possible the gathering of material for his books about Glacier Park, but this rapport deteriorated to the point where Schultz's requests for financial assistance were rejected when key officials learned of his intemperance and of his arrest in Alberta with liquor in his car and while drinking with a woman (Miss Donaldson) on an Indian reservation.[2]

From other close friends of Schultz and Jessica comes a somewhat less vivid picture. Schultz occasionally visited Ernest and Grace Miller at their Elk Horn Ranch and enjoyed a very friendly relationship with them. When Harry James quoted Stewart Edward White's comment in a letter to Mrs. Miller, she replied:

> Ernest and I have known Apikuni and Jess Donaldson since 1917 and Ernest maybe earlier. He and Ernest had a great many common interests—the West, hunting, the problems of the Indians, and they spent many long hours together. Sometimes they had a few drinks, but I do not ever remember seeing Apikuni intoxicated. Apikuni was by nature a very retiring person. The fact that a reasonable amount of alcohol was relaxing for him makes me feel that his consumption of it was an asset and to my knowledge never a problem.

According to Jessie, Schultz took his whiskey straight. It seemed to relieve the tension that accompanied the planning for a new book, when his mind would be working on the upcoming story with its complex of characters and set of circumstances, action, and dialogue. Drinking seemed to make him more willing to talk but had little effect upon him physically unless the drinking became protracted.[3] If it was more and more for a while, he got sick and Jessica would take him to the hospital, where the doctor prescribed three ounces a day. He did not get drunk; he just got sick.[4]

Jessica related an interesting incident that occurred at Fort Washakie, Wyoming, in the course of her employment on the reservation there. While recuperating from his in-

---

[2] Letter from Great Northern President W. P. Kenny to J. A. Lengby refusing to grant further assistance, December 27, 1929.
[3] "Adventuresome, Amazing Apikuni," 15.
[4] *Idem.*

jury of October 25, 1942, Schultz for some reason wanted to
go downtown to the hotel to chat with people. Jess had had
to drive to a nearby town on business, so he got into his
wheelchair, rolled down their driveway, and persuaded a
passing truck driver to take him where he wished to go.
There he encountered an Indian policeman, whom he asked
to get him a bottle of whiskey. The policeman asked someone else to take care of the errand and then reported the
episode to the reservation superintendent. When Mrs.
Schultz returned to town, the superintendent called her into
his office, told her of the incident, and said, "Jessica, this
cannot happen. Apikuni must not ask my police to buy his
whiskey for him." She smiled and said to herself, "As if telling Apikuni he must not do that would have the slightest
effect. Apikuni did as he pleased. Always."[5]

When Schultz fell and broke his right arm and left leg in
October, 1942, he was taken to Bishop Randall Hospital at
Lander, Wyoming, where he was to spend several weeks. He
proceeded to create consternation in that good Episcopalian
institution by demanding that he be allowed to have a private bar set up in a pantry across the hall from his room.
Later he insisted that his rapid recovery was due solely to
this accommodation. According to a letter from his wife to
Harry James,[6] when he wanted a libation he yelled, "Nurse!"
and every nurse on the floor came running.

"I want a highball," Schultz would announce.

"When did you last have one?" a nurse would inquire.

"What the hell difference does that make?" he would de-
mand indignantly. "I want one now."

"How many have you had today?" would be the stern
inquiry.

"What in hell do you care? *I want one now!*"

Whereupon, according to his wife, and without regard to
how many or how long before, he would get his highball
and become all smiles while the nurses would congregate in
the pantry all a-giggle.

Whether Schultz's use of alcohol had any effect upon his

---

[5] *Idem.*

[6] Harry James, "Apikuni as I Knew Him," *The Piegan Storyteller*, Vol. I,
No. 2, April, 1976, 4.

longevity would necessarily be speculative. He suffered long periods of hospitalization and disability following injuries at home and elsewhere, yet there is nothing to indicate that his accidents were alcohol related. But in any event, as his tolerant and understanding wife has explained, the use of alcohol did play a part in his work as an author, as well as in his personality.

Schultz's second addiction was also well known to his friends: the use of tobacco. As a matter of fact, he was never really at ease without a cigarette in his hand.[7] Even in his twenties he had become a chain smoker, the depth of his addiction being disclosed, perhaps unconsciously, in his own writings.[8] Like many westerners, he preferred to roll his own, and the deleterious effects of the noxious weed were yet to become known.

In the case of Schultz, the use of tobacco was a comfort, often a crutch, and sometimes a means to an end. Among the stories that Harry James has told in reference to Schultz and his use of tobacco is one about a meeting involving Apikuni and leaders of the Hopi tribe in the early 1920's. The meeting was held in an office adjoining the Santa Fe roundhouse at Winslow, Arizona, and the Hopis were, of course, total strangers to Schultz. To break the ice, he introduced himself to the group and passed out sacks of Bull Durham tobacco and packets of cigarette papers. Soon everyone was seated in a circle and busily smoking as the meeting got under way.

With many tribes, including the Blackfeet, the smoking of tobacco by means of a pipe has served as a ritual as well as a friendly social custom. It is unlikely, however, that its use for such purposes ever rose to the level of an addiction, as it did in the case of Schultz. If he ever gave the matter any thought, he undoubtedly considered his smoking habit to be a harm-

---

[7] This can be noted in many of his photographs.

[8] For example, in *My Life as an Indian*, 417, he tells of how Nätahki would worry about him when she did not hear the sounds of him at work nearby and on checking would be relieved to find him "sitting on a log, or lying on the ground, smoking, always smoking." On Page 97 of *Blackfeet and Buffalo*, Schultz has Nätahki remind him of how, had her uncle Red Eagle not given him some of the tobacco from his sacred elk-tongue bundle when none was available elsewhere, he "would have gone crazy."

less pleasure and may even have regarded it with special favor because of the ceremonial and social uses of the weed by his beloved Pikunis.

That Schultz had suffered from a third and more serious type of addiction was known only to a few of his intimate friends. This was his morphine addiction, from which he suffered for a time in his early seventies. It began with the back injury he suffered en route to Montana shortly after his 1931 marriage to Jessica Donaldson. Prolonged rest and repeated hospitalization had failed to provide relief from the intolerable pain undoubtedly attributable to a ruptured intervertebral disc. At the end of the summer, he and Jessie finally headed for the lodge of his son in the White Mountains of Arizona. When it became too cold there, they moved to a house near Tucson.

Since the condition was considered inoperable, the various doctors from whom he had sought relief as he moved from place to place had been prescribing morphine for pain relief. With the coming of spring there was no improvement, and the Schultzes decided to head for Berkeley by way of Los Angeles. En route they stopped for gasoline at a small desert town, where he disappeared for several hours, taking the keys to the car and leaving her frightened and worried about him. When he finally returned, it appeared that he had been trying to obtain medical relief.

Their next stop was at the home of her brother Gilbert in Los Angeles, where the daughter happened to be giving a dancing party on the evening of their arrival. That night, according to Jessica, Schultz told her that "he had something very ugly to tell me. He said that the medicines the doctors had been giving him were so strong that he could not get along without them. He was a complete victim."[9] He was referring to the morphine prescribed for the relief of his sciatic pain; it had now become a bigger problem than the pain.

Jessica was shocked by this statement from her husband because she had not realized what was happening to him or what powerful drugs could do to people. She discussed the

[9] Letter from Jessica to Harry James, August 22, 1975.

matter with her brother, who became very concerned and called the family physician. The latter happened to be the head of the California Narcotics Board, and after examining Schultz he talked with Jessica privately, saying her husband's condition had reached a very serious stage, one where at any time he was likely to kill himself and possibly her as well.[10]

Despite the gravity of the situation, the Schultzes continued their journey to Berkeley, where they moved into an apartment. En route to Berkeley, Schultz asked Jessica for his gun, saying that he had stood the pain as long as he could and that he intended to kill himself. Needless to say, she did not comply with his request and with the aid of a recommendation from a Berkeley friend was able to get him under the care of Dr. Clark Burnham. This doctor and his son, also a physician, treated the case intensively for the next several months. There was gradual improvement, and Schultz's visits, necessary daily at first, became fewer and fewer.

During this period there were many occasions when, but for the intensive medical care and Jessica's determination and inner strength, the situation seemed almost hopeless. The details need not be set forth, since the day finally came when he was pronounced cured and Jessica could say, "So ended the episodes that filled the year of our honeymoon. It was a victorious year even though it was an agonizing year."[11]

So it was that Schultz conquered the most serious of his addictions, one thrust upon him by uncoordinated medication prescribed by a series of doctors with no realization by either Schultz or Jessica that his pain-relieving medicine could itself create a life-threatening problem. The battle with morphine was won, but only with the help of a competent physician and a dedicated wife.

---

[10] Letter from Jessica to Harry James, August 22, 1975.
[11] Letter from Jessica to Harry James, August 22, 1975.

CHAPTER 31

Apikuni and His Pets

HUNTING was a sport that Apikuni enjoyed through-out his life, first as a boy in the Adirondacks, later in the Rockies and on the plains of Montana, and in his older years in the White Mountains of Arizona. Buffalo he had killed by the score, as well as many a Rocky Mountain goat and sheep. Always an excellent shot with a rifle, he was equally adept with a shotgun and brought down many ducks and grouse in Montana and wild turkeys near his shooting lodge in Arizona. On the other hand, Apikuni was a lover of animals and was almost never without a pet of some kind. His most unusual pets were from the wild kingdom, of species that seldom deign to associate with humans. Others were from the domesticated canine or feline families, and during his years with Apaki these were always a source of much pleasure to both of them.

Apikuni's first pet was acquired in 1881 when he was living at a Kipp trading post on the Missouri River some thirty miles above the mouth of the Musselshell.[1] While on a hunt one day with his friend Eagle Head, they captured a male wolf pup near the underground den it occupied with its parents and brothers and sisters. Apikuni gave the pup the Blackfoot name for wolf, Mahkwoyi, or Big Mouth, and quartered it in the trading post smokehouse, which happened not to be in use. Soon, however, it became so friendly and playful that Schultz freed it, and it became his close companion, following him wherever he went.

[1] *Blackfeet and Buffalo*, 136–37.

Hunting turkeys in Arizona. Courtesy Renne Library Collection.

When the dinner bell rang, Big Mouth was the first into the dining room. His appetite was enormous, and two or three pounds of buffalo meat was but a small snack for him. He soon knew his name and would come running from as far as he could hear Schultz call, "*Mahkwoyi, puksiput!*" ("Big Mouth, come here!") Speaking only Blackfoot to him, Schultz taught him to heel, to hunt out ahead, and to retrieve; and how proud he was, bringing a grouse or a duck that had been shot and dropping it at his master's feet, then rising, and with paws on the latter's shoulders, licking his face as he waved his bushy tail. No deer that had been merely wounded ever got away from Mahkwoyi; he quickly overtook and downed it, sometimes killing it before the hunters could arrive.

The dogs of the Indians who came to the trading post were mostly afraid of Mahkwoyi. Only rarely could he induce them to play with him. When they did so and in their excitement barked, he could only whine. He did not begin to howl until he was about a year old. Then, one evening, he answered the far-off howling of his kind and, very proud of himself, came running to Schultz for approval of his feat; when he got it, he howled again and again. He had seen his first skunk when he was about eight months old, immediately seizing and shaking it, then dropping it. The result was, of course, that he was drenched with its scent and got sick. Thereafter he gave skunks the right of way; with drooping head and tail tucked tightly behind, he circled past them.

Schultz once came near losing the young wolf. With his friend Eli Guardipee he went deer hunting, Mahkwoyi at their heels. They ended up nearly being trampled by a rampaging herd of buffalo. After the mad stampede, there was no trace of his pet. Schultz wondered whether Mahkwoyi had been crushed under the thundering herd or carried off on some cow's sharp horns, and his heart was low. But even as he mourned the wolf came swiftly from they knew not where, to leap up and lick his face, run circles around him, then leap onto him again. Schultz was overjoyed.

Among the many admirers of Mahkwoyi was Captain

Williams of the *Red Cloud*, one of the many steamboats plying the Missouri between Fort Benton and St. Louis. He
begged Schultz for him and eventually got him. However,
it was to Schultz's sorrow ever afterward, for the captain, in
turn, gave Mahkwoyi to the St. Louis Zoological Park and
there, sickened by confinement and doubtless from longing
for Schultz, he soon died.

While Schultz was at Fort Conrad on the Marias River,
where Kipp had a trading post, he was given a young beaver
by his friend Tail-Feathers-Coming-Over-the-Hill.[2] It was
the offspring of a mother beaver Tail-Feathers had trapped.
Though it weighed only five pounds, still it was old enough
to thrive without its mother's milk. The room occupied in
the fort by Schultz had for its floor the hard-packed earth.
He sank a washtub in it and filled the tub with water in
which the beaver could swim and drink. Daily he brought in
a bunch of willows for it to gnaw, their bark being its favorite
food. *Tsisk-stuki*, or Wood-biter, as the Blackfeet called the
beaver, soon became friendly with Schultz and would come
waddling when he called. He dearly loved to have his head
and belly scratched but was ever silent; as long as Schultz
owned him, he never made a sound of any kind. When
Wood-biter was quite tame, Schultz carried him to the river
often to let him swim about. The beaver enjoyed such outings, always returning when Schultz called.

The inner side of the Schultzes' bunk was nailed to the
wall of the room, its outer side supported by two thin cottonwood posts. As they were retiring one night, Schultz's
wife called his attention to the fact that the forward post
had been partly gnawed through at about its center. To
Schultz it looked as if the wood were too dry for any more
gnawing, but sometime during the night the bunk suddenly tilted down, tossing the couple onto the floor. In
alarm Nätahki cried out, "Enemies have come! Protect me!"
Schultz groped about for the candle, lit it, and pointed it
toward the beaver. The latter floated placidly on the surface of the washtub pond and stared at them with beady

[2] *Blackfeet and Buffalo*, 138.

eyes. "There's your war party," said Schultz. The beaver had gnawed the front post of the bunk clear through, causing the other one to give way also and the bunk to slope outward at a forty-five degree angle. When Schultz replaced the posts the next day, he encased them with lengths of stovepipe.

Schultz lost Tsisk-stuki when the beaver was about a year old. He had taken the beaver out for a morning swim in the river when some Indian children came running and yelling along the shore and frightened the animal. He dived, came to the surface in the swift rapids below, dived again, and that was the last that Schultz ever saw of him.

In the late 1880's after Schultz had built a cabin near the foot of Upper St. Mary Lake, he and his wife spent much time there, and their Indian friends sometimes came to visit. One morning in late May, 1889, Schultz and his friend Bird Chief, with rifles and fishing tackle, set out to spend the day on the upper lake. As they were nearing Red Eagle Mountain in their boat they discovered a band of mountain goats, nannies and their young, together with yearlings and two-year-olds, feeding at the foot of its steep slope. Several of them were on the narrow shore of the lake.[3] Some fifty or sixty yards to the north of the band were a big nanny and her little young one. None took any notice of the hunters until they were so near that their eyes could be seen. Then they suddenly turned and fled for the upper reaches of the mountain with the almost incredible swiftness of their sure-footed kind. Bird Chief suddenly said excitedly, "Apikuni! That lone she one! She left her young one! Hid it! Made it lie down among those big rocks."

That excited Schultz. He had seen mother antelope and deer, when frightened, somehow make their young lie down and lie still, then run from them, so he wondered whether this could be true of goats also. Hurriedly rowing the boat to shore, they sprang out, sped up the slope, and soon came upon the little one, lying motionless in a depression in the shale between some boulders. It did not struggle when he

[3] *Blackfeet and Buffalo*, 139–40.

picked it up and tried to suck his finger when he put it to its mouth. Said Bird Chief: "We have no milk for it; let it go." Schultz responded that there would be plenty for it, leaving Bird Chief puzzled. When they returned to the cabin, he had Bird Chief run in his horses, one of them a mare with a week-old colt. He held the little goat up to her teats and it soon took its fill of her rich milk. Thereafter, morning after morning, he continued to so feed it until it soon regarded Schultz, rather than the mare, as its mother, keeping close beside him. At dawn each day it would spring onto his bed and, kneeling, bunt him with its little head; and it would keep on bunting, urging that Schultz get up and provide its breakfast.

Of all the animals Schultz had known, he regarded the baby goat as the most agile and playful. Particularly was he impressed by one of its surprising feats. From a standing position, it could leap high in the air and be headed in the opposite direction when it landed. Unfortunately, after he had had it for several months it sickened and died. His postmortem examination revealed that it had eaten a poisonous kind of weed, causing its stomach to be bloody. Schultz carefully prepared it for mounting, and sent it to his friend C. Hart Merriam, who in turn presented it to the Smithsonian Institution, where, presumably, it still stands in a lifelike pose.

The last of Apikuni's wild pets was acquired in the early 1930's at his cabin in the White Mountains of Arizona. He always recalled with delight the morning when he and son Hart were at Butterfly Lodge and how Hart, stepping out the back door of the cabin, found a very young male coyote pup nosing about for something to eat.[4] Hart called his father; when they walked toward it, it did not run away but rolled over on its back, trembling and whimpering. It was very emaciated, and as Apikuni stroked its back he could feel every rib. Its youthful cinnamon brown hair was matted with its still unshed gray baby hair.

Apikuni went into the kitchen and returned with a plate-

[4] *Blackfeet and Buffalo*, 140–43.

ful of pancakes and bacon, which the coyote ate ravenously. Hart, having spent much of his life on cattle ranches where coyotes were shot, not fed, was somewhat dubious when his father announced that he was going to make a pet of this one. As it did not run off during the day but followed Apikuni everywhere he went, Hart was amused enough to help, making a leash out of a length of light chain with a leather collar attached to it.

Apikuni named the young coyote Smokey. Its appetite was astonishing; making up for lost time, it ate more than a dog twice its size and grew fast accordingly. Like a dog, Smokey would bury his excess food in holes he dug in the ground. He would soon come bounding to the end of his chain to meet them, wagging his bushy tail and leaping up to lick their faces. He whimpered with joy when they petted him, and when he was freed from the chain he ran hither and thither and tirelessly played with them.

Hart already had a dog, a purebred English shepherd named Zora, a fine turkey dog and retriever. The two animals liked each other, and with Zora around Smokey could be released from his chain, they thought. The two occasionally reconnoitered the ranger's home down the road a piece, but they never went as far as Greer, the little settlement a mile farther up the Little Colorado River. Smokey's days of free wandering were soon to end, however. The ranger had acquired a couple of dozen hens to provide eggs for the family, and Smokey promptly killed five of them, including a fifteen-dollar Leghorn rooster. Thereafter it was necessary to keep Smokey on his long chain except when he was taken out to hunt or for exercise.

Smokey loved his outings! Being far swifter than Zora, he was everywhere at once—a gray flash exploring every log, every hole that might conceal a squirrel, rabbit, or pack rat. One day he furiously pawed into a hole at the foot of a pine, brought out a skunk, and promptly killed it, then rolled and writhed on the pine-needle floor of the forest in a vain endeavor to rid himself of the horrible scent with which it had drenched him. That one experience was enough; thereafter he gave skunks a wide berth.

During the following year Smokey became a hunter and retriever par excellence. Striking the trail of a flock of wild turkeys, he would cautiously sneak in among them so suddenly that they would flutter up into the nearest trees and sit peering down at him, paying no attention to the approach of the hunters. Whining shrilly, Smokey alternately would look at Apikuni and up at the birds, urging that Apikuni hurry up and shoot them. He dearly loved the crack of the gun, and when a turkey dropped, he would seize it as it struck the ground and come running to drop it at Apikuni's feet. Again whining and looking up at the birds, he would urge Apikuni to shoot more of them.

The forested country near Butterfly Lodge abounds in lakes, the breeding place of many kinds of ducks. Numbers of canvasbacks breed in this rather far-south latitude, an anomaly probably accounted for by the altitude of eight thousand to eleven thousand feet. Smokey had his first duck hunt in the autumn of 1930. When three of a flock of mallards splashed down into the water, he plunged in after them. He got one by the neck, then swam to another and tried to take it, too, with the result that he lost his grip on the first one. Several times he tried to bring in two at once; then, failing and all but exhausted, he brought in one and rested. However, he had learned his lesson and thereafter brought in the others separately.

People came from far and near to see Smokey the tame coyote. He was friendly with all women but took instant dislike to several male visitors and would not let them come near him. He was very mischievous. Several times when Apikuni and friends were turkey hunting and had stopped to eat and rest, Smokey would seize their sack of sandwiches as they drew them from their game bag, run off a little way, drop it, and look back at them. Then, as they drew near and were reaching down for it, he was off with it again, only to repeat the ploy as long as an attempt was made to retrieve it. Eventually he would tear the bag open, devour the sandwiches, and come back grinning. He took great delight in teasing Mrs. Schultz, particularly when they were turkey hunting. Whenever she started creeping under or through a

wire fence, he would be on the other side, growling, seizing
the shoulder of her jacket or her sleeve and shaking it, but
he always ended up whining and licking her face.

One day in the fall of 1931 while Apikuni and Hart were
turkey hunting they raised three coyotes, and Smokey immediately went into hot pursuit. They sat down and waited
for him to return. Ten minutes passed, twenty minutes, half
an hour, and no Smokey. They began to worry that he had
deserted them to join up with his own kind. They lost interest in the hunt and turned homeward, plodding along sadly
and slowly. They had not gone far when Smokey dashed
swiftly onto their trail and leaped up on them, licking their
faces, and whining. Then he ran madly around and around
them, led off, paused, and looked back as if to say: "Well,
come on, let's hunt!" They were much relieved, as well as
happy, and decided that he was fully tame.

The same thing happened on two later occasions; that is,
Smokey took after coyotes they raised but soon came hurry-
ing back, as much as to say that Apikuni and Hart, not
coyotes, were his kind of people. Schultz wrote to a friend in
October, 1930, inviting him to come to Greer during the
hunting season, saying:

> I am sure you will enjoy hunting with my son and me and
> Smokey, our tame coyote. . . . The coyote is the most interest-
> ing animal that I ever met up with. Full of devilment. A fine
> hunter and retriever. I do wish that you could join us before
> the close of the open season, November 15.[5]

While Schultz and Hart were away from Butterfly Lodge
in the summer of 1932, they left Smokey in the care of a
neighbor. Not long afterward, they received this terse wire
from him: "SMOKEY POISONED LAST NIGHT. HE IS DEAD."

For a number of years beginning in 1929, Schultz and
Apaki spent each autumn at Greer with his son Hart and the
latter's wife. The period of their annual visit coincided with
the open season on turkeys, and both father and son were
ardent hunters. In addition to Smokey, they also had a series

[5] Letter of October 6, 1930, to Harlan Burket of Findlay, Ohio. See *The
Piegan Storyteller*, Vol. VII, No. 1, January, 1982, 2.

of cats that loved to participate in the sport. The first of
these was Mary, a huge black feline with a litter of black kittens, all of which came running at Schultz's whistle. Although Mary never wandered far from her master, she
sometimes spied the turkeys before he did. Then, according
to Schultz,

> her hair would stand on end and she would growl viciously.
> When I shot she would run up to the bird and fight it while it
> was alive, or chew its neck if it was dead. And like a dog,
> Mary was rarin' to go whenever I started out of the lodge
> with my shotgun.[6]

Mary's successor as Schultz's companion on the turkey trail
was a big tiger cat named Mutsi ("brave" in Blackfoot). In
speaking of this cat, Schultz said:

> Recently when Mutsi and I were out hunting, I shot a turkey,
> apparently killed it. Mutsi ran to it and started chewing its
> neck. Suddenly the turkey began a convulsive beating with its
> wings and flapping that tossed Mutsi in the air and ten feet
> from it. At that, with a howl of rage and all his hair on end,
> Mutsi sprang upon the turkey and bit and clawed it, raising a
> cloud of feathers into the air until the turkey died.[7]

Black cats seemed to be favorite pets in the Schultz family.
Hart gave one of his kittens to his father. It was named
Blackie and became very fond of Schultz Senior. So fond of
Blackie were the Schultzes that he was included as their trav-
eling companion as they drove from place to place, usually
perched upon the shoulder of the driver.

They advertised for a mate to Blackie, evidently while
they were in Tucson, and obtained a black female they called
Tucsonia. As a matter of fact, there were times when their
liking for pets extended, it would seem, somewhat beyond
the bounds of mere fondness. The facilities of one of their
houses included a large, old-fashioned bathtub with a
wooden rim or shelf about it. Joining Apaki in the bathroom,

---

[6] Excerpt from an article by Jessie Louise Donaldson, *Boonville Herald*,
October 30, 1930, made available through research by Matthew J. Conway.
   [7] *Idem.*

Blackie and Tucsonia would stroll, one after the other, along this ledge as she performed her ablutions. This bizarre bit of feline voyeurism was humorously referred to by the Schultzes as the "procession of the equinoxes."

Blackie, it seemed, took an interest in other lady cats besides Tucsonia and at times evinced a determination to get to know them better. When the Schultzes were spending time with Hart and Naoma near Tucson in the early winter of 1931–32, Blackie spent several evenings serenading a puss at a nearby home. Finally, enough old shoes were thrown at him from a window to drive him up a ladder and onto the roof of a nearby shed. When the Schultzes missed him, Apikuni spent two days looking for him, finally hearing of a home where they were about to shoot a big black tomcat. The Schultzes located the house and Jess took a hatbox up a ladder to the roof of the shed, persuaded Blackie to jump into it, then backed down the ladder and headed for home.

When Blackie mated with Tucsonia, they became the parents of two equally black male kittens named Blackie Longtail and Feathers. They were distinguished by the fact that Feathers had beautiful long hair, in spite of the fact that his father and mother were short-haired cats. Counting a little tiger cat that hung around the place, the Schultzes had five felines.

After the acquisition of Tucsonia, both she and Blackie traveled with the Schultzes. When they were on their way to Montana immediately after their marriage, both cats were with them. When Apikuni had to enter Mayo Clinic at Rochester, Minnesota, they posed something of a problem. Apaki had to rent an apartment near the clinic, but she did not dare let the cats outdoors. For exercise, she let them into the hall, where they had a good time chasing each other.

According to Apaki, Apikuni enjoyed seeing the cats stretch out on the floor completely flat and go to sleep. When he was tense, he said, it relaxed him to watch them. Actually, the Schultzes' household came to include six pets, the last being a dog named Jet that lived harmoniously with the cats. The animals never fought and seemed to enjoy playing with one another.

Although the dog was called Jet, the name had nothing to do with her color; rather, it represented a shortening of *Jet-propelled*. She had appeared at the Schultz home as a wet straggly puppy, white and with a black nose, soft little white ears, a big black patch on her side, and a tail that didn't seem to match the rest of her body. She immediately began to look after the Schultzes and to take care of the house, not letting anybody in if she didn't think the person belonged there. She was an ideal pet and gave the Schultzes the most joy they ever had from any dog.

CHAPTER 32

Omega Chapter

D ESPITE the fact that James Willard Schultz lived to a
ripe old age, he did not escape periodic bouts of ill
health. He was no stranger to hospitals in Arizona,
Montana, California, Nebraska, Colorado, Wyoming, and
even Alberta, Canada. He not only suffered substantial periods of discomfort, as well as disability, from both acute and
chronic illnesses, but in his later years he became the victim
of a number of major injuries that left him partly crippled
in his lower limbs. Twice he underwent surgery.

His long history of health problems began soon after he
went to the West Coast. He had not been in California long
before he began to experience a general feeling of malaise
that led him to seek a change of climate in Arizona. Although after a few months there appeared to be some improvement in his condition, he nevertheless wound up in a
Phoenix hospital with an ailment of undiagnosed character.
He spent the next few years in Southern California; however, it was after he returned to Arizona and moved into his
new hunting lodge in the White Mountains that he again experienced health problems. This was diagnosed as a heart
condition and caused him to be temporarily precluded from
hunting or physical work. For relief, a return to a lower elevation was prescribed.

His next ailment of consequence occurred in California
when he began to suffer from pyorrhea, which developed
into a systemic infection. Both his dentist and his doctor told
him that extraction of his upper teeth and a certain amount
of gum surgery were imperative. He submitted, although

reluctantly, to this rather drastic treatment with marked benefit but not without a period of temporary disability. This was in 1921.

During the 1920's, Schultz began to suffer from an arthritic infection of the hip which may or may not have been related to his earlier pyorrheal infection. By the time he visited the Canadian Blackfeet east of Calgary in the summer of 1928 the condition, which had flared up during the previous winter in California, an especially rainy one, was bothering him considerably. Taking note of his problem, the members of the Beaver Society decided to stage their healing ceremony for his benefit, in the course of which prayers were uttered for his health, for long life, for plenty. Long life he did attain, but permanent relief he did not, for in September, 1940, he was complaining that he was so crippled with rheumatism that he could not walk about and could sleep but little.

Lung infections from time to time were one of Schultz's nemeses. These included a bronchial infection from which he suffered in 1919, a pneumonia that confined him to a hospital at Macleod, Alberta in June, 1925, and an attack of influenza at Bozeman in the winter of 1928–29. In the spring of 1939 while at Browning, he suffered from a prolonged bout of influenza which had not entirely cleared up by the following August. In the light of hindsight, it may well be that his problem at the Phoenix hospital in 1906 also involved this type of illness.

During his last years at Browning and his early years at Fort Washakie, Schultz was afflicted with a variety of ailments of disabling nature. One was a neuritis that developed in 1939 and by August had him in Columbus Hospital at Great Falls. The condition was described as an inflammation of the spinal cord extending up its right side into the skull. In 1940 he suffered not only from the crippling rheumatism mentioned above but also from a virulent sinusitis that continued to bother him for most of the year 1941 at Fort Washakie.

In other words, as Apikuni grew older he developed an increasing susceptibility to a number of illnesses of an infectious type, ranging from pyorrheal to arthritic and from pulmonary to cardiac, not to mention the persistent sinusitis. Compounding all of these problems after he had reached his allotted threescore years and ten was the fact that he had also become accident prone and suffered painful and crippling injuries.

The first of the three devastating injuries he was to sustain during his sunset years was the back injury of 1931. Although there is no record that his condition was medically diagnosed as a ruptured intervertebral disc, the excruciating sciatic pain he suffered for months is typical of that type of injury In his case it became life threatening when it deteriorated into an almost overpowering case of morphine addiction. Altogether, it disabled him from his work as a writer for a year or more.

Schultz was well into his eighties when he suffered a double injury on October 25, 1942. On that day he fell at his home in Fort Washakie, suffering fractures of his left leg and of his right arm near the shoulder. Whatever the immediate cause of the fall, the injuries necessitated nearly three months of confinement at Bishop Randall Hospital in Lander, Wyoming. Not long after his discharge he wrote Harry James: "I now have two saw-horses at my bed and getting up, resting my hands on them, I walk back and forth frequently, and so I am slowly regaining my leg strength. Hope soon to do some story work with my typewriter."

He managed to type an occasional brief note to friends but never succeeded in doing any more story work. On September 21, 1944, he and his wife arrived in Denver, where she was to attend classes in social work for the autumn quarter at Denver University. That evening he fell again, resulting in a fracture of the left hip that necessitated surgery; he remained in Denver until December 9. In a note to Harry James, Schultz described the accident that caused his injury:

> The house was dark and so was the street. Apaki went to the house, rang the bell. No answer. I stepped out of the car, moved forward, fell from the sidewalk onto the paved road and broke my left hip bone. Result weeks in the hospital . . .

cost more than $450.00.[1] The surgeon nailed and riveted the hip bone together. Leg is now two inches shorter than the right one.

After this, his attention span became shorter and shorter. His eyes troubled him. Although he wrote to Harry James from time to time, the letters consisted of just a line or two and always referred to his frustration at not being able to concentrate and complete his unfinished stories. During these very difficult months the devotion of his wife and his son, Lone Wolf, were his chief source of consolation.

In addition to the difficulty caused by the hip fracture, Schultz became afflicted with a condition that would become more serious as time went on. This was a progressive coronary pathology that produced heart discomfort and forced him to give up writing, although his stories were still much on his mind.

Apikuni died on June 11, 1947, on an afternoon when four inches of snow fell on the Wind River Reservation. Apaki recalled that the Blackfeet had always said that it is sure to storm when a chief passes. In a June 22, 1947, letter to Harry James, Apaki told him about *Apikuni's death and burial:*

> Apikuni had a heart attack—one hour—the only one of its kind. He had had a rough winter and still every hour that he felt at all well he was yearning to write his stories—could not get his *Bear Chief's War Shirt* off his mind.
>
> Hart and his wife met me at Browning—Apikuni had wanted to go there—to the old burial-ground of Natahki's family near Red Eagle and the other old friends of his youth. When we arrived and talked to the Blackfeet I knew that it could not have been otherwise. He was truly at home.
>
> The service at the grave was the most beautiful I have ever attended—the prayers of the four old medicine men, a talk by Bull Chief in which he recounted Apikuni's deeds and placed two coup sticks at the side of the grave—the mourning song of his adopted mother, Insimaki, and the long wail

---

[1] For some reason he sent the hospital bill to Houghton Mifflin. The latter returned the bill but did send him two hundred dollars with their sympathy and good wishes for an early recovery.

*Buffalo fall above the burial ground where Schultz is buried. Courtesy
Renne Library Collection.*

that followed; then the peace of the burial ground. The long
open meadow land through which the cars traveled toward
the burial place was unplowed and dotted with flowers.
There were ducks and even geese on the small lakes. A sage
hen peeked out from under the bush. All the birds in crea-
tion were singing their songs.

Apikuni wanted no marker, only to be with those he had
loved in his boyhood. He is next to Pahtaki, Natahki's mother,
whose burial he described in *My Life as an Indian.* All the cars
and buses on the reservation were put into service and the
full-blooded Indians—all of them—came to the edge of the
bluff and descended the steep trail to the burial ground.

Memorial gravestone designed by Lone Wolf. Courtesy Renne Library Collection.

There was no interpretation—no need for it. Hart told me, "They say he has gone to the Sand Hills with his old warrior friends and there they will hunt buffalo together—shadow buffalo in a land of shadows—but he will be with them."

Later Apaki added details to this lovely description. The meadow she mentioned was one that led up to the top of the buffalo fall, at the bottom of which is the burial ground. She wrote again of the sense of welcome she felt that day "as the birds and the flowers and the little animals made themselves known as we crossed that meadow. The sun, too, cast a warm soft light."

Later it was decided to disregard Schultz's desire that his grave be unmarked. So many requests came from the readers of Apikuni's books that the Indian agent at Browning prevailed upon Mrs. Schultz and Hart to have a suitable marker set in place. Hart designed a very simple stone to symbolize his father's life with the Blackfeet.

Biographical Postscripts

CHAPTER 33

Hart Merriam Schultz: Lone Wolf

NÄTAHKI'S contributions to the pattern of her husband's life as an Indian included one that was unique:
she made him a father. Although married three
times, Apikuni was blessed with only one child, a son, born
to himself and Nätahki on Birch Creek close to the Joseph
Kipp trading post at Robare Crossing, Montana.[1] At the
time, Apikuni was working with Kipp at the latter's winter
trading post at Carroll, and Nätahki was staying with her
mother. The date of birth was February 18, 1882.[2]

Nätahki's mother was Pahtaki, who had been the wife of a
noted Pikuni warrior named Black Eagle, of which union
Nätahki had been the child. Black Eagle was slain when she
was a small child, reputedly because he had become too
powerful and too successful on the warpath. Whatever the
reason, his younger brother, Yellow Wolf, in accordance
with Blackfoot custom, became the husband of Pahtaki and
the stepgrandfather of Nätahki's son.

The young Schultz unwittingly acquired names under
three different cultures. While Schultz was away, Father
Prando, a Jesuit, named the infant Thomas, at which his
father, when he learned of it, was "more than put out." Nätahki's uncle, Red Eagle, a medicine man, took it upon himself to give the child the name of Lone Wolf "from a power-

---

[1] Dyck, "The Return of Lone Wolf," 20.
[2] Dyck, "Lone Wolf Returns"; reprinted in *The Piegan Storyteller*, Vol. III,
No. 2, 2.

ful vision that Sun once gave him."[3] Schultz himself was
satisfied with neither of the foregoing and proceeded to
name the boy Hart Merriam for C. Hart Merriam, the noted
physician and anthropologist who had been Schultz's boyhood friend in New York.[4] While the Pikunis wanted to honor
the lad with the name Black Eagle, after his famous grandfather, Hart never accepted or used it because he preferred
Lone Wolf.

Hart's early years were spent near Fort Conrad, at his parents' ranch on Two Medicine River and at the three schools
which he attended—and also despised. It was in these early
years that he experienced his first travois ride and that his
Grandfather Yellow Wolf taught him how to use natural col-
ors, how to prepare them, and how to draw animals and
people.

From his parents' ranch he was taken, along with neigh-
boring Blackfeet children, by soldiers to attend school at Fort
Shaw. There the children's long braids were cut off, their
buckskin clothes were replaced with white man clothing, and
if they were heard speaking their native tongue, they were
strapped with a leather belt. Later he attended the new
Catholic school at the mission on Two Medicine River. Before long the schoolmaster undertook to punish Hart and
another boy with a heavy wooden rule, so they joined forces
to beat him up, with the result that Hart was expelled by the
superintendent. Hart was delighted; when he arrived home,
his surprised parents decided that he could forget education for a while.[5]

In his twelfth winter, Hart's father enrolled him in Willow
Creek School on the reservation. His mother was unhappy

[3] While Schultz Senior stated that Lone Wolf had been given that name
by Nätahki's uncle Red Eagle (*Blackfeet and Buffalo*, 82), Lone Wolf himself
told Paul Dyck, his adopted son, that the name was bestowed upon him by
his grandfather, Yellow Wolf; see *Montana: The Magazine of Western History*,
Winter, 1972, 27.
[4] *Blackfeet and Buffalo*, 82.
[5] This information and much of that which follows is from Lone Wolf's
own story as told to and related by his adopted son, Paul Dyck, in "The
Return of Lone Wolf"; permission to use here granted by *Montana: The
Magazine of Western History*.

to see him go, but his father was eager for him to receive an education. Here again treatment was sadistic and discipline drastic. Finally, when the master banged one of the boys with the handle of a pitchfork, young Schultz and several of his schoolmates piled on the man and gave him a beating. For this they were all put in jail, and after Hart got out his father decided that it was time for him to come home for good.

Now a teenager, young Schultz soon found that life on the home ranch along the Two Medicine was to be a busy one for him. His father was frequently away carrying on his business of guiding wealthy easterners through the future Glacier National Park. Thus Hart had to learn, fortunately with the advice and help of an uncle, Last Rider, how to operate a cattle ranch. Last Rider became almost a second father to Hart, since it was he who took care of the family during Apikuni's long absences. Despite his love for his father, Hart's mother and her people were closest to him, and Nätahki often told him: "You will have to follow the white man's way so it is best to learn how to make a living here."

The ranch work left little time for painting. Nevertheless, during this period Lone Wolf sold his first watercolor to Jack Carberry, a clerk in Joe Kipp's store at Browning. Some thirty years later, Carberry returned the painting to Lone Wolf as a sentimental gift.

When Apikuni finally tired of the ranch and sold it to his old friend Eli Guardipee, it became necessary for Lone Wolf to look for work as a cowboy and bronc buster with the nearby cow and horse outfits. It was during this period of his life, after the age of eighteen, that some of the adventures and escapades in which he engaged took place. They were mostly the kinds of incidents that Lone Wolf failed to tell his friends about when regaling them in later years with stories of his early life.

As a young adult, Lone Wolf's pattern of defiance of established authority continued to assert itself. After his mother died, one of his cowboy cronies was Angus Monroe, a grandson of Hugh Monroe, and, as a matter of fact, they became close lifelong friends. According to Angus, Lone

Lone Wolf. Courtesy Schultz Society Collection.

Lone Wolf and Smokey after a turkey hunt at Butterfly Lodge, in Arizona. Courtesy Schultz Society Collection.

Wolf at that time was a wild young cowboy who was frequently in trouble with the law both on and off the reservation.

It is a matter of record that Hart was mixed up in several horse-rustling cases and sometimes had to lie low. When he and Angus rode one evening into the wild and wooly rail-road town of Cut Bank, just outside the reservation, they had little trouble buying drinks, despite the fact that in those days it was forbidden to sell liquor off the reservation to any-one with Indian blood. On the reservation, nobody, whether white or Indian, could possess liquor in any form. That Hart and Angus were half bloods was easy to see, but there were places that paid little attention to the law.[6]

On this occasion the two were in town having a good time when Hart got into a fight with a white man who knew the authorities were looking for Hart. After the fight had been broken up, the still-angry white man sent word to authori-ties that Hart was in town. By this time, Hart and Angus had taken a room in Slim Brown's hotel and were just preparing to bed down when they heard several horsemen ride up to the front of the hotel. Looking down from their room on the second floor, they recognized the sheriff and a deputy. Hart immediately ran to the rear of the floor, jumped down to the ground, and made a circle around to the place where he and Angus had left their horses. He struck out for the reservation and did not slow down until he was safely across Cut Bank Creek, the boundary. Once on the reservation he was free from pursuit because only a federal officer could arrest him there; the sheriff had no jurisdiction.

According to Angus, he and Hart traveled together to many of the early rodeos held in the area and competed as bronc riders. They also rode together for a number of years on the big Indian Department roundup each spring and fall. Angus recalls that he and his wife, Lily, were friendly with Hart and Hart's first wife, a full blood named Margaret Strong Woman, and traveled together on several occasions.

[6]The story of the adventures of Hart and Angus Monroe has been writ-ten by Gordon L. Pouliot and appears in *The Piegan Storyteller*, Vol. VI, No. 4, 11.

Margaret and Hart were divorced when Hart contracted tuberculosis. After Hart remarried, the Schultzes and the Monroes stayed in touch by letter and always saw each other when the Schultzes visited Blackfoot country.

Because of his lung condition, Lone Wolf was advised by doctors to seek a change of climate, and not long after his mother's death he headed for the Southwest, where he spent a part of each year thereafter. He started work at the Grand Canyon in 1906 as a cowboy, wrangler, and guide. While there he maintained his interest in painting and started working seriously as an artist. He had the good fortune to meet the great artist Thomas Moran, who took a liking to Lone Wolf, particularly when he learned that he was a Blackfoot from the Northwest. He recommended that Hart study at the Art Students' League in Los Angeles.

Lone Wolf lost contact with his father when the latter departed for the Far West in 1903, and it was not until 1909 that they were reunited. He came to live with his father, by then married to Celia, and attended art school in Los Angeles; however, the situation became intolerable because of Celia's intense jealousy. He moved on to study at the Chicago Art Institute for a time, yet he found that the white man's art schools were not his answer; he longed for the old way of life. Consequently he returned to Montana and resumed his work as a cowboy.

In 1916, Lone Wolf went to work at the Galbraith ranch on the Milk River not far from the Canadian border. Near the ranch a construction crew was camped while doing some track repair work for the Great Northern Railway. The camp foreman, Eli Tracy, maintained a home in Cardston, Alberta, where his children could attend school. His daughter, Naoma, who was in high school, often heard from her brother, who also worked with the crew, about the camp and the work. He mentioned a young cowboy named Lone Wolf, who was a spectacular rider and afterward could draw a picture of it.

One day Naoma persuaded her father to take her with him to the ranch in the hope of meeting such a remarkable horseman and possibly seeing him perform. His riding was indeed outstanding, and she was amazed by it. When her father introduced him to her, she was impressed by the good looks and soft-spoken courtesy of the young cowboy. Hart, for his part, thought she was the prettiest red-cheeked girl he had ever seen. They were infatuated with each other and in the days that followed managed to meet several times.[7]

Five months later, by prearrangement, Lone Wolf, leading an extra horse, met Naoma at the edge of the construction camp. From there they rode sixty-five miles to the ranch of Last Rider, his uncle. The next day, they rode on to Cut Bank, where they were married by a justice of the peace. It was a marriage that lasted fifty-four years, a romance that never ended.

During the summer of 1914, Hart had spent some time at his father's Arizona mountain cabin, which had been completed earlier that year. Father and son made some hunting trips together and Schultz Senior was pleased to learn of Lone Wolf's progress with his painting. It was during this visit that they selected a site on the premises where his father promised to have a cabin built for Hart.

The promise was kept, and his father was delighted when Hart and Naoma in the latter part of 1916 took possession of the cabin, which had been completed that year. From that time forward, Hart and his wife spent a part of each year there, and in the middle 1920's became sole owners of the entire property, a gift from his father. Over the fireplace in the main cabin after it became theirs hung a painting of the Grand Canyon by Hart, which he had given to Naoma as a wedding present.

In 1917, Lone Wolf held his first art show at Los Angeles. The *Los Angeles Times* carried the headline VANCE THOMPSON DISCOVERS WONDERFUL INDIAN ARTIST, AN ARTIST WITH A VISION. In the article, Thompson, who was art critic for the *Times*, wrote:

> It is a rare thing to discover an artist. I have seen the young painters pass in droves through the schools and salons of Paris, and in 20 years I can claim to have been the discoverer

[7] The rest of this chapter is based on Paul Dyck's article "The Return of Lone Wolf"; permission to use here granted by *Montana: The Magazine of Western History*.

of only one great artist. Now I like to think that I have, at last, discovered another and he is an artist who has authentic vision, sincerity and a brush which is already capable of doing precisely the thing he wants it to. . . .

Lone Wolf has courage . . . artistic courage which is the rarest of all. His strength as an artist is in his uncompromising realism . . . in his sincere treatment of the human form . . . in his intimate knowledge of the life he paints. You might call it quality, but whatever you call it, it is the one thing that keeps art alive, this son of the Blackfeet tribe has got it. He has got it. And to art lover and painter folk I want to say one thing. There is a new artist coming up the trail and the name on him is Lone Wolf. His pictures are signed with a wolf's head.

Collectors and enthusiasts of the Old West finally started to seek Hart out. During the summers he could be found on the east side of Glacier National Park at his St. Mary studio. In autumn he would move to his spacious studio at Butterfly Lodge in Arizona, while in later years he went to Tucson for the winter and spring. Charlie Russell made several visits to the summer studio, seeking advice on ethnological details and asking Lone Wolf and such old warriors as Bear Head to help solve the problems.

In 1920, E. R. Yarnell, of Florida, saw Lone Wolf's paintings at Glacier Park and brought them to the attention of his business associate, August Hecksher of New York City. The latter, an ardent art collector, was to become one of Lone Wolf's devoted patrons. He arranged for Hart to hold his first eastern exhibition in New York City and bought all of the paintings from that first show. He also introduced Lone Wolf to Babcock Galleries, which handled his work for years. With the New York show a sellout, Lone Wolf was besieged by reporters, and the city's newspapers lionized him.

Lone Wolf's works found their way into collections and museums of international importance. Among his early patrons were Mrs. Calvin Coolidge, Herbert Hoover, Owen Wister, Burton Holmes, Robert Colgate, H. S. Duryea, J. C. Kinney, and Dr. Philip G. Cole. It would be difficult to estimate the total artistic output of Lone Wolf, since some of his paintings came into existence before 1913, when the Santa

Lone Wolf (left), Stoops-over-Butchering, and Schultz at Big Sorrel Horse Ranch, Alberta. Courtesy Schultz Society Collection.

Fe Railway commenced buying his work. His best estimate, made near the end of his life, was that about five hundred of his paintings were extant.

The 1920–30 decade saw Lone Wolf venture into sculpture, this being a period which produced the finest bronzes of his career. August Hecksher purchased and donated *Camouflage* to the Brookgreen Gardens Collection of American Sculpture in Brookgreen, South Carolina, in 1929. Only one cast was made of *Buffalo Run*; this piece was purchased by Hecksher's son as a wedding present to his father, and upon the latter's death it was purchased by Evelyn Walsh MacClean, of Washington, D.C. This unique work is now in the collection of the Phoenix Art Museum in Arizona.

Many of the sculptures Lone Wolf executed throughout the years did not mature into finished bronze casts, for the 1930's brought lean times and casting costs were high. One by one, the clay models were lost. *Riding High* and *Keeper of the Moons* were the only two pieces which survived in Lone Wolf's personal collection. They were cast in a limited edition in 1967.

The early years of bronc busting, with all its bruises and broken bones, began to take their toll on Hart. Arthritis set in and Lone Wolf's artistic ability gradually diminished until there was only a limited market for his work. Yet to the very end of his life he stayed at the easel every day in a heroic effort to record the past.

Lone Wolf died on February 8, 1970, in Tucson, Arizona, a few days short of his eighty-eighth birthday. In keeping with a promise made to him, his ashes were interred on June 19, 1970, in the grave of his beloved uncle, Last Rider, on the old ranch, close to Cut Bank Creek, that held so many happy memories. On July 16, 1971, Lone Wolf's widow, Naoma, accompanied by his adopted son, Paul Dyck, and Dyck's wife, Star, went to Browning, where the Give-Away Feast of the Blackfeet was held in Lone Wolf's honor, the details having been arranged by Peter and Aileen Red Horn and George Kipp. Hundreds of Blackfeet people and visitors attended to view the photographs, paintings, and other memorabilia of Lone Wolf's life. It was a sign to all that Lone Wolf had returned and was remembered.

In retrospect, the similarities in many respects between the lives of Lone Wolf and his father are striking. As youngsters, both were obstreperous students, resentful of schoolmaster discipline, with the result that each suffered expulsion from school or was no longer welcome to return. Both lived adventurous lives on the Montana frontier, and each, although at different times, had a brush with the law and narrowly escaped capture by its zealous minions, who were hot on their respective trails.

Both father and son suffered from health problems which led each, independently and unknown to the other, to go to Arizona, where each was able to find relief from his ailment. From that state the paths of both men led to Los Angeles, where each was soon to score his first major success in his chosen field. Both, however, subsequently returned with frequency to Montana and Glacier Park, particularly to St. Mary Lakes, where Hart, as did his father decades before him, had a cabin he used in the earning of his livelihood.

Both men had an affinity for the high mountain country of Arizona, where both spent much time at the shooting lodge built there by Apikuni and later owned by Hart and where both were ardent hunters. And as the years wore on, both men suffered from arthritis to the degree that it became a handicap in their respective activities. In the end, each succumbed to a progressive cardiac impairment.

The son, like his father, lived to be eighty-eight years old, give or take a few weeks. Both passed away outside Montana, but, in conformity with their respective wishes, each was brought back to Montana for interment in the beautiful green valley that each had for so long called home.

CHAPTER 34

Jessie Donaldson Schultz: Apaki

ALTHOUGH Apaki played a major role in the life story of James Willard Schultz, her own career is worthy of at least passing note. For nearly forty years before she met him, as well as for nearly thirty years after his death, she busily carved out a name for herself. A woman of wit and warmth, of ingenuity and determination, she gave tremendous support to Apikuni throughout their years together, and the highlights of her unusual life, as set forth in her memoirs, make interesting reading.

Jessie Louise Donaldson was born at Minneapolis, Minnesota on August 17, 1887.[1] During her earlier years she answered simply to Jess but later adopted the more formal Jessica after a family friend named Jessica Wakefield. Her father was Gilbert S. Donaldson, an electrical engineer of Scottish extraction, who became a builder of electric light and power plants in Minnesota and Iowa. Her mother was born Annie Berryman, who had hoped to become a concert pianist but gave it up for marriage and five children.

Jessie, youngest of the five, was a year old when her mother died at the age of thirty-nine. Her father took her to New York to live with her grandparents, where she remained until she was seven and returned to Minneapolis to live with the rest of the family. The next few years were spent in Min-

---

[1]Robert H. Martin, a nephew of Jessie Donaldson, in an article entitled "Vignettes of Jessie Donaldson Schultz Graham," *The Piegan Storyteller*, Vol. II, No. 1, January, 1977, 11–13, has furnished the information on which much of this chapter is based, except as otherwise indicated.

neapolis and in McGregor, Iowa, where her father was constructing a power plant.

When she was ready for college, Jessie enrolled at the University of Wisconsin, where she was initiated into Psi Chapter of Kappa Alpha Theta sorority. When she later transferred to the University of Minnesota, she became affiliated with the sorority's Upsilon Chapter. She majored in history, receiving her degree from the University of Minnesota in 1913.[2]

College was followed by research work representing postgraduate study at the University of Minnesota and later by a summer session at the University of Michigan. At this point she suffered a rather severe attack of typhoid pneumonia, as a result of which her physician recommended that she live at a higher altitude. To comply, she went to Bozeman, Montana, in 1915 to live with her sister Jean and brother-in-law, George Martin, a professor in the Dairy Department of Montana State College, where, incidentally, Jean served as a substitute instructor in home economics.

For most of her first year in Bozeman, Jessica was too ill to do anything but rest. When she began feeling better, she spent some time on the homestead of a friend, Mildred Livingston, some forty-five miles out of Bozeman. Later she taught briefly at Harper School, just west of Bozeman, and for the summer and fall of 1916 and of 1917 at Grayling School, near the headwaters of the Madison River some fifteen miles from West Yellowstone. This turned out to be an adventure, with very few pupils and a climate that required skiing to school when the deep snow began in November.

Jessie had applied for a position on the faculty of Montana State College, and after being interviewed she was hired in January, 1918, as an instructor in the English Department, assigned to teaching freshman English.[3] Her

[2] Parts of the story of her college years are taken from an article by Jane S. Koford of Napa, California, entitled "Thetas You'd Like to Know." First published in the 1975–76 Winter Issue of *Kappa Alpha Theta Magazine*, Vol. 90, No. 2, it was reprinted in *The Piegan Storyteller*, Vol. I, No. 4, October, 1976, 13.

[3] Except as otherwise indicated, the rest of this chapter is based on the unpublished memoirs of Jessica Donaldson Schultz Graham, reposing in

early years on the faculty at Montana State have been described well:

Finding Montana State to be primarily a men's school, she set about organizing activities for women: a chapter of Mortar Board, a women's athletic association, a literary society (the Eurodelphian Society) and a literary magazine (the Bobcat), both now defunct, and most notably, the original chapter of Spurs, the national sophomore women's honorary and service society.

Jess was also an innovative and inspiring teacher, introducing new courses in technical writing and contemporaneous literature, the latter so popular that she taught an evening section for townspeople. The culmination of her career at the college was a tremendous dramatic production based upon Crow Indian history and ceremony. It was entitled "The Masque of the Absaroka" and when presented in 1927 brought together students, faculty, townspeople, and some twenty-odd Crow Indians from the reservation nearly 200 miles away.

The Masque was a great success and drew attention from far beyond Bozeman, but the head of the English department (her superior) forbade her to produce another one, remarking grumpily that she had turned the whole college into an Indian camp.[4]

With further campus projects of the masque type vetoed by her superior, Jessica began to toy with the idea of staging something of the kind in Glacier National Park. Realizing that a great deal of groundwork would be necessary, she went to the park early in the summer of 1927 but failed to make the headway she had hoped for. Nevertheless, the summer proved an eventful one for two reasons: she was able to attend the special Indian ceremonies at both Belly

the Museum of the Rockies at Montana State University, in Bozeman. Prepared by Mrs. Graham through the use of tapes and capably edited by Anne Banks, they are especially valuable because they set forth Mrs. Graham's personal recollections of her years with *Apikuni*, both before and after their marriage, as well as the trying period that led up to and followed her resignation from the Montana State faculty.

[4] The quoted material is from Anne Banks, "Gifts Reflect Indian Ways," *Bozeman Daily Chronicle*, March 25, 1979, reprinted in *The Piegan Storyteller*, Vol. IV, No. 3, July, 1979, 1.

River and Browning, and she became well acquainted with
James Willard Schultz, having attended both of these outstanding ceremonies with him. As a matter of fact, the
events of the summer of 1927 were to change the pattern of
her life. From the cloistered stability of her college years at
Bozeman, she was unknowingly embarking upon a pillar-to-
post type of life, years of uncertainty, frequent changes, and
at times hardship.

Jessica had arranged to take a sabbatical leave from her
teaching duties at Montana State College during the 1927—
28 school year. She had decided to spend her leave pursuing
studies in anthropology at the University of California at
Berkeley, where she already had devoted one summer to
courses in that subject. In the fall of 1928, her sabbatical
now concluded, Jess returned to the Montana State campus,
ready and eager to resume her teaching duties after spending the summer at Calgary doing research for *The Sun God's
Children*, the book on which she would collaborate with
Schultz. While in Calgary, she and Apikuni had a number of
opportunities to visit with the Northern Blackfeet.

Shortly after she returned to Bozeman in the autumn of
1928, Apikuni went there and rented an apartment near
hers. It was during that school year that Jess carried her full
assignment of classes and wrote her part of *The Sun God's
Children*. It was to be illustrated by Winold Reiss, a well-
known painter of Indians, particularly members of the
Pikuni tribe. When winter came, Apikuni's room became too
cold for him to work in it, so Jess invited him to use her
apartment during the day while she was busy at school. This
worked out well because he prepared the noon meal for
both of them.

The college year was almost over when Jess was called into
the president's office, where that dignitary and her department head were looking very solemn and began talking
about the situation with Apikuni, saying it was better for her
and Apikuni not to be in the same town. Jess was surprised
and shocked by this arraignment and dismayed to find that
her side of the matter was falling on deaf ears. To her ac-
cusers, her relationship with Apikuni, or what appeared to

them to be the relationship, was simply incompatible with her position as a member of the college faculty. She realized that she had little choice but to resign and she did so, indicating that although she loved the college very much she felt that it was for the good of everybody that she leave.

It was not until much later that Jess came to realize the circumstances that had produced her contretemps. During the winter months of her last year at the college, Apikuni had contracted influenza and the doctor recommended that he be in a warm place rather than in the frigid room he was then occupying. Jess graciously suggested that he could stay in her warm apartment and she would occupy his cold quarters for the period of his illness. The unanticipated result was, of course, that she would be seen coming out of his apartment each morning on her way to the college, passing the fraternity house next door; and when he was well enough to get up, he would emerge from her apartment. This innocent switch was apparently the source of her problem with the college authorities, a situation which she was given no opportunity to explain.

When Jess had recovered somewhat from her frustration and Apikuni from his anger over the unexpected turn of events resulting from the arbitrary action of the college officials, they found themselves facing an uncertain future so far as Bozeman was concerned. This was the community which she had called home for most of the years since her arrival there in 1915. Nevertheless, without a definite plan for the year ahead, they left Bozeman at the end of the college year, that is, in June, 1929.

The next five years were difficult for Jessica and Apikuni; and the story of their travail has been told in Chapter 24 and need not be repeated here. During the two years before their marriage in April, 1931, as well as the three years afterward, they were together every day and almost every hour. After the interminable job drought ended with her appointment as a community worker for the Federal Emergency Relief Administration at Choteau, Montana, commencing in September, 1934, Jess was surprised to be transferred to a similar post at nearby Browning only three

months later. Here she was able to continue in federal service until 1940, although in the meantime the FERA had
been replaced by the Works Progress Administration and
she had been transferred in 1937 to the jurisdiction of the
Indian Service.

For the Schultzes, the move to Browning was a turn for
the better. It brought them back to an area and people with
whom they were familiar, and it enabled Apikuni to be
among those of his old Pikuni associates who still survived.
Also, it put them in a position, by virtue of being able to dis-
pense federal aid in connection with her community-worker
duties, of being able to help their Indian friends in need.

The record Jess compiled during her years in Browning,
with the aid of federal funds perceptively applied, certainly
has to be considered one of the success stories of the Great
Depression. Before she arrived, there had never been a social or community worker on the reservation, so she had to
start from scratch. Fortunately, a new house had been built
for the Schultzes on the government square and she was assigned an office in a government building.

The task faced by Jess was not an easy one. She started
with a number of handicaps, one of which was that both
whooping cough and measles were epidemic on the reservation and some cases were proving fatal. There was no existing inventory of community needs, and she found that these
were people who did not want to accept relief. On the plus
side was the fact that the Blackfeet were basically a happy
people and willing to work. Jess decided there was something they could do to earn an income, and thus was laid a
base for the beginning of a crafts program.

Steps were taken to teach the women to spin and to sew.
The government furnished an expert spinner, and sewing
centers were set up. From sewing clubs, a craft cooperative
was formed and a craft shop was set up at St. Mary. Its program reached a point where many people were involved
and exquisite work was being done, much of it individu-
alistic. When government authorities observed what the Indians were doing, they offered special help in the form of
WPA-sponsored white-collar projects.

In the latter part of 1940, Jess was transferred by the Indian Service from the Blackfoot Reservation to the Arapaho and Shoshone Reservation at Fort Washakie, Wyoming. She was sent there specifically to develop a crafts program similar to the one that was operating so successfully on the Blackfoot Reservation. When the time came for Jess and Apikuni to leave Browning, it was one of the most difficult moments of their lives and they wept openly with sadness at having to leave the Blackfeet.

As they drove to Fort Washakie, Jess recalled two of the most thrilling events of her personal life. One was being taken into the Blood tribe through adoption ceremonies presided over by their chief, Imitaikwan, who gave her the Indian name of Apaki. The other highlight was being admitted to membership in the Matokiks Society, the women's secret society of the Bloods, the only white woman ever to be accorded that honor.

Jess had found that while her postgraduate degree in anthropology was helpful, she also needed other special training to become a full-fledged social worker rather than a community worker. Accordingly, she undertook attendance at the University of Denver in order to gain the additional training she desired. Several summers were required, culminating in the granting of her master's degree in social work in 1944.

Fort Washakie, where Jess was to spend thirteen years, was the headquarters of the Wind River Reservation, which was half-Arapaho and half-Shoshone. She evaluated the conditions and needs for this double reservation and initiated among the Arapahos programs for mattress making, bed construction, and quilt making. When these had been completed, she had the Indians undertake a crafts program specializing in beautiful drapes and spreads in a variety of original designs, such as cattle brands, stars, and constellations. Many large orders were received, including one from the governor of Wyoming.

Jess decided to start the Shoshones on a different kind of crafts program, since their women did exquisite beadwork, using their own designs. She also instituted a weaving program, with the government helpfully providing a professional weaver. The Shoshones even acquired their own store to facilitate the sale of products.

Wherever Jess worked after her marriage to Apikuni in 1931, she and Apikuni lived together, whether it was Choteau, Browning, or Fort Washakie, and the income from her work became of increasing importance to them, particularly in the years when his health became such that he could no longer write. After his death from a heart condition in June, 1947, she continued her work at Fort Washakie until her retirement in 1953 at age sixty-six. Even before his death she had begun to experience a mild heart ailment of her own.

When she retired, Jess moved to St. Helena, California, but continued to maintain her deep interest in Indians and in Montana (she always considered herself a Montanan), returning to that state for visits as long as her health permitted. In 1961 she was given an honorary doctor's degree in letters by Montana State University in recognition of her outstanding work with the American Indian.[5]

In 1966, Jessica married an old friend named Harry L. Graham. Thereafter they spent a part of each winter in Arizona, living in the desert country and enjoying its beauty. Graham passed away in 1973; Jessica survived until 1976.

Throughout her life, Jess kept busy with various projects—writing, painting, making pottery—and took an active interest in Indian affairs. She carried on an extensive correspondence with publishers regarding the publishing and republishing of Apikuni's books. In the early 1950's, she undertook to edit for publication a number of his magazine and newspaper articles which had never appeared in a bound volume. This compilation, further edited by Keith C. Seele, was published in 1962 as *Blackfeet and Buffalo*.

In her later years Jessica spent much time preparing her memoirs, dictating them on cassette tapes supplied by Leslie Drew, director of the Museum of the Rockies at Bozeman.[6]

---

[5] Information concerning Jessica's final years is from the article by her nephew, Robert H. Martin in "Vignettes of Jessica Donaldson Schultz Graham," 12–13.

[6] Drew left this position for another museum directorship at Lubbock, Texas, in 1977 and was succeeded at Bozeman by Michael W. Hager.

Apikuni and Apaki about 1937 at Browning's Indian Days. Courtesy Renne Library Collection.

Apaki in Indian costume. Courtesy Schultz Society Collection.

The tapes were typed[7] and edited[8] by volunteers on the museum staff, and the final draft was in Jess's hands for reading at the time of her death. The museum authorities have indicated their intention to arrange for the publication of her story if possible.

In honor of Schultz, Jess established a trust fund at the university at Bozeman, to be called the Indian Heritage Award, the income from which is to be presented annually, along with a bronze medal, to an enrolled Montana college student whose name appears on the Indian census rolls and who best interprets his or her tribal heritage with a one-thousand-word paper on the subject "My Life as an Indian in the Tribe."

Jess also established at Montana State University a trust fund in honor of her second husband. The Harry Lee Graham and Jessica Graham Art Fund is to be administered by the director of the Museum of the Rockies, and the proceeds are to be used to buy Indian art for the museum.

After Jessica's death in July, 1976, her ashes were placed next to those of Harry Graham in Santa Rosa, California.

As a matter of interest to readers, I am including here the Montana State University faculty document recommending that Jess be given an honorary doctorate:

Copy of Report of
Montana State University Faculty Committee
Recommending the Granting of an Honorary Doctorate to

JESSIE LOUISE DONALDSON SCHULTZ
Route 1, Box 611. St. Helena, California

Personal data:
Born, Minnesota, 1887
Education:
    B.A. University of Minnesota, 1913
    M.A. University of California, 1930
Came west for her health in 1915
    1915–1916 Taught Harper School, west of Bozeman

---

[7] Principally by Della Mills, a museum volunteer.
[8] Entirely by Anne Banks, also a volunteer.

1916–1918 Taught Grayling School, Gallatin Canyon
(Because of snow, taught June to December each year)
Service at Montana State College
Appointed Instructor, English Department, January, 1918
Became Assistant Professor, 1921
Served as Acting head of the Department, 1923–24
Resigned, June, 1929
Memberships: Phi Kappa Phi, Kappa Alpha Theta, Ma'toki (She is the only white woman to become an active member in this woman's society of the Blood Indians).
Publications: Her work has appeared in Ladies Home Journal; Woman's Home Companion; Popular Mechanics, various educational journals; Montana, the Magazine of Western History. She is the co-author of the book *The Sun God's Children*, a story of the Blackfeet.

In 1931, she married James Willard Schultz, who died in 1947.

Mrs. Schultz's contributions fall into three categories: Teacher, Organizer, Community Worker.

I. Teacher

A. An inspiring teacher, she had the ability to recognize the capacity of her students and to stimulate them to work to their full potential; she maintained at all times a rigorous standard and "wanted her grades at MSC to be the equivalent to any great university."
B. As a teacher she was responsible for the production of two outstanding dramatic presentations on the MSC campus.
1. In 1919 she wrote and directed an outdoor pageant depicting the history of the Gallatin Valley.
2. In 1927 she was responsible for the production of "The Masque of the Absoroka," depicting the cosmogony of the Crow Indians. An extremely ambitious production—and perhaps the most lavish one ever staged at MSC—this masque involved students, townspeople, and representative citizens from Montana and the nation.
C. To inspire her students in creative work, she established a magazine, "The Bobcat," in which appeared outstanding literary work done by undergraduates at MSC.

II. Organizer

Historical records show that from 1918 to 1923 a goodly number of organizations appeared on the MSC campus. In this climate Miss Donaldson served as an inspiration and fountain of ideas for many of these groups. While the impetus for many of these is not clearly known, the inception of some of these can be traced to Miss Donaldson. Three prominent organizations functioning today on the campus owe their existence to her. They are Mortar Board, Women's Athletic Association, and Spurs.

A. Mortar Board—In 1920, Miss Donaldson established Cap and Gown, a senior women's honorary society whose purposes included "scholarly attendance, participation in college activities, and character development." This group was founded with the idea of its becoming Mortar Board, a national organization, and this was effected in April, 1927.

B. Women's Athletic Association—Early in her career at MSC, Miss Donaldson recognized the fact that women's activities were confined to "pink teas," and that no attention was being paid to physical education. As a result, Miss Donaldson informally developed a program for the girls to include hiking, walking contests, and running contests. As the interest grew, an organization followed that in time became the Women's Athletic Association. And, an athletic program for women became established as an integral part of the curriculum.

C. Spurs—In March, 1922 an organization for sophomore women came into existence. Miss Donaldson believed that women in classes other than seniors should be actively participating in campus activities. Concerning this organization, former Dean of Women, Una B. Herrick, wrote; ". . . the sophomore organization, Spurs, was originated by Miss Jessie Donaldson. Miss Donaldson felt a lack of activity for sophomore women and also felt that if freshman women had a service organization to look forward to it would encourage interest in a higher standard during the freshman year." From a Ms. "Twenty Years at Montana State College," p. 87. In 1924, Spurs became a national organization, and Miss Donaldson as sponsor of the mother chapter at MSC had the privilege of installing chapters on several campuses. The initiation ritual for Spurs was written by Miss Donaldson.

These organizations for women, as well as the now-defunct literary society, Eurodelphians and its predecessor, Alpha Epsilon Theta, also established by Miss Donaldson, stem from the philosophy of Miss Donaldson and Mrs. Herrick. Until 1918, MSC seems to have been primarily a man's college. With the advent of these women and the correlated interest in women's suffrage, the place of women students on the MSC campus became firmly established.

Not only active in student affairs, Miss Donaldson was also instrumental in the establishment of organizations for women in Bozeman. Pan Hellenic and AAUW both had their inception during Miss Donaldson's early years and she was a prime mover in the development of both of them. With Miss Freida Bull and Miss Helen Brewer, Miss Donaldson helped organize the Faculty Woman's Club on the campus.

III. Community Worker (Mrs. Schultz)

A. In 1937 she became Community Worker for the Blackfeet Indians at Browning.
B. There she established a craft shop and in cooperation with other artists in the Bureau of Indian Affairs she worked out the designs and patterns for the articles to be made by the Indians. These were the authentic Indian designs.
C. Through her efforts, she established an outlet for the crafts, which she always insisted be of the highest standards. This outlet eventually became a cooperative which she taught the Indians to operate the proceeds from it raised the income substantially for the Blackfeet Indians. In time this movement embraced all of the Northern Plains Indians and, as such a cooperative, it is still functioning.
D. In the craft shop she established an excellent lending library to serve the Blackfeet people.
E. She fostered Indian artists. Victor Pepion, a Blackfoot artist of considerable repute at the time of his death in 1956 and who did the murals in the Plains Indian Museum, credited his start in painting to Mrs. Schultz.
F. At the same time, she did social welfare work and helped the Indians budget their money to cover their needs.
G. She conceived the idea and laid the groundwork for the features of the Plains Indian Museum, now a state-wide attraction at Browning, Montana.

H. From 1941 until her retirement in 1953, she held the same type of position at the Wind River reservation in Wyoming.

I. There she worked with the Shoshoni and Arapaho Indians and repeated the successful work that she had begun with the Blackfeet. Beginning afresh in some fields, she started the Indians weaving by using wool from their own sheep. She discovered the old vegetable dyes used in primitive times and taught the Indians how to utilize them.

J. In speaking of her work, M. A. Johnson, Assistant Area Director, Bureau of Indian Affairs, Billings, wrote: "Mrs. Schultz sincerely loved the Indian people with whom she worked and was always very sympathetic and understanding when trying to assist with their personal and family problems." Letter dated January 27, 1961.

Retirement

Since her retirement in 1953, Mrs. Schultz spends the winters in California and the summers in Montana. She has been busy writing, and organizing her husband's notes from which a book-length publication *Reminiscences* is scheduled to appear this spring from the University of Oklahoma Press. She has also been instrumental in having other books of her husband's republished. Her interest in Montana State College continues as evidenced by her frequent visits to the campus in the summer and her occasional lectures to classes in history and literature being conducted during the summer session. Therefore, for her outstanding work as a teacher and for her creative leadership in establishing women's organizations at Montana State College, for her deep insight and understanding of Indian people as shown by her achievements with the Plains Indians; for her knowledge of human values as manifested by her love of and ability to work with people, we recommend Jessie Donaldson Schultz for your consideration to receive an honorary doctorate from Montana State College.

Verne Dusenberry, Chairman
Lois Payson
Martha Palffy
Sarah Vinke
Doris Willson

Appendix

Books by James Willard Schultz

PUBLISHED DURING HIS LIFETIME

Order of Publication	Title	First Issued	Original Price	Publisher
1	*My Life as an Indian*[1]	1907	$1.50	Doubleday, Page & Co., New York
2	*With the Indians in the Rockies*	1912	1.25	Houghton Mifflin Co., Boston
	Same	1925	1.75	Houghton Mifflin
	Same	1925	2.00	Houghton Mifflin (Riverside Bookshelf Edition)
	Same	1960	2.50	Houghton Mifflin
3	*Sinopah*	1913	1.10	Houghton Mifflin
4	*Quest of the Fish-Dog Skin*	1913	1.25	Houghton Mifflin
	Same	1923	1.00	Grosset & Dunlap, New York (Boy Scout Edition)
	Same	1960	2.50	Houghton Mifflin
5	*On the War Path*	1914	1.25	Houghton Mifflin
6	*Blackfeet Tales of Glacier National Park*	1916	2.00	Houghton Mifflin
7	*Apauk*	1916	1.25	Houghton Mifflin
8	*Gold Cache*	1917	1.25	Houghton Mifflin

	Title	Year	Price	Publisher
9	*Lame Bull's Mistake*	1918	1.35	Houghton Mifflin
	Same	1921	1.00	Grosset & Dunlap (Boy Scout Edition)
10	*Bird Woman*	1918	1.50	Houghton Mifflin
11	*Running Eagle*	1919	1.50	Houghton Mifflin
12	*Rising Wolf*	1919	1.50	Houghton Mifflin
13	*In the Great Apache Forest*	1920	1.75	Houghton Mifflin
14	*Dreadful River Cave*	1920	1.90	Houghton Mifflin
15	*War Trail Fort*	1921	1.75	Houghton Mifflin
16	*Trail of the Spanish Horse*	1922	1.75	Houghton Mifflin
	Same	1925	1.65	Houghton Mifflin
	Same	1925	2.00	Houghton Mifflin (Riverside Bookshelf Edition)
	Same	1960	2.50	Houghton Mifflin
17	*Seizer of Eagles*	1922	1.75	Houghton Mifflin
18	*Danger Trail*	1923	1.50	Houghton Mifflin
19	*Friends of My Life as an Indian*	1923	3.00	Houghton Mifflin
20	*Sahtaki and I*	1924	1.65	Houghton Mifflin
21	*Plumed Snake*	1924	2.00	Houghton Mifflin
22	*Questers of the Desert*	1925	1.75	Houghton Mifflin
23	*Signposts of Adventure*	1926	3.00	Houghton Mifflin

Books by James Willard Schultz, *Continued*

Order of Publication	Title	First Issued	Original Price	Publisher
24	Sun Woman	1926	2.00	Houghton Mifflin
25	William Jackson, Indian Scout	1926	1.75	Houghton Mifflin
26	Son of the Navahos	1927	1.75	Houghton Mifflin
27	Red Crow's Brother	1927	1.75	Houghton Mifflin
28	In Enemy Country	1928	1.75	Houghton Mifflin
29	Skull Head the Terrible	1929	1.75	Houghton Mifflin
30	Sun God's Children (with Jessica L. Donaldson)	1930	3.00	Houghton Mifflin
31	White Beaver	1930	1.75	Houghton Mifflin
32	Alder Gulch Gold	1931	1.50	Houghton Mifflin
33	Friends and Foes in the Rockies	1933	1.75	Houghton Mifflin
34	Gold Dust	1934	2.00	Houghton Mifflin
35	White Buffalo Robe	1936	2.00	Houghton Mifflin
36	Stained Gold	1937	2.00	Houghton Mifflin
37	Short Bow's Big Medicine	1940	2.00	Houghton Mifflin

1	*Blackfeet and Buffalo* (edited by Keith C. Seele)	1962	University of Oklahoma Press, Norman
2	*Why Gone Those Times?* (edited by Eugene Lee Silliman)	1974	University of Oklahoma Press
3	*Floating on the Missouri* (edited by Eugene Lee Silliman)	1979	University of Oklahoma Press
4	*Many Strange Characters* (edited by Eugene Lee Silliman)	1982	University of Oklahoma Press
5	*Bear Chief's War Shirt* (completed and edited by Wilbur Ward Betts)	1983	Mountain Press Publishing Co., Missoula, Mont.

[1] *My Life as an Indian* was republished in September, 1914, by Houghton Mifflin Company of Boston and sold for $1.50 per copy.

357

Dates of Publication of Schultz Books and Serials

Title of Book and/or Serial	Date of Publication — When Both Serial and Book	When Book Only	When Serial Only	By Whom Serialized
In the Lodges of the Blackfeet	1906			Forest and Stream
My Life as an Indian	1907			} same
Indian Winter	1911			Youth's Companion
With the Indians in the Rockies	1912			} same
Sinopah, the Indian Boy	1913			
Quest of the Fish-Dog Skin	1912 1913			Youth's Companion
On the War Path	1914 1914			Youth's Companion
Blackfeet Tales of Glacier National Park		1916		
Apauk, Caller of Buffalo	1916 1916			American Boy
The Gold Cache	1916 1917			Youth's Companion
Lame Bull's Mistake	1917 1918			Youth's Companion
Bird Woman		1918		
Running Eagle		1919		
Rising Wolf, the White Blackfoot	1918 1919			American Boy
In the Great Apache Forest		1920		
"The Sacred Buffalo Hunt"			1917	American Boy

Title					Journal
"The Warring Tribes"				1920	American Boy
The Dreadful River Cave	1918	1920			National Stockman and Farmer
The War Trail Fort	1920	1921			Youth's Companion
The Trail of the Spanish Horse	1921	1922			Youth's Companion
Seizer of Eagles	1921	1922			American Boy
The Danger Trail	1922	1923			National Stockman and Farmer
Friends of My Life as an Indian			1923		
"The Wolfers"				1923	American Boy
Plumed Snake Medicine	1924	1924			American Boy
Sahtaki and I	1922	1924			National Stockman and Farmer
Questers of the Desert	1925	1925			American Boy
Signposts of Adventure			1926		Frontier Magazine
Sun Woman	1926	1926			American Boy
William Jackson, Indian Scout	1926	1926			Youth's Companion
Son of the Navahos	1926	1927			American Boy
Red Crow's Brother	1927	1927			
In Enemy Country			1928		American Boy
Skull Head the Terrible	1929	1929			
The Sun God's Children (with Jessica L. Donaldson)			1930		
White Beaver			1930		
Alder Gulch Gold	1931	1931			American Boy

Dates of Publication of Schultz Books and Serials, *Continued*

Title of Book and/or Serial	Date of Publication — When Both Serial and Book	When Book Only	When Serial Only	By Whom Serialized
"The Peace Trail"			1931	*American Boy*
The Raiders	1932			*American Boy*
Friends and Foes in the Rockies ⎬ same	1933			
At the Sacred Rock	1933			*American Boy*
Gold Dust ⎬ same	1934			
"The Sacred Otter Bowcase"[1]			1935	*Boy's Life*
Beaver Woman's Vision	1935			*American Boy*
White Buffalo Robe ⎬ same	1936			
Stained Gold	1937 1937			*American Boy*
Warring Medicines	1934			*American Boy*
Short Bow's Big Medicine ⎬ same	1940			
Posthumously Published: *Floating on the Missouri*	1902 1979			*Forest and Stream*

[1] Published in condensed form in *Blackfeet and Buffalo*

360

Schultz Stories First Appearing in
Youth's Companion

Date Published

MEMOIRS OF A WHITE INDIAN

"The Buffalo Hunt"	November 3, 1910
"An Adventure with Ap-si"	November 24, 1910
"The Making of a Warrior"	December 8, 1910
"The Punishment of Afraid Eyes"	December 29, 1910
"The Passing of Back-In-Sight"	January 5, 1911
"A Message to the Mandans"	January 26, 1911
"A Day's Hunt"	February 16, 1911

MORE MEMOIRS OF A WHITE INDIAN

"Because of Apsi's Song"	February 15, 1912
"Rivois' Tale of Hardship"	February 29, 1912
"The Story of Pita"	March 14, 1912

NEW STORIES OF APSI

"The Night Struggle"	March 25, 1915
"Trouble at Flatwillow"	April 8, 1915
"A Hunt with Skunk Hat"	April 22, 1915
"High Bear and Real Bear"	April 29, 1915
"The Warning of the Gods"	May 13, 1915

OTHER STORIES

"A Medicine Animal Hunt"	March 27, 1919
"A Council and a Chase"	July 3, 1919
"Skunk Cap's Medicine"	September 25, 1919
"The Bad Luck of Low Horn"	December 25, 1919
"Puh—Poom"	July 5, 1923
"Laugher, the Tale of a Tame Wolf"	December 2, 1926
"Medicine Fly"[1]	May 19, 1927
"A Bad Medicine Hunt"	July 7, 1927

[1] A Schultz story by this title appeared in *Forest and Stream* on August 11, 1900, and was reprinted in *Why Gone Those Times?*

Schultz Stories and Articles First Appearing in the *Great Falls Tribune*

Name of Story	Tribune Date	Where Reprinted	Page
"Trouble to a Certain Extent"	October 8, 1899	*Many Strange Characters*	49
"Winchester Jack's Double"	December 17, 1899	*Many Strange Characters*	103
"To Old Mexico"	March 4, 1900	*Why Gone Those Times?*	53
"He Was No Hunter"	August 4, 1901	*Many Strange Characters*	93
"A Woodhawk's Christmas Dinner"	December 22, 1901	*Many Strange Characters*	115
"The Fatal Sign"	August 24, 1902	*Why Gone Those Times?*	205
"Fire at Fort Benton Courthouse"	October 8, 1933	*Blackfeet and Buffalo*	172
"Old Bison Drives"	March 31, 1935	*Blackfeet and Buffalo* (under the title "Plenty of Buffalo Meat")	306
"Last Trading Camp of the Pikunis"	April 7, 1935	*Blackfeet and Buffalo*	26
"Final Hunt on the Great Herds"	November 3, 1935	*Blackfeet and Buffalo*	37
"A Bride for Morning Star"	March 8, 1936	*Blackfeet and Buffalo*	347
"The Thunder Pipe"	March 22, 1936	*Open Road for Boys*, April, 1939	
"We Name Some Mountains"	October 18, 1936 October 25, 1936	*Blackfeet and Buffalo*	91

362

Other Schultz Stories and Articles From Various Sources

Story or Article	Source and Date	Reprinted	Page
	FOREST AND STREAM		
"Hunting in Montana"	October 14, 1880	Not reprinted	
"The White Buffalo Cow"	April 21, 1881	Not reprinted	
"Elk Hunt by Moonlight"	June 30, 1881	Not reprinted	
"Life Among the Blackfeet"	November 29, 1883 to January 24, 1884	Excerpt printed in *Blackfeet Lodge Tales*	269
"To Chief Mountain"	February 3, 1885	Not reprinted	
"White Goats and Bull Trout"	December 30, 1886 to January 6, 1887	Not reprinted	
"A War Party"	June 19, 1890	Not reprinted	
"To Tan a Hide"	June 23, 1892	Not reprinted	
"Little Plume's Dream"	October 13, 1894	*Why Gone Those Times?*	39
"Medicine Fly"	August 11, 1900	*Why Gone Those Times?*	217
"The Eagle Creek Wolfers"	January 5, 1901 to January 19, 1901	*Many Strange Characters*	3
"Beaver Bill's Close Calls"			
Part II	July 4, 1903	*Many Strange Characters*	59
Part I	October 12, 1907	*Many Strange Characters*	64
"Lone Elk's Search"	March 9, 1907	*Why Gone Those Times?*	235
"The Peril of Lone Man"	December 28, 1907	*Why Gone Those Times?*	21

WIDE WORLD, LONDON			
"On the War-Path with Redskins"	September, 1899	The Piegan Storyteller, January and April, 1979	
OUTING MAGAZINE			
"Winter Hunting of Goats in the Rockies"	January, 1901	Not reprinted	
"Hugh Monroe's Pistol"	January, 1907	Many Strange Characters	125
"A Memory That Endured"	October, 1909	Many Strange Characters	81
PACIFIC MONTHLY			
"Why the Moquis Perform the Snake Dance"	August, 1908	Not reprinted	
BOONVILLE HERALD			
"Sign Language of the Redskins"	August 30, 1917	Not reprinted	
SUNSET MAGAZINE			
"The Case of the Hopi"	October, 1921	Not reprinted	
"America's Red Armenians"	November, 1922	Not reprinted	

Other Schultz Stories and Articles From Various Sources, *Continued*

Story or Article	Source and Date	Reprinted	Page
	OUTLOOK		
"Indian Names in Glacier Park"	July 28, 1926	Not reprinted	
	YOUTH'S COMPANION		
"Laugher, the Story of a Wolf"	December 2, 1926	*Why Gone Those Times?*	179
"A Bad Medicine Hunt"	July 7, 1927	*Why Gone Those Times?*	163
	LOS ANGELES TIMES MAGAZINE		
"A Blackfoot Tragedy"	March 27, 1932	*Blackfeet and Buffalo* (under the title "Cutnose")	225
	BOY'S LIFE		
"The Sacred Otter Bowcase"	July, August, and September, 1935	*Blackfeet and Buffalo* (condensed version)	179
	OPEN ROAD FOR BOYS		
"He Sang the Victory Song"	September, 1937	*Blackfeet and Buffalo*	155
"Thunder Pipe"	April, 1939	Not reprinted (first appeared in *Great Falls Tribune*, March 22, 1936)	

	AMERICAN BOY		
"Smokey, a Good Coyote"	February, 1935	*Blackfeet and Buffalo*	140
"The Duel"	April, 1941	*Blackfeet and Buffalo* (under title "Three Bears' Combat for a Wife")	194
	CAVALIER		
"The Duel"	February, 1958	Duplicate of story in *American Boy*	
	ST. NICHOLAS		
"Last Years of the Buffalo"	July, 1934	Reprinted in *Cavalier*, and *True Western Adventure*	
"The Sacred Rock Vision"	January, 1936	Reprinted in Ginn & Co. 1936 textbook *Too Many Bears and Other Stories* and in *The Piegan Storyteller*, Vol. II, No. 2	8
"Skunk Cap's Medicine"	May, 1937	Reprinted in Ross Peterson & Co. textbook *Best Short Stories for Boys and Girls*, 1938, previously published in *Youth's Companion*, September 25, 1919	

Other Schultz Stories and Articles From Various Sources, *Continued*

Story or Article	Source and Date	Reprinted	Page
	GINN & CO.		
"A Warrior and His War Horse" ("The Gray Colt") from *The Attack and Other Stories* (edited by B. R. Buckingham)	About 1936	Reprinted in *The Piegan Storyteller*, Vol. II, No. 3	3
	SPECIAL COLLECTIONS MONTANA STATE UNIVERSITY		
"The Loud Mouthed Gun"	Previously unpublished	*Why Gone Those Times?*	65
"Trouble for the Gros Ventres"	"	*Why Gone Those Times?*	81
"The Black Antelope"	"	*Why Gone Those Times?*	99
"The First Fire Boat"	"	*Why Gone Those Times?*	115
"The First Elk Dog"	"	*Why Gone Those Times?*	129
"The Famine Winter"	"	*Why Gone Those Times?*	145
"The End of Laugher"	"	*Why Gone Those Times?*	191
"Hero Bradley"	"	*Many Strange Characters*	35
"Three Suns' War Record"	"	*Blackfeet and Buffalo*	264
"The Faith of Ahko Pitsu"	"	*Blackfeet and Buffalo*	338

Bibliography

MANUSCRIPT MATERIALS

James, Harry C. Unfinished typescript dealing with the life of James Willard Schultz. Roland R. Renne Library, Montana State University, Bozeman.
Schultz-Graham, Jessie Donaldson. Typescript of memoirs. Museum of the Rockies, Montana State University, Bozeman.
Sheire, James W. "Glacier National Park." Typescript (1970) in Glacier National Park Library, West Glacier, Montana.
Vaught, L. O. "History of Glacier National Park." Typescript in Glacier National Park Library, West Glacier, Montana.

CORRESPONDENCE, DIARIES AND PAPERS

Conner, Stewart W. Letter to Jessica Schultz, February 16, 1961.
Grinnell, George Bird. Diaries and Papers. Southwest Museum, Pasadena, Calif.
Great Northern Railway. James Willard Schultz Correspondence Files. Minnesota Historical Society, St. Paul.
James, Harry C. Correspondence with various persons.
Overholser, Joel F. Letters to Warren L. Hanna regarding James Willard Schultz.
Schultz-Graham, Jessie Donaldson. Letters to Harry C. James, October 22, 1947; November 25, 1955; May 22, 1974; August 22, 1975.

GOVERNMENT PUBLICATIONS

Scott, W. F. "The Pulitzer Case." *Second Biennial Report of the State Game and Fish Warden of the State of Montana, 1903–1904.*

NEWSPAPERS

Boonville (New York) *Herald.*
Bozeman (Montana) *Daily Chronicle.*
Fort Benton (Montana) *River Press.*
Great Falls (Montana) *Tribune.*
Rocky Mountain American.

PERIODICALS

Forest and Stream.
The Piegan Storyteller. Edited by David C. Andrews. Vol. I
and continuing. [Contains information on James Willard
Schultz contributed by hundreds of people who knew him
or possess information about him.]

BOOKS

Cooper, James Fenimore. *The Leatherstocking Tales.* Edited by
Allen Nevins. New York: Pentheon Books, 1954.
Curtis, Edward S. *The North American Indian.* 20 vols. New York,
1907–30.
Dary, David A. *The Buffalo Book.* Chicago: Swallow Press, 1974.
Francis, John W. *Sport Among the Rockies.* Troy, N.Y.: Privately
printed, 1889.
Grinnell, George Bird. *Blackfoot Lodge Tales.* New York: Charles
Scribner's Sons, 1892; Lincoln; University of Nebraska
Press, 1962.
———. Foreword to James Willard Schultz. *My Life as an Indian.*
New York: Doubleday, Page & Co., 1907.
———. *Pawnee Hero Stories and Folk Tales.* New York: Charles
Scribner's Sons, 1889.
Hanna, Warren L. *Montana's Many-Splendored Glacierland.* Seat-
tle, Wash.: Superior Press, 1975.
Hanson, Joseph Mills. *The Conquest of the Missouri.* New York:
Rinehart, 1946.
Hodge, Frederick W., ed. *Handbook of American Indians North of
Mexico.* 2 vols. Bureau of American Ethnology Bulletin 30.
Washington, D.C.: U.S. Government Printing Office, 1906.
Laut, Agnes C. *Enchanted Trails of Glacier National Park.* New
York: Robert M. McBride & Co., 1926.
Long, William J. *American Literature.* Philadelphia, Pa: Richard
West. Originally published 1913.

Renner, Frederick G. *Charles M. Russell.* New York: Harry N. Abrams, in association with Amon Carter Museum of Western Art, 1966, 1974.

Schultz, James Willard. *Blackfeet and Buffalo.* Edited by Keith C. Seele. Norman: University of Oklahoma Press, 1962.

————. *Floating on the Missouri.* Edited by Eugene Lee Silliman. Norman: University of Oklahoma Press, 1979.

————. *Many Strange Characters.* Edited by Eugene Lee Silliman. Norman: University of Oklahoma Press, 1962.

————. *Why Gone Those Times?* Edited by Eugene Lee Silliman. Norman: University of Oklahoma Press, 1974.

Stimson, Harry L. *My Vacations.* N.p.: Privately published, 1949.

Wechsberg, Joseph. *The Merchant Bankers.* Boston: Little Brown, 1966.

ARTICLES

Adams, Donald J. "Speaking of Books" (*New York Times* column), item on James Willard Schultz, 1967.

Banks, Anne. "Gifts Reflect Indian Ways." *The Piegan Storyteller,* Vol. IV, No. 3, July, 1979.

Coryell, Hubert V. "James Willard Schultz." *St. Nicholas,* July, 1934.

Dusenberry, Verne. "An Appreciation of James Willard Schultz." *Montana: The Magazine of Western History,* Winter, 1972.

Dyck, Paul. "Lone Wolf Returns to the Soil of His Indian Forebears." *Montana Post,* Vol. 8, No. 4, November–December, 1970.

————. "The Return of Lone Wolf." *Montana: The Magazine of Western History,* Winter, 1972.

Fritz, Harry W. "The Best Books About Montana." *Montana: The Magazine of Western History,* Winter, 1982.

Gilmore, Tom. "St. Helenan Tells of Life with Indians." *Napa (California) Register,* July 22, 1975.

Grinnell, George Bird. "The Crown of the Continent." *Century,* September, 1901.

————. "Maps of St. Mary and Swiftcurrent Regions." *Century,* September, 1901.

————. "The Rock Climbers." *Forest and Stream,* Vol. XXX, 1887–88.

———. "To the Walled-in Lakes.'" *Forest and Stream*, Vols. XXV—XXVI, 1885–86.

Hesslip, Thomas. "Notes on a Visit with Lone Wolf." *The Piegan Storyteller*, April, 1980.

James, Harry C. "Apikuni's Ageless Audience." *Montana: The Magazine of Western History*, Autumn, 1960.

———. "Apikuni as I Knew Him." *The Piegan Storyteller*, April 1960.

Koford, Jane S. "Thetas You'd Like to Know." *Kappa Alpha Theta Magazine*, Vol. 90, No. 2, Winter, 1975–76; reprinted in *The Piegan Storyteller*, Vol. I, No. 4, October, 1976.

Martin, Robert H. "Vignettes of Jessica Donaldson Schultz Graham." *The Piegan Storyteller*, Vol. II, No. 1, January, 1977.

Miller, Grace. "How Apikuni Met Jessie Donaldson." *The Piegan Storyteller*, Vol. VI, No. 1, January, 1980.

Pouliot, Gordon L. "The Story of Angus Monroe." *The Piegan Storyteller*, October, 1981, January, 1982.

Schultz, James Willard. "America's Red Armenians." *Sunset Magazine*, Vol. 49, November, 1922.

———. "The Case of the Hopi." *Sunset Magazine*, Vol. 57, October, 1921.

———. "To Chief Mountain." *Forest and Stream*, Vol. XXV, December 10, 1885.

———. "White Goats and Bull Trout." *Forest and Stream*, Vol. XXVII.

Schultz-Graham, Jesse Donaldson. "Adventuresome, Amazing Apikuni." *Montana: The Magazine of Western History*, Autumn, 1960.

———. "Apikuni's Pets." *Boonville* (New York) *Herald*, October 30, 1930.

Vestal, Stanley, "An Appreciation of James Willard Schultz." *Dallas* (Texas) *News*, July 10, 1930.

White, Stewart Edward. "The Plight of the Blackfeet." *Sunset Magazine*, October, 1921.

Index